How Physical Principles Guide Our Behavior

Ran Tel-Vered

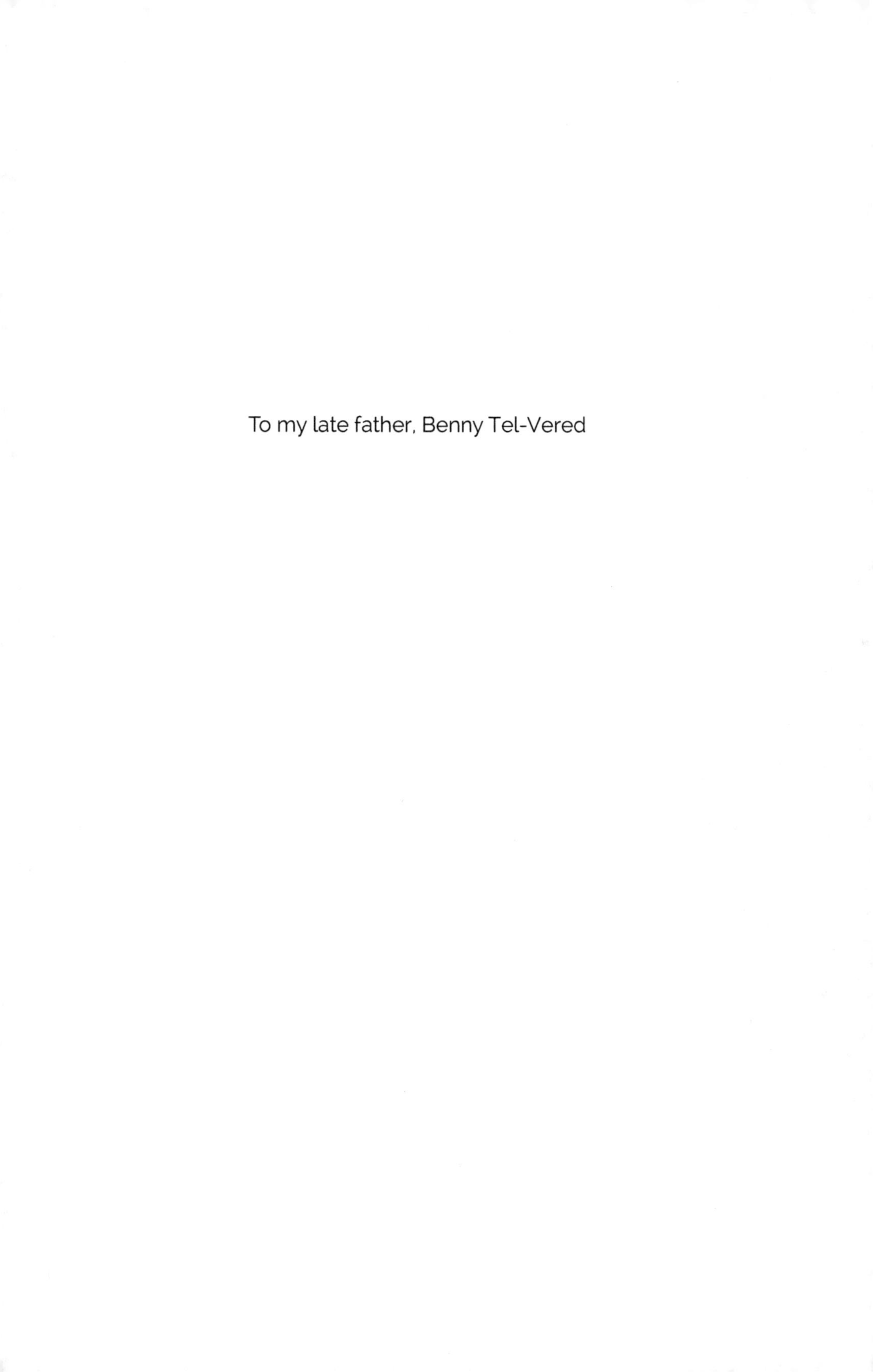

To my late father, Benny Tel-Vered

Table of Contents

Preface

This book aims to describe some elementary yet fundamental relations between beliefs, structure, and human behavior and suggests their interconnected potential evolution in nature. Several initial thoughts concerning these ideas came to my mind a few years ago during a wonderful road trip in South America. Back then, long bus rides exceeding 10 hours each became a fertile ground for immersing myself in a deep escapist state, slightly detached from the struggle of life, and this attracted me to these fairly abstract concepts. Looking from a broad perspective, engaging in this thinking matched well with my natural inclination to repeatedly search for order patterns, as an essential strategy used by all humans in dealing with different fears and challenges. Unsurprisingly, through some sort of an "evolutionary process" affected by many personal and external factors, my initial thoughts have drifted and changed considerably since that trip, to the point of being crystalized into the current form presented in the book. Now, in my native field of studies I am not a philosopher, pure physicist, anthropologist, neurobiologist, or algorithm developer, and yet this book concerns all of these to some extent. I believe that if I had to dedicate all of my free time to fully mastering all the disciplines, I could never have published my own insights. In fact, several subjective experiences during the early writing stages have even led me to actively decide to minimize dependency on ideas and thoughts contributed by others. This obviously does not mean that I have not been exposed to relevant literature (as evident from the various citations enclosed throughout the chapters of the book) but rather that I have persistently limited my search for additional information to briefly reviewing very specific topics whenever certain ideas crossed my mind. Adopting such an approach is clearly risky when presenting my own interpretations, as I may never fully know whether my postulations overlap or coincide with previous contributions by others or, even worse, have been consensually rejected/contradicted. Yet it gives the authors who follow this direction the power to unorthodoxly flow with their relatively less biased ideas and, occasionally (even if rarely), create "belief mutations" that can add to the global, orthodox understanding of this or another topic. With that said, I hope that those who desire to read this book will find different "unpaved trails" of ideas and points of view within the writings that can stimulate further thinking and trigger progress in the field.

I wish to thank the dear people who have accompanied me along the rocky—yet filled with sheer pleasure—road of writing. From my precious mother, Yardena; my phenomenal brother, Gal, and his amazing family; to my dear cousins and good friends. Your part in my life is priceless and I am lucky to have you with me. Above all, I am indebted to my beloved wife, Kiti. Your unconditional love and endless support and understanding facilitate my dreams.

Introduction

Why do we spend so much time and effort on attempting to expand what can be perceived as our resources and possessions when all the components preset in our life environment tend to reduce excessive potential energy? Possible answers to this question are fairly common. One of them combines, for example, basic principles of biochemistry and thermodynamics in suggesting that, among other reasons, recruitment of resources is required for the sustenance of the low entropy, outstandingly ordered structure of our bodies, from which different life functionalities emerge. A possible incentive for this sequence of occurrences is the expected increase in the universal entropy facilitated by the internal human conversion processes as well as by many of the interactions of the human with his or her external environment obtained throughout this state of life. Considering that, we may add and ask several other profound questions like, Is it possible that fundamental physical laws, also standing for instance behind such biochemical life reactions, pervaded through evolutionary processes into the mechanisms that shape our perceptions regarding the environment we live in? What about the potential subsequent assimilation of these laws to our decision making regarding interactions with the perceived objects? Has evolution deliberately shaped our mind structures and functions to shift our awareness from these hypothetical mechanistic guidelines towards the intuitiveness associated with our struggles, desires, and urges? May one of the reasons for this possible distraction strategy be the benefit of nature from us missing the chance to realize that our core function is to serve as disposable fine structures to its predetermined evolution dictated by physical laws?

This book deals with the two thoroughly interlinked concepts of belief and physics. Being canonically accepted nowadays, we regard the scientific discipline of physics as a belief in the full sense of the word, as its principles and concepts may be transferred between humans by means of communication, accepted or rejected through a struggle with other beliefs, memorized or forgotten, or their formulation might change with time, and so on. In parallel to that, we favor to adhere to the physicalistic approach which identifies every universal occurrence, and in this case the belief, as a product of a physical process (holding a foundation that can potentially be explained by physics) that is driven and shaped by certain laws of nature. The alleged reciprocal relations between physics and belief are expected to raise the philosophical question of which one is based on the other, an issue that will continue to accompany us throughout the attempts to address the fundamentals of human perception and the behavior it evokes. With this in mind, we already note that regardless of our specific beliefs in their essence, the core laws of nature will be considered here to be immutable by beliefs, an idea which implies a certain universal hierarchy between the terms. Unsurprisingly, various challenges are expected along our ambitious path of upcoming interpretations. Some of these concern, for example, limitations over our observations, knowledge, and the ability to objectively explore perception and different belief-related matters. Another inevitable ontological problem stems from the questionable veridicality, reflecting in this context the degree of authenticity of a correlation between possibly existing "real" or "pristine" and perceived worlds. Due to such obstacles, we will frequently be coerced into assumptions which dictate the hypothetical nature of this work, also emphasizing our desire for a further empirical/theoretical validation and development of its contents. The first chapter of this book, aiming to provide a valuable toolbox of concepts for the reader, to be used in the subsequent stages, will discuss several matters revolving around the fundamental question, Can we draw a connection between beliefs and properties which are apparently being reflected from spacetime? The chapter will also address questions such as, Is it possible to distinguish the individual human's body, mind, and external world, as components of an objective general spacetime whose existence might be affected by, yet can possibly also be independent of, perception? And what are the hereditary-dictated goals of the human and how do they behaviorally project at the individual level? Some aspects of these "genetic targets" will be scrutinized from an energetic standpoint referring to the investment of efforts (and time) in their realization.

The second chapter proceeds to describe integrated "sensoresponsive" pathways in the human. These are associated with a primary conversion process, which is presumably responsible for the generation of life functionalities in the forms of spatial perception and perception-based behavior. In contrast to conventional macro-level physiological (neurobiological) descriptions, the conversion process will be approached from a reduced mechanistic standpoint, describing the sequential physical formation of correlated structural-functional projections from sensing to response. Two basic questions accompanying this part are: Is it possible to ascribe for a certain individual a human energy based on the transient structural distribution states of his or her body and mind contents? And what is the possible connection between such an energy function and several major events in the individual's life? Further described in Chapter 2 are several key aspects of the "individuality dimension", a hypothetical measure reflecting a systemic microscopic-level progression through physical-structural changes during the formation of functionality—in this case, in the human. Some of the interlinked concepts discussed in Chapter 2 form a basis for the central and most significant part of the book, the third chapter, describing the prominent contribution of the individual's mind to the sensoresponsive conversion process. The chapter starts by suggesting a sequential and circumstantial correlation between the sensory information that we absorb from the external environment, our phenomenological sensation experiences, and cognitive interpretations given to the stimuli. These are followed by addressing questions like: How do we determine and grade the relative (genetic) meaningfulness of patterns perceived and identified within this information? How do these meanings relate to our decisions and perception-based behavior? What is the role of the self and its perception in the assessments? Is it possible that the mind mechanisms directing such an activity encode certain combinations of fundamental physical laws standing behind the causal-circumstantial construction and evolution of nature? The fourth and final chapter of the book attempts to expand the postulated descriptions from the individual level to groups of communicating and collaborating people. Accordingly, we ask: Are the hypothesized individual energy perception and behavior patterns which follow it conserved in larger human assemblies? And how does the human struggle affect the group organization and energy-related operations? Following these discussions, Chapter 4 continues to address several aspects of our collective evolution and its by-products from a physicalistic-deterministic united standpoint.

While this book describes common inherent mechanisms which are believed to operate in all humans regardless of their race, gender, or personal beliefs, it also persistently emphasizes the uniqueness in the dynamic structures and specific responses of each individual. Intuitively accepting that personal differences do exist, it is easy to understand that no theory can encompass and pinpoint the specific responses of all humans to a certain trigger, yet we believe that our experiences in life may assist us in exploring their common mechanisms and psychoenergetic/socioenergetic patterns. Finally, along the convoluted pathways between physics and beliefs, we wish (note that in order to avoid a writing style that may sound arrogant at times, this book will only employ plural-form expressions such as "we believe" or "we wish") that our hypotheses and mechanistic interpretations herein would become a fertile ground for new thoughts and insights by all curious readers whose life trajectories have led them here.

Chapter 1

Beliefs, Spacetime, and the Individual Human

1.1 Spacetime and its perception: An ontology of belief and existence

The sensation that follows the act of reaching out and successfully holding an object perceived to be located in a given place can be regarded as a recurring and reproducible experience which seemingly evidences the presence of the object in our vicinity. Observations of this kind impart us with an *intuitive belief* in the existence of a *spacetime* with which we carry out different interactions throughout our lifetime. The nature of spacetime has been contemplated by humankind since the ancient times. Philosophical questions kept arising throughout the years, asking if this spacetime only exists in our mind as a *phenomenological conscious experience (PCE)*, or if, alternatively, we sense unique parts of a reality whose existence is absolute and independent from our experience of it. Naturally, we also wonder whether our perception itself contributes to the evolution of spacetime. Regardless of these ontological and epistemological views, from early on in our lives we assimilate an intuitive belief in the existence of a medium in which we are present and to which we respond. The term "intuitive belief" was coined to symbolize in this context an exceptional degree of consensus among humans that is based on recurring and similar personal experiences. Clearly, holders of this belief may add their own interpretations of the essence of spacetime and view it, for example, as transcendent, controlled by God(s), or they may not believe in the existence of any form of deity. Yet, regardless of any of these beliefs, people will continue reaching out with their hands and grasping identified objects, as they believe in their nearby tangible presence. Naturally, this apparent simplicity does not reliably reflect the phenomenological and other challenges which ought to be taken into consideration by every serious debate dealing with spacetime from a belief-centered standpoint, and especially by our discussion, which aims to explore some of the bilateral relations between physics and beliefs. One major difficulty arises from our inherent mechanistic reliance when perceiving elements of spacetime on present states of personal beliefs. This implies that perception and beliefs are not only inseparable but also that the former is essentially individual and subjective, as beliefs vary to a certain extent from one person to another. One conclusion which can be drawn in this regard is that no matter how advanced humanity becomes in "decrypting" the laws of nature and in finding causal explanations for the observed spacetime, due to our hereditary functions which force us to perceive it behind projections and beliefs, such attempts are always doomed to be biased by the latter. This unbreakable dependency in humans will be generally referred to here as the *inextricability limitation*. In this context, we accept the limitation as directly projecting on some aspects of *veridicality*, to which we refer here as a potential congruence between certain states of objects as they are perceived in spacetime and their hypothetical existence—possibly in a "pristine" form—in the absence of perception. Whereas the inextricability limitation seems to undermine the possibility for high degrees of veridicality and even the prospect to ever realize how far this correlation extends, it still does not necessarily contradict our basic intuitive beliefs and does not prevent us from assuming that spacetime perception can be based at least on the grounds of a "relative veridicality" which may be further associated with a physical correlation.

From our own observations of ourselves and other humans, we may express several beliefs about beliefs. First, we realize that beliefs can change over time and that they are not necessarily unified and/or identically assimilated globally. Additionally, we accept that beliefs can be transferred and distributed among individuals via *communication* events involving human-based information exchange. Despite their strong potential, communicative interactions do not necessarily lead to assimilation of new beliefs. One example is the present book and its function as a possible means of mediation between perceptions. Unlike the consensual intuitiveness associated with the belief in spacetime, this book reflects a broad collection of personal beliefs held by the author. The extent of assimilation of these by any given reader of the book will naturally depend on, among other factors, the author's ability to articulate those beliefs efficiently for this purpose and on the array of beliefs held by the individual who delves into the reading. Such examples of conditions that must be met before a successful distribution of beliefs can take place imply subjective and other limitations of human communication. Differences in beliefs, also concerning the interplay between an individual and his or her external spacetime and even about beliefs themselves, make it hard to unify them into consensual perceptive "truths" shared by many individuals, thus making their canonization difficult. One related idea is that while a similar inextricability limitation applies to all individuals, a "microscopic" subjectivity emerging from unique variations in their own structures keeps contributing to differences in their perceptions of spacetime elements and to their responses to them. These differences, which later on in this book will be associated with the systemic property of "individuality dimension", pose a significant challenge to bridging beliefs. An additional difficulty which will be further addressed in this chapter relates to our ability to refer to and describe humans separately from the "general spacetime" in which they are believed to be contained and comply with its physical laws and dictates. In view of these challenges, it is possible to consider this book as a combination of personal beliefs about spacetime and its contents which cannot be regarded as truer, better, or more accurate than any others, including those held by any of its potential readers. Thus, in order to possibly convince them of our truths, all that we can do is try to raise questions and come up with ostensibly causal explanations (occasionally hypothetical but always striving for reduced subjectivity and high consistency) for them, hoping that the readers would be willing to examine the concepts presented in a similar, albeit not identical, manner.

Let's return briefly to the question of veridicality and ponder the connection between reality and its perception. As noted, belief- and subjectivity-related, as well as other intrinsic limitations, prevent us from knowing if spacetime exists in a different, "more pristine", form compared to its PCE sensation and perception reflections. Given these obstacles, it can be assumed that we are forced to explore nature by constantly making comparisons between spacetime objects as they appear to be experienced by us and beliefs as dynamic personal and/or shared reference points. One important form of reference may rely on the fairly intuitive idea of *structure* originating from our *observations* of nature. To explain the process of observing, we need to refer to two frequently separated localities in spacetime: an "observing region" that in our case is believed to be associated with spacetime content distributed in a given human, and an "observed region", which is the focus of the observation and which under specific circumstances may also be ascribed to parts of the individual "observer".[1] We will regard the observations as fundamentally contributing to spacetime perception and doing so by causally changing spacetime content which is internally localized in the observer, thus forming projections that serve as building blocks for some of his or her PCEs and perception. The structure, associated with each of the observed regions and related to the circumstantial changes that led to their state of existence, can be viewed in this context as a set of (perceived) "reference" characteristics which is used to define local content distributions and can be related to the intuitive concept of order. Additionally, it is possible to distinguish between direct and indirect observations, with the latter referring to the mediated induction of structure changes in the observer by means of foreign objects that can measure the observed region and relay the results to him or her. From a general viewpoint, observations reflect certain properties which can often be associated with the structures of the focused regions observed. The properties observed are in many cases consistent and, depending on the physical nature of the observation, may be cross-verified. A simple example of this is the cup of coffee that some of us drank this morning. Its sight, texture, smell, and the sound made by drinking it, combined with the sensation of the warmth and typical taste are all apparent in this case to our cross-verified patterned perception of the coffee cup in spacetime, even in the absence of any knowledge of its exact structure and composition. Fortunately, due to the ability of our systemic functions to form *patterned perception* that is often combined with reasoning, we are endowed with the potency to use partial observation information to perceive spacetime objects. Among other implications, this trait helps us recognize, for instance, different cups of coffee following the sensation of only a few of their

---

1 Also considered are observed regions at which the observer does not deliberately or consciously direct (direct or indirect) sensory systems in order to actively initiate the observation.

interactive characteristics. The profusion of observations of (physical interactions with) spacetime objects strengthens the beliefs in the existence of a *spatial content*, which is, at least on the absolute physical level, unevenly distributed in the surroundings of the observer and farther away in space. On these grounds we also assume that (part of) the spatial content supports observable properties which are accessible and assessable from different scales and dimensions, including time. This allows us to refer to distributions of the content which are delimitated by observable-perceivable "borders" as *local structures*, and to associate them with beliefs regarding relative locations, compositions, stabilities, and so on. Now, throughout the years and in parallel to global scientific and technological advances, humanity has been improving its capabilities to observe spatial content and has accordingly refined the conventional definitions of the word "structure". Beyond the presumption that the properties of the content correlate with its structure and composition, *reductionism theories* suggest that macroscopic-level features, including those observed and perceived, rely on their respective microscopic structure foundations. Supported by certain indirect evidence, we also consider the possibility that *fundamental structures* limit the downscale convergence of the building blocks of nature's content. These various perspectives and assumptions suggest that despite all the aforementioned challenges, humanity has developed different beliefs in spacetime content and its properties. The beliefs extend far beyond the environmental boundaries set by direct sensations, and we intuitively tend to believe in their validity even if the observation and perception functions of humankind have somehow ceased to exist.[2]

The next question to be asked is, Can we perceive the entire structural information assumed to exist in the spacetime content which we directly observe? Hypothetically, if we could do so, we might be able to claim that an "ideal" projection of the observation has been formed in the human observer on the grounds of assimilation and our structure-based beliefs.[3] Generally speaking, we assume that the

---

2 In a similar way to assuming that spacetime existed in the absence of human observations prior to the appearance of humankind on Earth (leaving the question of extraterrestrial humans open to debate).

3 While such a hypothetical scenario does not overcome the inextricability limitation (also preventing us from knowing the true limits of the "entire structural information"), it could have been associated with the highest degree of veridicality.

scenario is impossible for several practical and theoretical reasons. First, perception of external spacetime content is believed to emerge from biased projections of physical interactions between external stimuli and sensory body units. Added to these are different objective physical and physiological limitations which only allow the sensing of a very limited part of spacetime content and its physical characteristics. Moreover, as the cognitive assessment processes on which perception relies require focusing and involve patterned recognition of the projected contents, a considerable amount of spatial information typically remains unprocessed and thus unperceived. We should also highlight the physical uncertainties which avert the ultimate definition of structure and hence any absolute-level correlation between contents. These descriptions imply that our observations correspond to "reduced information" projections of spacetime content in the human from which approximate patterns are derived. Later, we will assume that the perception and the processes leading to it and following it constitute an unfolding causal and circumstantial correlation between physical states in nature. The existence of an abundance of spacetime content whose physical properties are hidden from our perception supports the idea that a genuine veridicality, in terms of a high degree of structural correlation, can never be claimed. Yet, such difficulties will not hold us back from trying to explore the perception of spacetime. Inspired by our multi-sensory abilities and certain beliefs, we suggest that perceiving spacetime is solidly bound to physical grounds and does not happen without a cause or in total absence of veridicality. Accordingly, we presume that spacetime does contain a certain kind of "veridical content" and that parts of it are being observed and experienced by us while shaping our beliefs and perceptions.

We now wish to present several more premises related to beliefs. The first claims the existence of a *specific structure-belief connection* in spacetime. Consistent with our previous references to this term, we identify "structure" as sets of (preferably consensual) order (distribution)-defining patterns ascribed to spatial contents often with respect to specific observation scale and conditions. On the other hand, a "belief" is regarded here as an expression of a certain specific PCE in conjunction with the local physical event which has allowed its immediate expression. As will also be emphasized in the next chapter, we refer to the latter as a *transmission process* ("transmitting" in the sense of "screening" or "projecting on a screen") of certain local content distributions formed in every individual. The content distributions will be regarded as *beliefs-encrypting structures (BES)* that are obtained via designated *conversion processes*, some of which related to the observations made by the individual. Next to be hypothesized is the *belief locality assumption*, suggesting that core processes involving the BES, including their transmission as beliefs, occur in a specific body element found in every individual which is associated with the *mind*. We believe that minds also exist in various other living species, and we will later refer to them in the anatomic-physiologic context of the brain organ. The BES transmissions are assumed to emerge from specific structural changes in the mind and to contribute to numerous phenomenological expressions evoked in the individual's *consciousness*. Our ability to focus *attention* and experience specific PCEs, in an analogous way to concentrating on a specific pattern displayed on a screen, will promote our *awareness* to them (whereas, from a broader perspective on the concept of awareness, we might still remain aware to temporarily unfocused PCEs). Adhering to these ideas, we assume that the dynamic processes related to the formation, accumulation, change, and transmission of the BES as beliefs have a strong impact on the individual's perceptions and perception-based behavior throughout his or her life. Another early assumption suggests that besides the perception of the individual's self, every human possesses two *core perceptions*: a *classical spacetime perception (CP)* and an *energetic perception (EP)*. These participate in a methodological interpretation of spacetime and prediction of some of its changes and are believed here to play a prominent role in the sensoresponsive behavior of the individual whose mechanisms will be set out in the next two chapters.

The premises and preliminary definitions presented so far continue with the conversion processes which are believed to constitute the physical foundation for perception. Adhering to canonical "sensoperceptive" physiology, we describe a situation in which certain spacetime contents, among which some may compose the individual, act as *stimuli* to different functional units in his or her body. Under apt conditions, the successful conversion[4] of the stimuli-activated body "inputs" into mind "outputs" and their consequential transmissions in the consciousness will allow the observation-sensation of spacetime elements and their perception. These systemic processes are further viewed as critical to the generation of decisions shaping the individual's perception-based behavior. Now, some of the biophysical pathways of conversion are believed to engage mind structures that participate in functional reactions attributed to *cognition*. Accordingly, the assessment of spacetime observations and formation of respective perceptive interpretations to them make use of cognition, with the latter utilizing BES reservoirs in the form of memories. We will distinguish between *transient cognitive assessments (TCAs)* that are mainly tailored to the specific inputs which trigger the assessments and *overarching cognitive assessments (OCAs)*, which frequently rely on beliefs encompassing more general properties observed from spacetime.[5] Typical beliefs which appear to be valuable for the OCAs concern stability, repetitiveness, causality, relativity, orientation in space, as well as others. The transient and overarching assessments are thoroughly intertwined and can help generate predictive elements that depend on their combined contributions. People accept, for instance, that in the absence of external intervention, objects that they have recently left in a nearby room continue to exist there. Such estimations rely on a fundamental *assimilation* of beliefs (as BES stored in memory arrays) following experiences with past events. In the absence of "higher quality" updated inputs, these are often regarded as reliable and holding the potential to be probable, as in the case exemplified. Based on the above assumptions, we argue that the systematic observation-assessment-assimilation mechanism plays a prominent role in perceptions and predictions that take part in the destined fate of the human.

So far, we have insinuated the existence of a structure-based connection between spacetime, beliefs, assessments, perceptions, and behavior. We assumed that the perception of spatial elements

---

4 The comprehensive use of the term "conversion" will refer to transduction processes involving effective physical and structural changes to the individual's content along the way to producing functionality outputs from the stimuli-based inputs. The functionalities produced will be correlated to different traits observed in the human.

5 It should be noted that both kinds of assessments employ top-down processing (see next chapter) and can be applied to interactions with occasional-coincidental stimuli.

combined with predictions of their changes occur in specific and separated localities in spacetime corresponding to minds, and they are being facilitated through circumstantial changes in their own structures. A related idea is that for us to experience some sort of intuitive elementary veridicality, even only as a vague projection of the existence of a "real" spacetime, a structural-physical correlation must exist between the source of the stimulus, the body imprints it generates, and their respective cognitively processed and transmitted products in the mind following the conversion process. From a physical perspective, perceiving an object as a *source of stimulus* in spacetime requires a great deal of carefulness in regard to what is being converted. While often being able to perceive an object he or she is directly interacting with, in many other cases the individual indirectly perceives objects via sensing their *carriers*. The latter can be attributed either to content, as matter or radiation which has left the sources via different physical processes and reached the individual, or to spatial content that has interacted with the sources along its circumstantial migration in spacetime and continued in its movement pathway towards the human (with or without his or her active intervention). Regardless of the events that lead the carriers to the individual, we regard these carriers as mediators conveying a certain projective information about the sources. During the migration stage, some of the properties of the carriers are likely to be affected by interactions with the external medium, and upon reaching the individual, the stimuli they provide may differ from the hypothetical "pristine" projections of the sources, also reflecting the history of changes during the migration. Despite the conservation of a causal physical-structural correlation along this path of consecutive changes, we believe that perception requires the extent of the accrued structural changes during the migration to be limited to a certain degree in order for the cognitive processes to be able to meaningfully interpret the sources and their properties.

A brief glimpse of the conversion process takes us back to the problem of subjectivity. Assuming hereditary-based "unity" in the conversion mechanism among different individuals, observing in this case the same local content in spacetime, we expect that any apparent differences in their perceptions of this content may arise due to possible variations in the structural characteristics of the object or its carriers upon arrival to the observers and activation of the conversion processes, and/or due to possible differences in the individuals' internal structures that affect the conversion and its products. Among the factors relevant to the second reason, we also find the long-term incremental and circumstantial assimilation of BES corresponding to individual experiences in spacetime. Additionally, internal structure differences may account for variations in subjective sensation experiences between individuals associated with *qualia*. Naturally, these perceptive and sensation differences between humans ostensibly oppose the genetically unified nature of their mechanisms and negate any objective basis for considering true veridicality. Returning to the idea that absolute-level perceptual differences are inevitable, we may ask the following question: Can we still "accurately" describe spacetime, and among its dynamics the conversion mechanism that enables our human perception, while it is being differently perceived by each of us? One potential way to minimize subjective gaps is by getting the BES arrays assimilated in the minds of the people communicating the observations and interpretations closer to one another. Through adopting the concepts of projective-correlative conversion of observations and their dynamic assimilation, we expect that such an effect can be achieved via repetitive and selective exposure of individuals to similar beliefs concerning different aspects of spacetime. Communication processes that are frequently associated with *teaching and learning* hold, for example, a potential to increase the "objective" similarities within certain mind structure distributions amongst humans. These cannot eliminate the qualia but may establish a solid ground for common beliefs also concerning the nature of spacetime processes. Before discussing some of these beliefs, we wish to dedicate a few words to human communication.

Communication has many facets ranging from direct and indirect interactive exchange of information between individuals and groups to self-transfer of information over time. From the standpoint of the individual receiving the communicated information, the event may be regarded as a plain sensation of a spacetime observation. This idea will remain valid also in view of a possible claim that "communication stimuli" are encoded in a way that makes their interpretation and assimilation slightly different from other sensory triggers and as such have the potential to accelerate "patterned" processing and perception. Intuitively, communication can also lead to an evolution of ideas and beliefs.[6] With these ideas in mind, we emphasize that drawing BES arrays closer to one another requires a prolonged investment of efforts and overcoming potential states of incompatibility and resistance. A fruitful transfer of beliefs can be viewed as a successful "copying" of certain BES arrays between minds, which is by itself imperfect yet does contribute to increasing structural similarity and reducing certain gaps between the participants. One possible implication of this process is the formation of human assemblies consisting of two or more individuals who are gathered around non-identical yet similar BES and beliefs. Clearly, communication also has the power to change and even replace beliefs. As a consequence, one may dissociate from groups that are united by beliefs, and in fact we assume that a considerable part of human behavior can be explained on the grounds of communication-mediated dynamic "struggles" between existing and new beliefs (see Chapter 4 for further reading). Interestingly, we may identify spatial content, which is related to communicative information and is external to any mind in spacetime, and refer to it as a potential BES "extension" or "non-affiliated" BES. This idea does not contradict the belief locality assumption as the PCEs of the BES and their processing are still confined to the mind. Nevertheless, it reflects in a way the evolving capabilities of humankind to provide a variety of communicative relay and storage solutions to belief-related information—and among them this book.

We now return to discussing our options in fairly describing natural processes. Limited by our individual subjective observations, perceptions, and communicative expressions, we realize the need to adopt a discipline such as *science* and conform with certain principles believed to stand behind it. Science urges its believers to adhere to strict rules regarding, for example, the methodological execution, assessment, and reporting of observations, and it does so with the utopian aim to reduce the extent of subjectivity involved in these actions. Towards this goal, science seeks to carry out targeted

---

6 The pioneering work of Dawkins in this area should be acknowledged: R. Dawkins, *The Selfish Gene*. Oxford: Oxford University Press (1976), which paved the way to the study of memetics— for example, R. Brodie, *Virus of the Mind: The New Science of the Meme*. Integral Press (1996); S. J. Blackmore, *The Meme Machine*. Oxford: Oxford University Press (1999).

observations and predict their outcome as well as to provide causal interpretations for observations and the ways they have evolved to appear and/or will continue to evolve.[7] Again, these all are desired to have a minimal footprint of subjectivity. In order to pursue these goals, a collective acceptance of certain general rules combined with complying to implementation of different practices are required on the part of the believers.[8] As adhering to these rules and practices never leads to fully subjective interpretations of nature, we accept that at best we can aspire to provide explanations to observations through a *semi-objective lens* compromising between fundamental scientific ideals and compulsory subjective limitations. Accordingly, we will adopt a status of *side observers* who examine, analyze, describe, and try to distribute beliefs which are not necessarily specific to our own experiences. These beliefs will generally be described as applying to a given "individual", bearing in mind that they are expected to apply to us as well.

Assuming that the mind plays a major role in the conversion process leading to perception and behavior in the human, we will now introduce its fundamental part in it from a preliminary, bird's eye viewpoint. The interpretations and their complementary presentation in Figure 1.1 are deliberately aimed to match the simplicity desired at this stage, and will be followed by more comprehensive descriptions in the next two chapters. Assisted by the belief-locality assumption, we view the individual's mind as a *latent system* operating in the human body (see later in this chapter), which is generating from within its own boundaries consciousness, awareness, and other functions to maintain a crucial part of the living functionality. In accord with the previously mentioned ideas, we accept that the generation of certain elements of the human functionality also relies on the stimuli and on structural changes associated with all, including mind-unrelated, conversion processes in the individual. Adopting fundamental scientific guidelines combined with physicalistic and materialistic views (while

---

7 One can accordingly view science as a macroscopic scale doctrine emerging from many contributed beliefs which have been copied between individuals' minds and became linked through means of communication.

8 Contrary to the widespread tendency to view science as being exact, due to its persistently progressing nature, subjectivity at different levels, and because of inherent uncertainties related to the physical properties of spacetime content and its observations, these views seem to be distorted.

intentionally excluding various panpsychism-related interpretations from the discussion), we approach the nonconsensually resolved dynamic mind construction via a generalized time-dependent *structure function*, $k_{mind}(t)$. Throughout this book, structure functions (alternatively called "content distribution functions") will refer to reduced parametric projections of several subjects of interest. Based on our previous approach to "structure" and by linking it to physical characteristics that are reflected from ephemeral or sustained ordering of content, we will regard the structure functions as representing time-varying distributions of the contents of the focused systems. Despite the generalized form depicted for simplicity reasons for the structure functions, we embrace a reductionist viewpoint and consider them as based on the entire set of calculable physical interactions between the respective contents' elementary microscopic ingredients, including their biases with respect to circumstantial interactions with the external environment.[9] In parallel to that, we assume that several unit arrays producing designated functions operate within the structure of the mind, and as such we may also ascribe respective structure (sub) functions to them. Accordingly, for the preliminary, basic description of mind operations that are presumably participating in the formation of perception, we will now refer to several dynamic arrays and their corresponding structure functions. Among these we find the entire array in the mind that is genetically designated and expressed to direct the local conversion processes, and to which we assign the dynamic mind "functionality/toolbox" function $k_f(t)$. This constantly changing array, to which we further ascribe the mind-contributed systematicness[10] behind sensation and cognition, is believed to contain the hypothetical mind units and is assumed to be affected by the body-based regulation of the physiology supporting the transformations

---

9 Naturally, we use scientific interpretations of structure functions to correlate them with the physical properties observed from their objectives in the general spacetime (k^{tot}_{st}). In the specific case of the mind, we will assume that at present its content has not been fully and consensually resolved and, thus, it will be regarded as latent within local structure distributions of the human body (such as the brain whose biophysical nature is allegedly better understood by us). These challenges do not restrain us from assigning to the mind a non-empirical structure function which should have a physical foundation in general spacetime As long as the mind shows signs of contribution to the living functionality of the individual, we can hence define: $k_{mind} \in k_{individual} \in k^{tot}_{st}$, where in this context $\in$ represents "belongs to".

10 The term "systematicness" will be used herein to refer to a combination of the inherent systemic dynamics ($k_f(t)$) guiding the conversion processes and the functionality emerging from it.

entailed. We specifically highlight the structure function $k_{BES}(t)$, corresponding to the distribution of the BES in memory unit localities following their assimilation via past conversions. As stated before, attributed to some of these is a critical role in determining the outcome of the conversion, say of a stimulus whose initial footprint in the system is marked by $k_{input}(t \equiv 0)$, to the respective product k_{output} (Figure 1.1).[11] Under the right conditions, core transformations involved in the $k_f(t)$-regulated conversion attempt to correlate the structural projection k_{input}, generated through the impact of the stimulus to the existing

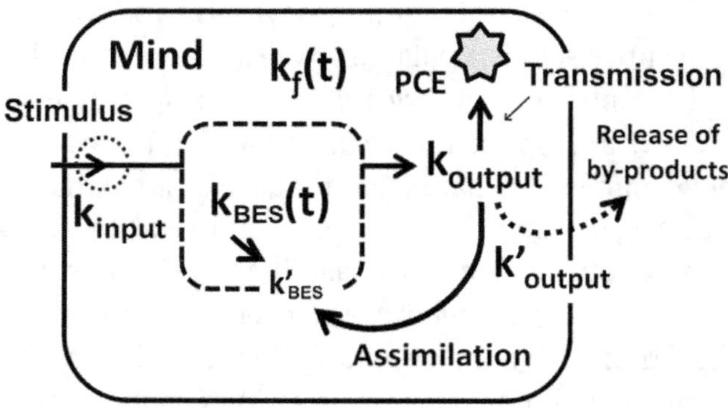

Figure 1.1: A simplified mechanistic depiction, employing different structure functions, of the most elementary mind systematicness facilitating the conversion of triggered inputs into sensation and perception outputs on the way to forming conscious observations.

array of encoded beliefs, k_{BES}, in order to assess the nature of its source in spacetime. This cognitive "processing" (comparing) activity is believed to entail several consecutive steps producing different intermediate products and PCEs which are regarded as essential for the formation of perception and decision making (see Chapter 3). An

---

11 These various structure functions refer to content distributions inside the mind and thus can be alternatively marked as $k'_{mind}(t)$, $k''_{mind}(t)$, and so on. This is also the case for k_{output}, which retains its terminology as an output despite the possibility of staying confined to the latent boundaries of the mind (as highlighted in the figure and in parallel to accepting that some related physical processes may involve emissions outward from the mind). Hence, for now we regard the term "mind output" as a systemic inner product, as in k'_{mind}.

assimilation of the perceptive products yielded, k'_{output}, into the BES memory arrays then establishes a new reference state, k'_{BES}, acting as a standard for the next cognitive assessments. Examining this basic, highly simplified mechanism, we realize that dynamic functions like k_{input} and k_{BES} play a role in determining "what will be experienced"; k'_{output} implies "what may follow as a consequential response", while the "entire toolbox" k_f function addresses "the way in which the experience and response are formed". It should be reemphasized that k_f and k_{BES} are dynamic, and that their changes are as important to the process as their momentary distribution states.

Before moving on, we would like to clarify a few points regarding the preliminary mechanistic interpretation. The first concerns the "functionality" structure function. As expected, due to hereditary replication, we regard the elementary structure-function traits of $k_f(t)$ as common to all humans. This does not contradict variations in the mind content distributions $k_{mind}(t)$ from one individual to another. This situation is comparable, for example, to all of us having the same nose functionality, which is yet structurally different in every person. Naturally, differences between humans also exist in other structure functions, and among them it is especially eminent in k_{BES}, as its respective content is being constantly reshaped by external environmental triggers. Another point to consider is that the simplified mechanism deliberately "secludes" the mind as a human experience and interpretation function while ignoring its physical interactions with the external body surroundings. By doing so, we ignore for now the conversion processes preceding the formation of k_{input} and proceeding the evolution of the k'_{output}-related products in the body.

We now return to the basics of science. In abiding by parts of this broad discipline, we share some "local" similarities in the overall k_{BES} distribution function with other believers. Naturally, we wish that the reader would also share these beliefs with us. The common scientific principles and practices unite a community of believers around them, allowing an exchange and distribution of different observations, interpretations, and occasionally also possible ways to harness these to our (genetic) needs. Such practices are carried out through conventional procedures which employ more-or-less unified "languages", while seeking to find order in nature.[12] This is exemplified by the use of *scientific operators* such as in the generalized expression given by Equation 1.1.

$$(1.1) \quad O_{sci}(k'_{st}) = \kappa_{sci}$$

O_{sci} is an example of a scientific operator which can be shared among different believers. It represents a natural law or a series of laws targeting a spacetime content corresponding to the structure function k'_{st} (in scientific practices k'_{st} often refers to an observation, namely $k'_{st} \equiv k_{observ}$), which can be correlated with a subjective mind projection k_{input} in a certain individual. κ_{sci} marks the O_{sci}-dependent solution or interpretation of the observation. It reflects to the mind of its believers, who do not necessarily need to witness the observation directly, some of the latter's *properties* and/or, for example, the probability to be observed. The properties would occasionally coincide with the projective physical imprints experienced directly or indirectly from the observed structure. Now, we should consider that O_{sci} relies on shared specific beliefs, whereas many other assessments which are not necessarily scientific, relate to other types of beliefs. This statement can be generalized as $O_{belief}(k'_{st}) = \kappa_{belief}$, where $O_{sci} \in O_{belief}$ in some people. Naturally, the choice to rely on specific operator(s), O_{sci} and/or O_{God}, for example, is tightly coupled to the personal distribution of the BES arrays, yet we also believe that it is always carried out through the strict, genetically hardwired systematic perception mechanisms. It is notable that the implementation of the operator requires a fair degree of awareness, which often entails the cognitive function of *concentration*. Among the basic scientific guidelines and principles adopted, we embrace physics as a fundamental discipline that aspires to explore and understand the nature of spacetime via following and contemplating the dynamic interactions between its content ingredients. This brings us to another favored viewpoint in this book, which is physicalistic, suggesting that the entire spacetime and its global and local evolution, and thus also any PCE and belief occurring within it, are based on ongoing physical processes (which

---

12 Standardized communication cannot avert possible discrepancies in interpreting observations. One factor which plays a role in these discrepancies regards the relatively lower matching parts in the k_{BES} functions of the followers which have been shaped by their previous individual experiences (e.g., regarding resembling k_{input}s).

are believed to be causal). One important dimension in this regard is the *time* and its connection to structures and beliefs. Time is commonly accepted as a pivotal element in physics. Its perception is often intuitive to us, possibly due to being indirectly deduced from the spacetime perception indicating subsequential changes in observed situations. Accordingly, it is assumed that the perception of time becomes deeply rooted in our experience-acquired beliefs concerning causal dynamics in spacetime, and which contribute immensely to assessing, predicting, and perceiving changes. A further significance of the time factor stems from the fact that beliefs, including those that are scientific, are subject to changes. With this in mind we accept, for example, that the ever-flowing flux of discoveries is advancing physics through time, although it may occasionally seem to the side observer as if they are stagnating or even following a path of regression.

Nowadays scientific development relies significantly on governmental and industrial capital invested in research. Typically, after being internally and externally criticised, the successful findings facilitated by these funds are often distributed as innovative beliefs. Such practices lead to an ever-growing volume of descriptions and interpretations, attempting both to understand transitions and reactions between dynamic states in nature and to provide causal explanations which are linked to scientific laws, or even to define or redefine them. Consequently, the communicated knowledge serves as a bountiful source for the incremental progression of several distinct, yet connected, established scientific fields. Now, it is clear that all of the details regarding all past and present discoveries and inventions cannot be fully contained in the minds of the science proponents, and that the majority of the information is kept in the external "BES extensions" suggested earlier. We also accept that the distribution of different scientific beliefs between followers occasionally leads to debates which are either being resolved with time or remain unsettled. This question of correctness in scientific disputes will be further addressed here shortly. The aforementioned ideas indicate our desire to abide by various scientific interpretations and guidelines in explaining perception and perception-based behavior. We believe that any attempt to do so must consider a basic bidirectional ascription between human beliefs and physics as a fundamental scientific discipline. Namely, physics is based on a collection of evolving beliefs in spacetime which themselves stem from physical processes in spacetime. From our "semi-objective" outer observation viewpoint, which is bound to this and other belief limitations, we will attempt to describe the conversion processes generating the functionalities of interest in humans.

The idea that spacetime content can be converted to human functionality raises basic questions regarding the nature of the processes in the external-to-the-mind (EM) space preceding and contributing to its triggering. Ahead of the later discussion regarding a possible conceptual distinction between the individual's body and mind contents, we emphasize our compliance with broadly accepted (neuro)physiological interpretations, suggesting that a preliminary conversion stage in the medium attributed to the individual's EM body is essential to experiencing direct sensations and perceptions of EM spatial contents. At this stage we already believe that part of the conversion leading to the experiences takes place in the mind, and thus may assume, upon separately addressing the body and mind as *distinct reference sites* (DRSs),[13] that the transformations are divided between them and require "crossing" their ill-defined physical boundaries (see an extended description in Section 1.3). Given these assumptions, we accept the formation of an unfolding conversion pathway between external-to-the-individual (EI) space, EM body, and mind DRSs is exhibiting different dynamic projections, advancing directions, and physical properties along its trajectories. In this description one may also consider some dynamics in the EI space affecting the stimuli even prior to its triggering the EM body responses that will possibly lead to the mind-processing stage. An important property which we may tailor in this regard to EI contents and seems to be relevant to our discussion is their *basic conversion potential* to induce perception and even awareness in the individual. Some elementary conditions that must be fulfilled before this potential can be possibly realized are for the external content to reach, directly or through mediating carriers, the individual and to initiate a proper structural response in his or her body, allowing the triggering of the conversion process. Relying on anatomy and physiology, we identify the body parts designated for this external activation with the frontal sensory systems. Unsurprisingly,

---

13 We refrain from using the term "entities", as it may imply some sort of independent existence which we believe does not apply in this case.

in the case of EI stimuli, which stays for now in spotlight of our discussion, the success of this triggering stage is crucial to the human functionality of interest. Furthermore, it is not only the arrival of the stimulus and its timing that are essential to realizing the conversion but also the physical-structural *compatibility* between the stimuli and the sensory units. As a matter of fact, this compatibility is believed to be both mandatory and critical throughout all the different proceeding stages of the conversion process. Now, based on our observations and scientific knowledge, we accept that the vast majority of the universal EI content lacks a practical conversion potential since the combined probabilities of its arrival to our sensory systems and potency to successfully interact with them turns out to be negligible. Among the causes preventing the interactions and activation one may highlight, for instance, inherent physical-structural incompatibilities that can be permanent or transient (sometimes requiring synchronization), improper stimulation intensity, insufficient stability, and so forth. At this point we also emphasize the persistent demands for compatibility required in all subsequent steps of conversion of the stimuli inputs to the sensation, perception, and behavior outputs in the human body and mind trajectories. Interestingly, some structures that lack conversion potentials—such as neutrino particles constantly passing through our body in immense ($\sim 10^{14} \cdot \text{s}^{-1}$) quantities and yet, due to their physical properties, have no capability to interact with it—may still be perceived through indirect measurements. The latter detect and report interactions between such entities and other contents that hold a potential to be affected by them and signal these events to us, now in an interactable manner. We assume that in certain cases a present assessment of a given conversion potential might change with time. This can happen, for instance, following circumstances which facilitate the removal of accessibility restrictions to stimuli or hypothetically through long-term evolutionary modifications to our human structures. Our ability to distinguish between spatial contents supporting or lacking conversion potentials enables us to contemplate the hypothetical existence of a *general spacetime* that is valid for its entire content, extending beyond what can be observed and perceived by humans over the course of time. The contents in this general spacetime can be divided at any instant into "perceivable" versus directly and indirectly "hidden" from perception. Among the hidden constituents we may also accept the existence of "dark" content, whose presence is speculative and even probable yet has never been experienced and currently seems immeasurable. Relying on scientific observations, we also accept that immense parts of the general spacetime are correlated with voids containing sparse content at nearly perfect vacuum conditions.

The speculated existence of a general spacetime leads us further to discussing the perceptive concepts of "true" and "false" regarding our interpretations of the states of its locally observed content. To approach this subject, we will examine a well-known case in human history which exemplifies a chronological evolution of beliefs in spatial dynamics. It has long been known that our ancestors noticed dynamics of celestial body movements in the night sky but were not quick to conclude its nature and, as a part of it, that Earth is rotating on its axis—let alone that it is revolving around the sun. Despite certain important, yet of limited impact, early contributions by a few Greek philosophers, until the Copernican revolution of the 16th century AD, the majority of humankind believed in the geocentric model, which claimed the existence of a stationary Earth at the center of the universe. Later observations and calculations, including the extraordinary contributions by Galilei, have eventually established Copernicus's heliocentric interpretations, which have been refined and canonized with time, and are commonly believed still today. Therefore, it is not surprising that almost all of us who live in the modern times adhere to the heliocentric model and regard the ancient geocentric descriptions as a ridiculous "mistake". But are there absolute truths in general spacetime? We have good reason to believe that the biophysical conversion mechanism operating in us humans has not been significantly changed between the eras related to the past and current beliefs and, consequently, the elementary causal correlation between spatial dynamics and its perception has never changed. Clearly enough, the replacement of the astronomical beliefs involved new insights, which were also based on technology-matured observations concerning the spatial dynamics and their interpretations. Yet it also relied on another critical process, which is the successful distribution of "new" beliefs, a process whose efficiency depends on several other human factors. Based on our hypothesis that will be presented later in this book, for existence of an energy perception, we assume that the fate of this distribution is significantly determined by the human struggle over "genetic needs", in which communication often plays a pivotal catalyzing or inhibiting role in the mass assimilation and canonization of certainties (or lack thereof). We also remember that from the individual-level standpoint, changes in existing beliefs and particularly their entire replacement by new ones require overcoming inner organizational resistances in his or her mind. From the historical perspective of the geocentric-heliocentric case exemplified, for instance, we know that, among other factors, resistances stoked by religious beliefs and power-related considerations impeded at first the canonization of the "innovative" astronomical interpretations. Taking it back again to the individual level, we suggest that the probability to reassimilate beliefs depends on both the intrinsic distribution state of the BES in one's memory, reflected in already-present beliefs, and the predicted and assessed self (genetic) benefits related to the new belief and the implications of its acceptance. It is hence not surprising that, as in the exemplified case, a "conservative"[14] human environment led by prominent influencers (see Chapter 4) who attempt to maintain their power within an ongoing struggle provides a strong resistance to changes that might diminish it.[15] Significant changes in beliefs and even their "full replacement" indeed occur and extend from the individual level to the masses. Nevertheless, we reemphasize the essential need in these cases for external circumstances in favor of the BES copying, overcoming compatibility obstacles during the transfer, and at a later stage also an efficient distribution to a critical mass of believers to promote canonization. Looking backwards from our present days on the heliocentric-geocentric dispute, we can argue that in the spirit of the time the claim that the sun revolved around the Earth served as a *reference point for the truth*. This suggests that the truth is a belief as well. As we do not think that back in those days the celestial trajectories were significantly different than now,

---

14 It is interesting to postulate an analogy between the human trait of conservatism and certain mind dynamics acting in the reorganization of the BES memories. The systemic operations may act in stabilizing the arrays against abrupt changes that challenge, for example, genetically favored states and might be considered as taking part in some sort of a mental homeostasis.

15 As implied, communication holds an additional potential to catalyze/inhibit and thus divert the "struggle" between beliefs. It may reduce or enhance resistances through mind activity reorganizing susceptible BES channels while exerting a change in, or alternatively preserving and consolidating, existing beliefs.

we use our historical and scientific perspectives to assume that what has changed with respect to the circumstantial progression is in fact the reference point for truth (which for now is believed to be heliocentric). As suggested, this clearly correlates with the copying and reorganization of some BES mind arrays which have gradually led to the global replacement of these beliefs.[16] In other words, any truth which we adhere to in interpreting spacetime observations is a belief that holds a potential to change and be defined as false in the future. With this in mind, we want to add a few more insights that seem to be relevant to the belief-replacement process discussed. The first intuitively emphasizes that humans do not need to physically meet for this process to take place, as it can be remotely communicated and might even utilize external "BES extensions". Another thought is that the reference point for truth may also remain split between groups and lack global consent and canonization. The size of the group in this case does not imply or correlate with an "absolute truth" which, according to the claims above, does not exist anyway, also due to the chance of being contradicted. This argument remains valid even if we tend to establish a (belief-based) connection between the prevalence of beliefs and their truths. We also assume that the causal conditions required for belief replacement and distribution, including specific energetic-genetic incentives and the need for structural compatibility between the communicators (which may occasionally lead to the reference drifts), are bound to a deterministic progression of the general spacetime.

Despite the necessity for several conditions to be met and coincide in spacetime for them to occur, changes of truth reference points are more frequent than it may seem. In fact, such events do not even require groups of humans and canonization, as they keep appearing at the individual level. This happens transiently, for example, whenever we change our minds regarding the identity of an object after reobserving it. Assuming that the structure of the object has not been significantly changed between the observations, we may attribute the differences in its assessments to a series of *perception-shifting factors* that can rapidly change over time. Among other causes, these

---

16 We note that the term "global replacement" remains a statistical generalization as every individual or a group of humans who desires to do so may align themselves with the former reference point for truth.

include the structural state of the observer's frontal sensory units and their orientation in relation to the external object being observed, duration of exposure to the stimulus, and a range of influences on the internal—body and mind—conversion process. Significant discrepancies between subsequent assessments may also arise due to the predictive nature of the spacetime perception. As was previously noted, we believe that a part of the cognitive assessment focuses on attempting to foresee changes in the observed environment. Unlike in the case of the initial exposure to the object, during the successive "update" assessments the mind already possesses some preliminary information for comparison, which can then be employed for revalidation. This may increase the vigilance and enhance the accuracy of identification, thus affecting the outcome of the newer assessments. Also to be mentioned in this context is the existence of "sensation illusions". In the next chapter, which reviews certain physical aspects of the conversion process, we will assume that under specific conditions a careful selective exposure to different EI stimuli can lead to structurally close body projections eliciting nearly indistinguishable cognitive expressions. The awareness of such events in our lives makes us at times question the reliability of our perceived environment and under certain circumstances even regard some of our experiences as based on sensing illusions. These instances tend to further bring about PCEs related to *suspicion*, which presumably play a role in increasing the resistance of the BES arrays to changing. In parallel to that, it is also intuitive to assume that by increasing the update frequency of the observations and assessments we may better notice the impact of some of the shifting factors and short-term anomalies on perception. In view of these and other concepts, one may conclude that our accrued experience in interpreting spacetime and predicting its dynamics urges us to believe in our capabilities to "reliably" assess it, and on the other hand to accept our occasional "failures" in doing so (also due to the occasional experience of illusions). With this in mind, our discussion returns to disputes between humans and their different reference points for truth. Let's assume a case in which a group of friends has been shortly exposed to a certain object. One individual identified it differently than all the rest, who were united in their assessments. Upon communicating their interpretations to the individual, he or she doubted his or her identification and accepted the friends' impression without further verifying the observation. Now, it is clear that this scenario is replete with subjectivity related to each of the different individuals' personal conversion processes. In a general sense, the case demonstrates that belief replacement may possibly arise solely due to a communicative mediation which is favored in some situations over direct sensory updates. The example may also imply potential correlations between the number of influencers, and/or their extent of mutual agreement concerning the observation,[17] and the probability of accepting their reference for truth. Nevertheless, we reemphasize that the reliability of a "collective truth" is not necessarily superior to an "individual truth", that it is not fully objective even if some subjective factors can be balanced out, and that conforming to it does not automatically guarantee any genetic benefit to a certain individual. It almost goes without saying that the individual may insist on adhering to his or her own truths and refuse to adopt the majority's views[18] or that the latter would ever get canonized. Clearly, the exertion of external forces may also push individuals to change their personal beliefs. In another plausible and prevalent case, discrepancies in beliefs will motivate the individual to update his or her sensory observations and to reexamine objects from a viewpoint contemplating between different reference points of truth. All these point to the tremendous potential that lies at human communication to influence and change beliefs.

1.2 Spacetime content and some of its properties

In Section 1.1 it was claimed that our sensation experiences allow us to postulate an existence of spacetime outside our own bodies containing non-uniform content. Scientific beliefs based on practical observations may further extend the limited reach of the sensations and suggest that the heterogeneity of the content also applies to distant spacetime regions inaccessible for direct, non-mediated, human sensation. The global "anisotropic" heterogeneity, at least on the micro level, allows

---

17 For example, a variety of interpretations among the rest of the observers is likely to have affected the chances for the individual to shift his or her reference for truth.

18 As in the case of the tragic imprisonment of Galileo Galilei who refused to apostate his observations and belief in the revolution of the Earth in orbit around the sun as a part of the heliocentric model.

describing local structures as distributions of spacetime contents from different observation points. Adopting scientific views, we accept that the content, including in the form relevant to our direct sensation, is composed of matter and radiation and holds a scale-dependant particle/wave nature. As was previously mentioned, among other scientific disciplines physics seeks to causally explain the properties of spacetime content and its structural changes. This typically involves understanding dynamic interactions taking place between contents and the interlinked forces they exert on each other.[19] Needless to say, physics deals with a wide range of direct and indirect observations and postulations, which are carried out on different scales and from different investigative points of reference. The observations often match previously recognized laws of nature and interpretations, while in some other cases they may contribute to revising them or even formulate new laws. The fundamental assumption of a causal connection between forces/interactions and structural states allows us to ascribe to many observations a history of changes that have chronologically led to their current state. Accordingly, we may assume that the spatial content has been distributed to its present heterogeneous construction and composition through a long-lasting progression of physical processes. The heterogeneity is also evident from observations indicating the persistent dynamic dispersal in spacetime and the circumstantial change in the properties of sources and carriers. The relative distributions of the sources and their effective interactions with their surroundings provide an important factor in their potential motion, reaction, expansion, and collapse. Processes like these are frequently accompanied by release of matter and/or radiation carriers and may entail interactions with other components of content. Science suggests that during their motion, carriers will circumstantially undergo different processes such as absorption, transmission, reflection, scattering, conversion, and so on.

Next, we wish to emphasize that we conform with some known principles of causal determinism[20] and choose to approach the general spacetime as a materialistic and physicalistic system, whose causal evolution is governed solely by physical events that leave no

---

19 With their fundaments in the four elementary forces of nature.

20 For example: C. Hoefer, Causal Determinism, in *The Stanford Encyclopedia of Philosophy*, edited by E. N. Zalta (2009).

room for transcendental contents and dynamics. While we are aware of the long-lasting controversial debate revolving around these views, we are not discouraged from complying with them[21] due to the lack of a consensual point of reference for their truth. As we believe that the human body and mind constitute an integral physical and corporeal part in the general spacetime, in a similar manner to the rest of the contents; we also expect them to comply with its deterministic dictates. Therefore, we favor the belief that all events taking place in every individual's life, including his or her experienced PCEs and expressed behavior, result from an unfolding physical progression involving a unique dynamic interplay with the effective EI space.[22] One possible implication of this view is that, contrary to our PCE expressions leading us to believe that many of our thoughts, decisions, and actions constitute a reflection of "pure" self-choices and desires, they are all physically dependent on, and deterministically dictated by, the universal evolution of general spacetime. Controlled by external-internal biases which direct us towards these functional outputs, the idea of free will turns accordingly into a very convincing illusion (and an intuitive belief). With that in mind we wish to emphasize that while the deterministic dictates have led to our evolution as living humans who share structural-functional traits like conversion and sensation/perception mechanisms, they have also separated our lifelong trajectories of interactions with spacetime which reflect in our own individual uniqueness.

Two relevant concepts that deserve a brief mention at this stage are *fundamental spacetime components* and *emergence*. Our intuitive daily experiences with matter lead us to believe that many objects can be "broken down" into smaller and smaller components from which they are composed. Science further addresses these beliefs, suggesting, as

---

21 And with several aspects of related interpretations, such as "Laplace's demon", for example (also discussed in M. Van Strien, "On the Origins and Foundations of Laplacian Determinism". *Stud. Hist. Philos. Sci.*, **45**, 24–31 (2014)), which, despite being essentially non-practical and de-batable, does leave a taste of causal determinism, especially when applied in some modified forms to systems of reduced degrees of freedom which are far easier to follow.

22 In addition to the diverse literature relevant to these ideas, we would like to mention the concepts of co-evolution/co-adaptation, which have been suggested in coupling the human to the environment and scrutinizing the evolution process under a global structural determinism. For example, H. R. Maturana, and F. J. Valera, *The Tree of Knowledge: The Biological Roots of Human Understanding.* Boulder, CO: Shambhala Publications (1992); J. Proulx, "Some Differences between Maturana and Varela's Theory of Cognition and Constructivism". *Complexity: An International Journal of Complexity and Education*, **5**, 11–26 (2008).

we all know, that certain forces/interactions describable by general spacetime physical laws hold these components of matter together. Looking in this case at the spacetime content from a reductionist top-down standpoint, science sets a lower limit for the scaled-down convergence. This limit is ascribed nowadays to elementary subatomic particles which are regarded as undividable fundamental components and are theoretically unified by the standard model of particle physics. As expected, the elementary particles are believed to constitute the building blocks for the general spacetime content as well as to lay out the forces shaping its construction and dynamics.[23] Naturally, one should also be aware of some basic limitations concerning the descriptions of such entities. Since the physical approach to content at the lower dimension scale (aiming to derive, for instance, some of its physical functions) often requires assessments of statistical distributions, the uncertainties involved in these probabilities introduce theoretical obstacles to the accuracy of top-down and bottom-up descriptions of nature and its evolution. Besides these challenges, we can mention other complications, such as stochastic processes, whose relevancy to the matter is open for scientific and philosophical discussion. Considering that the physical causes behind such difficulties play an inevitable part in the evolution of spacetime, we will nonetheless apply a reductionist viewpoint, as limited as it is, in depicting the conversion systematicness of the individual. Let's move on now to the well-known concept of emergence. Emergence is believed to account for situations where interactions between an abundance of micro-level components of spatial content become expressed in new properties (and among them, functionalities) observed from their combined macro-level assemblies. We accept that these occurrences do not yield "something out of nothing"[24] and, as such, pose no concern to violating energy conservation principles. Interestingly, some believe that the consciousness and its PCE expressions correspond to emergent properties arising from the neural activity in the central nervous system.[25]

---

23 At least regarding the part of the content as we know it.

24 For example, R. M. Galatzer-Levy, "Emergence". *Psychoanal. Inq.*, **22(5)**, 708–727 (2002).

25 For example, S. R. Brown, "Emergence in the Central Nervous System". *Cogn. Neurodyn.*, **7(3)**, 173–195 (2013); T. E. Feinberg, J. Mallatt, "Phenomenal Consciousness and Emergence: Eliminating the Explanatory Gap". *Front. Psychol.*, **11**, 1041 (2020).

Next, we ask whether all possible contents should be taken into account upon attempting to predict spacetime evolution.[26] In case we seek an ideal/optimal answer and refer to the entire universe, the answer has to be positive. Based on our beliefs in causality and determinism, physicalism, and reductionism, a hypothetical solution encompassing all possible macroscopically observed changes and reflecting all emergent properties, must account for the entire spacetime content. Nevertheless, since the global evolution depends on forces and interactions, the practical contribution of local contents which are almost entirely isolated from other environments to its dynamics might be doubted. A clear example for such a case concerns the sparse content found in cosmic voids (with an average density of ca. one hydrogen atom per cubic meter). Such isolation remains extreme even when considering, for example, the interactive potential of incidentally crossing particles and radiation in these regions, or other minor effects. While it is clear that the basic physical principles also apply to the isolated content in the voids, the severe limitations over its interaction with the external spacetime contents suggest that the entire universe is not an "interactive continuum" and, as such, its contents evolve asymmetrically, from within "localities", rather than as an integrated whole. Now, despite the negligible density of the intergalactic voids, these widespread regions do possess in total a large mass which should be considered by any model attempting to assess the dynamics and evolution of the universe.[27] The idea that effective interactions and significant forces only arise when certain physical conditions are met in spacetime has a critical significance in our attempt to understand human nature. In fact, there is no real need to wander far into outer space in order to acknowledge that interaction fields are also limited in the relatively dense (in this case) environment of our lives, the same environment which triggers conversion mechanisms to yield perceptive interpretations. Unsurprisingly, obstacles over interactions affect the structural organization of the content in

––––––––––––––

26 Acknowledging that any ambitious attempt to realistically calculate this impossible challenge is expected to suffer from limited accuracy and reliability due to the previously mentioned and other limitations.

27 It should be noted that the reported density was measured indirectly and reflects an averaged value, as we cannot communicate directly with (all) these atoms in order to formulate a precise distribution function. This compromise also exemplifies the need to invest energy in communicating with isolated content and trade it with (precision of) information.

nature. One basic instance for that refers to the need for proper local energetic conditions to overcome *potential barriers* before activity/reactivity can occur there. Taking all these into account, we assume that while causal determinism is universal, from an effective macro-scale standpoint (which still considers the energy conservation and spatial restrictions playing in quantum effects such as tunneling, for example) that also concerns the human functionalities, it dictates a multi-site evolution towards specific pathways in compliance with distinct physical barriers. We will refer to this idea as *restricted-contingent deterministic evolution*. Now, whereas the concept of causal determinism might be doomed to remain hypothetical and controversial, its restricted-contingent aspect is more intuitive and can be recognized in our daily experiences. With that said, many individuals adhere to beliefs that contrast the restrictions imposed by nature's barriers. They do so by having faith in what may appear from our reference point for truth perspective as physically impossible interactions and reactions which supposedly control their lives. We will return to these beliefs in Chapter 3 and address their origins in light of the psychoenergetic views to be presented.

We move on now to briefly discuss the universal property of *energy*. In its scientific context, energy typically appears as a measure accompanying structural changes or reflecting the potential of structures to change. These are frequently correlated to physical and other perceived interpretations of the changes and the processes enabling them. Quantitative energy measures are normally obtained through conducting scientific observations and measurements and/or from analysis of past observations/postulations. As the measures ideally correlate with possible transformations between different states of content, they may further be connected to their structures, motion, stability, or potential to elicit a further change. Indeed, physics considers energy to be a universal property which is strongly linked to the local and global spacetime evolution through a variety of scientific beliefs. Based on evidence and concepts that have been collected and developed over the years, one can nowadays use a broad selection of formulated physical laws to provide energetic solutions ($E'_{k'st}$) to defined distributions of content (k'_{st}), as generalized in Equation 1.2.

$$(1.2) \quad H'(k'_{st}) = E'_{k'st}$$

Being a special case of Equation 1.1, this equation exemplifies an assessment in which a specific energetic operator ($H' \in H_{sci} \in O_{sci}$) is selected for the observation. Before introducing some of the challenges involved in the assessment, we emphasize that in many cases its reproducibility and accuracy can be satisfactory for practical human needs, including engineering purposes. Yet, an absolute accuracy can never be reached. Two prominent reasons for that relate to our incompetence in precisely defining the structural distribution k'_{st} and in providing an all-encompassing, perfect H' to solve it. Defining k'_{st}, for instance of an EM content objective, is a projective and subjective challenge that often requires preliminary measurements. Yet, the latter are known to involve objective physical limitations (and subjective others) which are expected to bias the results.[28] All these factors lead to inevitable compromises on the precision of the assessments, yet go hand in hand with our patterned perception of nature, and, as mentioned, currently satisfy most of our engineering needs. Also to be noted is that some of the means to assess k'_{st}, as well as the scientific operators used in its energetic assessment, are not necessarily tenacious and may develop and improve with time.

As was stated above, energy estimations can be used in many cases as a predictive measure for content changes in spacetime and sometimes also for speculating their respective properties. This leads us back to the contingent evolution of nature. The claim that spacetime is developing via multiple events in which potential barriers (to be referred to by "activation energies", E_a) are being crossed allows us to generally regard the activated transformations producing the changes as *reactions*. To describe reactions, we use the basic chemistry notations separating, typically on the grounds of time and structure, the reactant content k_R from its respective converted products k_P, according to Equation 1.3:

$$(1.3) \quad k_R \longrightarrow k_P \ (\text{when } E_R \geq E_a)$$

---

28 As claimed by different quantum mechanical interpretations originating from the Copenhagen interpretation and discussing the idea that observations may cause a quantum superposition collapse, namely in the potency of systems to simultaneously retain multiple eigenstates until measured; for example, R. Omnès, *The Interpretation of Quantum Mechanics.* Princeton, NJ: Princeton University Press (1994). Two common arguments that accompany these interpretations are that our perception follows a series of collapsed eigenstates of reality and that the observations and measurements which allow that, including direct observations which involve the individual's consciousness, exert a consequential impact on the evolution of spacetime. Accordingly, upon their assessment, one may choose to correlate k'_{st} with collapsed wave functions.

Clearly, the specific properties of the reaction, including the entropic changes it entails, number of interacting-reacting components involved and their nature, possible existence of intermediate steps, degree of conversion with respect to the initial amount of k_R, symmetric factors, or its rate depend on the nature of its content and the effective environmental conditions present. Accordingly, we may view the energetically/entropically regulated and restricted evolution of the entire spacetime as being simultaneously carried out through countless, subsequent "Equation 1.3-like" specific reactions (between different reactants), some of which are discrete, but all depend on meeting certain essential conditions at their "active sites" of occurrence. Among these conditions one may typically highlight different-level compatibilities in the reactants' intrinsic structures which at times lead to affinities to react, a close vicinity needed for effective preliminary interactions, and presence of sufficient energy, beyond E_a, to drive the conversion process. When certain observational conditions are also met, we, as external human observers, may sense some of the changes, barriers, and products, and ascribe to them belief-biased identities and qualities. As expected, science goes even a few steps further and uses its massive collection of direct and indirect observations data to establish correlations between structural changes, as reactions of spacetime contents, and their projected energetic states[29] (and distributions in the entropic sense). Scientifically interpreting these correlations also enables us to predict directionality of reactions. It is well-accepted, for example, that nature tends to spontaneously develop in pathways which reduce local potential energy excess and/or increase the degrees of disorder and stability via broadening energetic distributions of products. Such inclinations and the related physical laws that were found to describe them allow us to estimate and predict reactions' pathways, rates, barriers, ways to accelerate or inhibit them, and so forth. Now, as we view the biophysical mechanism leading to our perception as an integral part of nature's progression, these assessments are expected to be applied to it as well. As this idea appears to be intuitive from a physicalistic perspective, we will later postulate a correlation between (energy-oriented, for instance) basic

---

29 One common example is the thermodynamic evaluation of energy changes caused by reactions upon considering physically equilibrated states of the reactants and the products with their surroundings. Such changes typically correspond to differences between the energy-projected solutions of the products $H'(k_P)$ and the reactants $H'(k_R)$.

laws of nature and the operational mechanisms of cognition that supposedly yield perception. Interestingly, the universality of energy and its total conservation may assist us in simplifying and relating descriptions of the various conversion processes generating the human sensoresponsive functionality to be discussed in the next chapter. That is, the cumbersome need to continuously elaborate many complex physical, chemical, and biological processes can thus be replaced by a "bird's eye", reduced yet seamlessly flowing, projective view that is united by the global scientific "language" of energy transitions. As will be shown, this simplified description will encompass several physical and physiological processes which delineate a "cyclic" directionality between the EI spacetime, the EM body, and the mind. Further relevant to our discussion is the physical quantity of *frequency*. Considering its fundamental relations to spacetime content and energy,[30] we may regard frequency as universal as well. The microscopic-level intersection of structures and frequencies might imply on a possible, emergence-corrected, correlation[31] between structure (see chapt. 1, n. 9) and frequency functions and the use of the latter in describing universal contents and some of their structure-related properties. One possible implication of this assumption is that every local change in spacetime can alternatively be expressed by changes in frequency functions. And from a different perspective, it might be that every fruitful reaction between contents requires a resonant compatibility between their frequency functions, or at least no strong dissonance, as a contingent prerequisite to its feasibility.

Also of interest is the concept of *functionality*. We perceive objects as functional upon believing that they produce an impact which serves a certain purpose behind its execution. In this context, we further refer to *functional systems* as constructions generating functionality in an organized and systematic manner. Methodologically converted "outputs" of functional systems can be cognitively processed by human observers, who ascribe them with an "essence" linked to beliefs regarding the specific purpose that they serve. While the perceived functionality does not necessarily benefit the observer, his

---

30 One example is the fundamental Planck-Einstein equation. It is further interesting to think that correlating spacetime contents to frequencies brings out some aspects of time dimension to the former.

31 Acknowledging the uncertainties related to the determination of both.

or her estimations of it typically entail an inevitable subjectivity that is often normalized, also linguistically, by patterned categorized beliefs. Let's consider a few examples. The functionality of a pen as a basic writing tool is widespread among humans. Our experiences indicate a common practice in which investment of energy in pressing down and moving an object identified and classified as a "pen" over a structure recognized as a "substrate" in a way that its tip touches the latter and discharges an ink component generates a new structure whose impact is externally experienced as a "drawing" and sometimes interpreted as "writing". Clearly, this description does not necessarily imply that every repetition of these events forms a drawing, that this is the only recognizable functionality of the pen, or that there are no other objects and dynamics[32] in spacetime that can yield similar results. It should also be noted that in this example both the absorbing substrate and the external force exerted by the human as the "stimulus" for the process are mandatory for the drawing functionality of the pen.

Next, we refer to the ink and the cap components assumed to be included in the pen. Despite the fact that it can be replaced, by virtue of its role as a "sensation marker" projecting (assisted by light) the formation and the pattern of the drawing onto the mind of the observer, the ink holds an integral and essential part in the pen's systematic operation, which leads to its perceived functionality as a tool for writing and drawing. This is clearly evident upon the dysfunction of the tool in the absence of ink. Unlike the ink, the cap is being temporarily moved by the individual to cover or expose the tip of the pen, and its functionality is basically identified with avoiding the ink from drying up while the pen is not in use. These examples highlight our ability to perceive different sub-functional processes/elements contributing their *componential functionality* to the macro functionality observed, and which refers in the case under consideration to generating the drawing. This concept is clearly also valid when describing, for instance, the componential contributions of different body organs to

---

32 Patterned recognition and categorized descriptions of objects and dynamics contribute to concealing their uniqueness, which is frequently evident in perception of functionality. For example, we ascribe the same functionality to different pens possessing various structures and topological or other characteristics. This is also the case for a pen whose exact structure has been modified between uses, yet its linguistic and perceptual identities are retained. Furthermore, the functionality of any given pen may be tailored to the present situation defining its use. These can be circumstantially associated, for example, with writing, trading, tearing things, using it as a bookmark, and so on.

the emergence of the overall human functionalities observed.[33] At this stage we would like to briefly refer to the implementation potential of functionality. While tending to rely on accrued experiences that demonstrate more or less a similar outcome from repeatedly triggered functional systems, we identify a general human inclination to ascribe *potential functionality* to objects, which might differ from their present observation (applied) *practical functionality* or unfunctional state. A pen placed on a table and perceived by a human observer as a writing tool serves a good example for this.

We are also interested in the perceived characteristic of *complexity*. Among different modern approaches to complex systems,[34] we aim to address the concept of *physical complexity* through employing several examples that involve comparative assessments. Let's examine two local content constructions, "AA" and "AAA", composed of a variable number of repetitive units of the ideally identical ingredient "A". Assuming a fair definition of the structure distribution functions of these contents, we may use Equation 1.2 to assess their relevant energetic solutions from as many scientifically applicable and multi-scale perspectives as possible and compare their E^{AA} versus E^{AAA} descriptions.[35] One way to assess the physical complexities of the contents is by analyzing the length of their communicative—verbal or written—energetic descriptions. The longer description expected, in accord with the above-mentioned conditions, for E^{AAA} as compared to E^{AA} suggests that, due to the energetic implications of its additional ingredient, AAA is the relatively more complex construction. To decrease complication (see below), we assume that the descriptions are optimally carried out in the most succinct and efficient way possible.[36] We also acknowledge that the

---

33 The driving force behind the generation of these functionalities can be discussed from different perspectives. At the most fundamental level, we may associate it with the energetic/entropic propensities of the general spacetime, while viewing the generation of life functions as contributing to the evolution of nature.

34 For example, Y. Bar-Yam, General Features of Complex Systems, *UNESCO Encyclopedia of Life Support Systems*, EOLSS UNESCO Publishers (2002).

35 Or, more practically, to a certain high degree of elaboration and precision. The use of an energy projection was preferred due to its universality. By directly comparing possible structural descriptions of k^{AA} and k^{AAA} distributions, some intra-/interactive aspects, which might be regarded as important to the physical complexity, would have been lost.

36 Among the ideal conditions preferred, we require the human performing the comparison to have a knowledge of the scientific assessments and to be able to conduct them swiftly in order to minimize the probability of significant structural changes occurring in the meantime.

assessments involve a great deal of subjectivity even if the comparison is being carried out by the same person. An additional challenge is posed by the scientific operators which are, as stated before, limited, belief-related, and sometimes "meta-stable" throughout the evolution of science. Nevertheless, these should suffice at the level of objectivity-seeking determination of relative physical complexities. To refine the results, the assessment might be repeated among a group of motivated and qualified individuals who possess, or can be imparted on with (on site) adequate scientific knowledge to separately assess the objectives compared. The most comprehensive yet "efficient" descriptions of the assemblies would then be decided, and their lengths would be compared. A strict implementation of the conditions above is expected to yield a decent correlation between the length of the descriptions and the physical complexities of their objectives. The results can also serve as a database reference for similar future assessments and comparisons. Moving on to a different example, we now aim to compare the assemblies AA and AB. Evidently, this case explores two content ingredients with non-identical compositions. In the absence of the analysis suggested, we would probably regard AB as the more complex content since we tend to intuitively associate this characteristic with its heterogeneous asymmetric nature. Yet, from the viewpoint of the physical complexity, we must also consider the forces acting internally—inside and between the different components—and occasionally also their interactions with the external environment. Hence, one should also consider situations in which, compared to the second "A" component in AA, the presence of the "B" unit in AB is associated with more modest physical effects, as is expected to be evident from the energetic assessments suggested. Generally speaking, the estimation of complexity in daily life situations does not need to rely on similarly performed calculations, yet it probably exploits the aforementioned TCAs and OCAs as well as the cognitive skills of recognition and comparison involved in the "classical" spacetime perception. These may entail Gestalt psychology or other related principles assisting the rapid patterned assessment of key characteristics related to the observed content. A striking difference between the approaches can be demonstrated by comparing, for example, the complexity of a bucket filled with grains of sand and a little creature such as a fly. From the quantitative physical assessment point of view, the static organization of the vast amount of sand grains, each with its unique composition and orientation in the assembly, seems to be more complex than the fly's construction regarding its far fewer building blocks. Nevertheless, due to the detectable emergence of life functions in the fly (which are indeed based on complex biophysical dynamic reactions absent in the lifeless sand and that might not be reflected through the formerly suggested "static" methodology), it is often regarded as the more complex object in the comparison. Indeed, one may refer to *complexity of dynamic processes* in nature and, later on, we will focus on this exact property in regard to the human conversion processes. Interestingly, the associative linkage made between complexity and functionality holds a potential for some profound questions. A physiological failure which differentiates a dead creature from a living one within a short time interval is an example for two highly complex states of content with only one sustaining complex functionality. In a somewhat related example, we compare the two content assemblies, AB and AAABAAA. The "A" and "B" components are respectively ascribed in this case with inert and reactive characters towards a certain external factor. Now, as AB contains fewer building units, at first glance it seems to be the less physically complex assembly. Yet, as implied by the formulas, on the grounds of its structurally enhanced reactivity due to the relatively more facile access of exterior substrates to the "B" unit, AB appears as the more complex content in terms of potential functionality. The various examples indicate our wish to keep the definition of complexity versatile as we may take advantage of the human arsenal of cognitive tools and scientific beliefs to explore it in different situations from various standpoints. The use of complexity and functionality in characterizing spacetime content, and especially regarding dynamic processes, is of importance to this book and also to the next section, which deals with a conceptual differentiation between the individual's body and mind.

Next, a distinction will be made between physical complexity and *complication* in the sense of *convolution*. Similar to complexity, complications can be scrutinized from different perspectives, and we specifically prefer to relate them here to efficiency losses. It was recently suggested that one way to estimate physical complexity may require succinct yet detailed and accurate projective descriptions of spacetime content. In accord with our human capabilities, such assessments are expected to yield descriptive parts, sometimes valid by themselves, which are not optimized in terms of the required criteria. Any excessive elaboration of the physical projection can thus be regarded as a decrease from the "peak efficiency" attributed to the optimal estimation. This situation resembles two computer programs that use similar logic principles in yielding an identical output from a single input, yet their codes vary in length due to unnecessary excessive additions in one of the two, which could have been eliminated without impacting the computation results. The excessive code, in analogy to the excessive description in the more complicated case, for example, consumes additional energy[37] that is ostensibly invested "in vain", and from another point of view, computational resources and cognition-oriented work have been seemingly wasted on the excessive compositions. The cumbersome nature of these cases is accordingly identified here with complication. In analogy to complexity, we can also associate complications with spacetime patterns which are perceived as being hard to solve or interpret, namely requiring an extra investment of energy and/or time in doing so. Interestingly, from the viewpoint of our limited lifetime, these can be regarded as a loss of "potential functionality" or as decreasing our "functional efficiency". One may also realize that while functionality and (physical) complexity are frequently perceptually correlated, we tend to associate a lower degree of complication with the former.

At this stage we would like to introduce a hypothetical characteristic that will be attributed to functional systems and referred to as their *individuality dimension* (*ID*). Prior to the forthcoming discussion, we already note that the ID will be ascribed with high importance as a potential physical-based causal linkage between stimuli impacts, core perceptions, and human behavior. Having that in mind, for now we aim to generally explore the individuality dimension in regard to any "standard" input/output conversion system supporting functionality, irrespectively of humans and their lives. To this end we will employ several "ideal" assumptions, which might be utterly hypothetical and impractical yet might help our descriptions later. In defining the ID, we assume that spacetime contains conversion systems (circumstantially being sensed and perceived plainly as "objects"), whose structures causally change upon interacting with certain external triggers referred to as their "stimuli". Under proper conditions, the arrival of a stimulus to such a system will activate a "reception" reaction, marking

---

37 Which may also be indicated following the integration of electric computing power over a longer processing duration.

it with a local structural impact referred to as an "input" projection. A conversion process of this impact may then begin, whereby subsequent transformations within the system's structure will finally yield an output response ascribed with a certain identified functionality. We further assume that the entire process, from triggering to functionality, is being monitored by an "ideal ID detector" that can follow the physical-structural progression at a reduced microscopic level and can transduce it to our minds. Therefore, the individuality dimension is defined as the specific, time-dependent, highest possible informative structure or energy distribution function of the system during the generation of the functionality. By assuming a trajectory based on a finite number of consecutive conversion reactions (stages) starting with the triggered inputs and ending with the functional response outputs detected, the ID is further expected to project the "trail/s" of the transformative progression within the system.[38] The trajectories formed abide by the restricted-contingent progression principles required for the unfolding interactions and reactions accompanying the conversion process. As part of the "ideality" of the ID monitoring, we assume that the detection efficiency is optimal at all times and that the obtained projections are of high reliability and accuracy. Also, we deliberately omit from the description any possible physical uncertainties and disturbances to the measurement, including collapse of wavefunctions to single eigenvalues and the system's eigenstates due to the observations (see chap. 1, n. 28), ineradicable background noises, technical limitations to the sensing, and other related challenges. These defy practicality and suggest that IDs will always remain hypothetical characteristics of conversion systems. Ahead of the discussion to follow, we may already accentuate that the ID is a reflection of changes complying with the general physicalistic and deterministic dictates of nature, and that at high intrinsic complexity levels of the conversion system its ID projection is also expected to demonstrate a transformative *uniqueness*.[39] In living systems, for example, some of the factors contributing to such levels

---

38 From which measurable macroscopic properties can circumstantially emerge (such as those associated with human physiology).

39 This complexity-uniqueness connection does not contradict the possibility for relatively simpler systems of fewer conversion stages to be unique as well, especially upon reckoning with their microstructural levels.

of complexity are the diverse conversion tracts and their structural-functional branching, formation of multiple output functionalities, time-related effects and synchronization between transformations, among others.[40] Nevertheless, we still assume that the systematic conversion which forms the functionality takes place in a finite, albeit sometimes large, number of restricted-contingent, sequential, and coupled steps. This poses a theoretical, contrarily to practical, limit to the system's possible structural divergence.[41] In view of these ideas, we believe that the uniqueness of a stimulus-triggered complex functional system can be expressed within a wide, yet theoretically confined, *variation spectrum* of its intrinsic structural-physical systemic conversion states. This idea has certain implications relevant to our later discussion regarding interpretations of human responses to stimuli among different individuals. Another assumption concerns a functional system whose conversion reactions are susceptible to a broad range of influences. We expect that the accumulated impact of the latter will shift the conversion (within the broad variation spectrum of its feasible states) while generally decreasing its plain "linear nature", "robot-like" response expectancy. Accordingly, we will refer to this effect as "nonlinear". Regarding complex functional systems, we also believe that certain parts of their conversion routes can occasionally show higher susceptibility to certain influences in comparison to others. This, we suspect, particularly applies to the human mind.

Following the introduction of the above-stated definitions and assumptions, from this stage on, we will focus on the ID of the human being and associate the paramount functionality relevant to this projection with the broad concept of life and its genetic dictates (or with any sub/componental functionality of our choice within this range, such as perception and/or perception-based behavior). The upper dot notation, for example, in "$\dot{x}$", will be employed to indicate

---

40 As might be expected, we believe that some of these evolve from an externally biased expression of non-identical genetically encoded core structures. The human ID footprints are thus inherently coupled at any given observation time to the complexity of the living individual. It should be noted that within these we also find specific mind structures, such as BES, which effectively contribute to the conversion.

41 Interestingly, another factor which can be viewed as obstructing this divergence in living systems such as humans is the homeostatic activity attempting to counteract destructive shifts from genetically directed equilibria.

individuality, suggesting in this case that the element "x" takes a physical part in, or reflects a perceivable property related to, the human conversion process yielding functionality, and which can be described by a respective ID projection. It should be emphasized that when referring to a certain "x" and describing its nature or function at a given moment, it might not yet be clear whether it will practically contribute to the entire functionality. Accordingly, we will occasionally need to refer to "x" as a potential to turn into "ẋ" and address its present questioned compatibility in the system to continue contributing to a possible generation of functionality. Attempting to write with a pen whose cap has not been removed, thus preventing the transfer of ink to a sheet of paper or trying to see the environment with one's eyelids closed are examples of "failed" states of delimited compatibility in terms of producing functionality. This section aimed to combine our intuitive belief in the existence of spacetime with several naturalistic/scientific concepts in order to highlight certain perceivable properties and attribute them to local contents presumably existing in the former. Whereas some properties are sensed and perceived by directly observing "accessible parts" of nature, others involve interpretations based on mediated information. The beliefs in general spacetime and its perceivable properties lead us next to a short discussion addressing the human individual as an integral part of nature which is simultaneously functioning in observing it and responding to it.

1.3 Distinct reference sites for an individual human

It is common knowledge that due to their persistent exchange of energy and matter with the external environment, human beings are regarded as open thermodynamic systems. As one can understand, this scientific term and its implications take a natural part in the physicalistic materialism abided by here. Holding such uncompromising monistic views and considering the above thermodynamic statement, we ponder whether it is possible at all to discuss the human as a distinct functionality, observing spacetime and physically interacting with its content while being an inseparable part of it. This "half-objective" question revolves around *a conceptual distinction* between two belief-based references to content—the individual and the entire spacetime—under conditions where the human cannot be deemed as a physical entity independent from the latter (from an energetic standpoint, for example). This challenge leads us back to the aforementioned possibility to conceptually differentiate the individual from his or her respective outer spacetime content, and to similarly perform an artificial separation between the individual's mind and external body. In accord with the distinctions, we refer to the EI spacetime,[42] EM body, and mind,[43] as different DRSs united under our monistic views which encompass all general spacetime elements. It should be noted that while there is a fair amount of asymmetry in the distinction, mostly due to our conspicuous incapability to perceive almost the entire EI spacetime, it can still be supported among other factors by intuitive "Descartesian" insinuations such as regarding the *self* and its perception. The self will be referred to here, and in more depth in the first section of Chapter 3, as an *own reference function* that is both shaped by and used in the systematic assessments establishing the individual's core perceptions (and which relates to specificity in the organization patterns of certain mind assemblies). Earlier in this chapter we postulated that two individual core spacetime perceptions are the "classical" perception (CP), allowing the human to recognize and believe in his or her surrounding and in some of nature's properties and structures, and the energy perception (EP), enabling the individual to ascribe significances to CP-identified spacetime objects and dynamics mainly with respect to their potential contribution to realizing his or her direct or projected goals. To these we now add the *perception of the self* as another systemic core element that subjectively reflects a dynamic set of cognitive self-assessments whose PCEs occasionally reach the individual's awareness.[44] Experiencing our own self, it can also be analogized to some kind of mind-situated singularity to which the sensed EI spacetime and many of its interpretations are

---

42 Based on our sensory experiences and their interpretations, also regarding functionality, we indubitably expect the EI world to further include other distinct objects such as other individuals and living creatures' minds.

43 The mind is viewed at this stage as a spatial content that is organic to the body and contributes to the overall human functionality in certain ways, some entailing PCEs which potentially emerge from causal changes in its structure.

44 The perception of the self will be correlated in Chapter 3 to the individual's self-narrative. The latter resembles in a way a frequently updating, life-long autobiographic movie in which he or she is intermittently taking the roles of player, camera man, director, producer, and (occasionally critical) observer.

ostensibly converging into or relative to. Such personal—yet shared by all humans—PCEs may be perceived as intuitively supporting the distinction without violating the integrated existence of the individual in general spacetime.

Schematically illustrated in Figure 1.2(A) is the idea that from the viewpoint of every human, his or her own EI spacetime consists of other individuals (see chap. 1, n. 42) who share with him or her comparable conversion systematicness and basic functionality (f_{human}). These common traits are broadly accepted as being established by heredity-based genetic expressions in the forms of anatomy and physiology (GEAP). We have recently postulated that similarities in GEAP among humans may relatively limit the wide "variation spectrum" of their internal structural dynamics of conversion, and thus also the divergence in observed human responses, upon interacting with given spacetime stimuli.[45] The limited variation spectrum concept allows us to generalize our mechanistic descriptions from the specified individual level to the entire humanity. It should be noted that to some extent we also share certain biophysical mechanisms and behavioral traits with other living species whose functionalities are marked by the generalized $f_{non\text{-}human}$ notation in Figure 1(A). With that said, we believe that the human susceptibility and adaptations to a variety of biases and flexible capabilities to implement functionality which occasionally demonstrates outstanding complex features, are exceptional among all known living species. Unsurprisingly, it is suspected that the contributions of the mind to shaping this functionality play a key factor in its complex nature. As science indicates a high degree of structural and dynamic organizational complexities in anatomical body units like the central nervous system and especially the brain, we suspect that there might be a connection between the latter and the latent mind, whose complex functions possibly emerge from. Millennia-long debates over the concept of the mind, its physical or transcendental essence, existence as a separate entity or an integral body organ, and possible

---

45 Nevertheless, it should be reemphasized that due to the immense complexity of the entire GEAP-based human assembly, the accumulated specific structural changes in every person during life, and the physical variations in the interactions between humans and their external environments, a case of an absolute structural identity between individuals is highly improbable. Consequently, we also regard each individual's transient internal constructions, experiences (including self perception and qualia), and responses to the external surroundings (and thus also local contributions to the evolution of general spacetime) to be unique at the absolute level.

body-mind interactions between such identities, have been persistently occupying philosophers' and scientists' minds despite never being fully resolved. Many associate the mind with PCEs reflecting feelings, emotions, thoughts, memories, and other transmitted conscious expressions. As was previously mentioned (see chap. 1, n. 25), some suggested that these express a biophysical emergence originating from the neural electrochemical activity taking place at the central nervous system. Committed to compliance with the materialistic approach, we favor to correlate here the mind with body (brain) processes whose exact structural changes and features, including the possibly emerged (neuro)physiology, will be considered latent.[46]

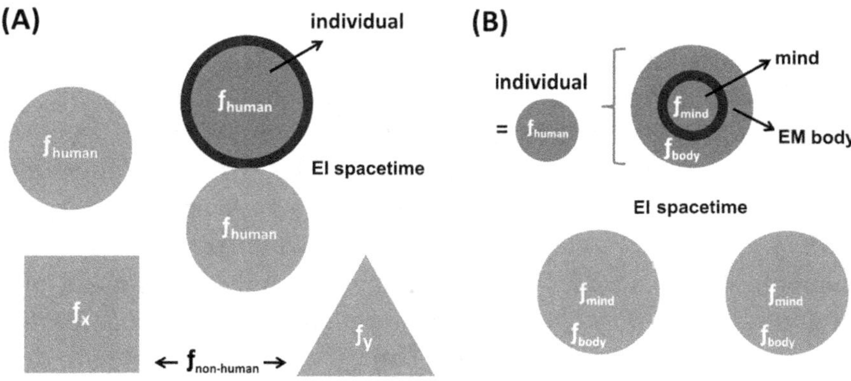

Figure 1.2: Schematic illustrations of the functional distinctions (marked by thick lines) made in perceiving each of the "EI spacetime/individual human" and "EM body/mind" pairs, highlighting (A) the existence of comparable other human (f_{human}) or different ($f_{non-human}=f_x,f_y,...$) functionalities in the individual's external spacetime and (B) the fundamental functionality differences between the mind (f_{mind}) and its external body (f_{body}) in every living individual. While the comparable f_{human} functionalities result from hereditary functions between humans, their expressions are naturally diverged as every living individual's body and mind possess unique structures reflected by his or her transient ID.

---

46 Certain theories are known to postulate latent mind processes and units, not necessarily in the context of their distinction from the body, and among them some written by my father Benjamin Tel-Vered. For example: B. P. Tel-Vered, *Theory About the Perception Schemes: A Hypothesis about the Essence of the Mind.* Self-published (2001), and here: https://sites.google.com/telvered.com/www-telvered-com/benny-tel-vered.

As such, the mind is believed to integrate massive amounts of data from all relevant DRSs and to form the above-mentioned PCE expressions on the way to systematically directing the individual's perception-based behavior. The decisions to regard the mind as latent and approach its structure and/or physiology accordingly are based on significant and unresolved gaps in understanding its overall functioning and the precise nature of the PCEs accompanying its activity. From a wide perspective, some of these obstacles might be related to the inevitable inextricability limitation mentioned earlier. Of course, this does not contradict an abundance of theories proposed in the area, aiming to provide possible physical, physiological, and mechanistic interpretations to the mind, but which have never been turned into a consensual "truth" overcoming the diverse controversial aspects of the dispute. Adhering to the materialistic beliefs, we do assume that the mind originates from body content, yet based on the uncertainties and gaps in its understanding and definition, it can still be conceptually differentiated from the brain, probably its most fitting and natural anatomic unit to associate it with.[47] This possible structural congruence yet conceptual distinction will be referred to herein as the *assumption of mind/brain correlation* and abbreviated as "mind/brain". Even if only symbolic and semantic, the distinction between the individual's mind and external body will aid the exploration of the mind-conversion processes by avoiding some of the complexities associated with their possible anatomic and physiological descriptions.

The two coupled pairs, "EI spacetime/individual (body and mind)" and "EM body/mind", show some relative resemblances. One similarity, for example, concerns the suspected dependence of the individual on the EI spacetime and the mind on the EM body. In both cases the continuous functioning of the former "site" requires a seamless external matter/energy supply from the latter, which is reflected by transitions from the EI spacetime, through the EM body, to the mind.[48,49]

---

47 Supported, for example, by current capabilities to monitor in-vivo brain regions and correlate local neural activity with processing changes triggered by specific stimuli as well as with the accompanying PCEs experienced throughout these reactions.

48 We acknowledge that part of the energy transferred is being allocated to the preservation and maintenance of the overall GEAP construction essential to the production of functionality.

49 Assuming a mind/brain correlation, it is commonly accepted, for example, that neural cells that might play an active role in the functionality produced by the mind rely on EM body supply and convert it to free energy at their mitochondria organelles.

Furthermore, the directionality behind the dependency is relentlessly evident during a sustained deprivation/absence of external supply from the EI spacetime. Under such conditions, the consequential damage to the highly organized body and mind assemblies— typically as irreversible structural changes—is expected to result in discontinuation of the individual's abilities to further recruit essential energy resources. Without a third-party intervention, prolongation of this state will disrupt and then cease the individual's body and mind functions, hence causing him or her to die. Incidents like this may hint that one major purpose of the mind is to direct the body to recruiting external energy. We believe that such actions are required for the realization of several human goals, which will be identified in the next section as "genetic" (they can also be alternatively referred to as "hereditary goals" by those who prefer to make the distinction). Looking from a broad perspective, this corresponds to an interesting situation where, in a spacetime—whose contents spontaneously tend to change/react in manners and paths that locally minimize their potential energy—the mind is systematically directing the individual to conserve and even enhance his or her potential energy resources (see also a related discussion in Chapter 3). Acknowledging the investment required for the recruitment processes, spacetime's entropic gains through sustenance of active metabolism and some behavioral responses in living organisms, and that possession is in the end a belief-based interpretation, we accept that such mind-directed reactions to the environment do not violate the universal energy conservation and comply with the fundamental laws of nature. Considering the causal energetic dependencies in the life-sustaining EI spacetime→EM body→mind trajectory, it is interesting to think about these DRSs as bidirectional relays, both transmitting and receiving (with an exception forbidding a direct transition from the EI spacetime to the mind; see Chapter 2). This energy transfer pathway can further be viewed as cyclic, with mind/brain outputs contributing both directly and through body responses to the local development of the EI spacetime (see chap. 1, n. 28). Another distinction that can be made in accord with our assumptions is between the *individual's mind energy*, as a projection of his or her mind content which may be regarded as hypothetical due to its challenging definition behind the latency, and his or her respective and similarly hypothetical *EM body energy*. Now, despite the points of resemblance between the two pairs of sites, they also show some asymmetries. For example, contrary to the existence in the EI spacetime of every individual of multiple humans with fundamentally similar functionalities, prominent functionality differences always exist in every EM body/mind pair, shown in Figure 1.2(B). At this point we would also like to note that our premise regarding the latency of the mind in the body does not necessarily disprove, for example, a hypothetical situation in which several minds are ascribed to a single human. Preferring to avoid such potential complications, we adhere to Occam's razor principle,[50] which lets us simplify the discussion through reducing it to a single-mind scenario. In this part we have conceptually distinguished the human from his or her external spacetime and his or her mind from its outer body. The attribution of these presumably physically connected spacetime contents to separately addressed DRSs will later allow us to examine interactions and reactions occurring in and between them and to follow their restricted-contingent energy transfer patterns throughout the generation of living human functionality and its physical impact on general spacetime.

1.4 Genetic goals and the foundations of human functionality

The earliest biophysical indications for the beginning of the individual human's life can be associated with the fertilization process, which leads to the assembly of a zygote with 46 chromosomes which are equally contributed by the merged sperm and egg cells.[51] In this genetically encoded construction, to be referred to by the structure function $k_{inherited}$, we favor seeing the *individual's nucleus of life*, a local content which contains a hereditary "action plan" designated to motivate the individual to fulfill several *genetic goals*. Being inherited to all its individuals through a unified replication mechanism, the genetic goals

---

50 For example, J. Feldman, "The Simplicity Principle in Perception and Cognition". *WIREs Cogn. Sci.*, **7(5)**, 330–340 (2016); P. Domingos, "The Role of Occam's Razor in Knowledge Discovery". *Data Min. Knowl. Disc.*, **3(4)**, 409–425 (1999).

51 The main indications for the initiation of life-related activity correspond in this case to the self-organization processes observed in the zygote right after its formation and from which the embryo is eventually developed. As basic characteristics of this activity are absent prior to the merging of the ingredient cells, we tend to view the zygote as the incipient assembly implementing construction-conservation living functions in every human.

are not only important at the individual level but were first and foremost meant to serve the evolution of the entire human species. Parallel to the ongoing interactions between $k_{inherited}$ and the *effective EI spacetime* (k_{st}^{eff}),[52] which corresponds at this initial stage to the mother's womb, the nucleus's bioorganic components, including relevant remnants from the development of the egg, will start executing the genetic instructions for implementing the first steps of the action plan aimed to assemble the body arrays (from which those ostensibly related to the mind will also soon emerge). We correlate the beginning of this activity with the initiation of the *individual human time* at $t_{observed}=\dot{t}_0$. An execution of genetically regulated meiotic divisions at this stage further marks the beginning of a *construction-conservation functionality* (*CCF*), which allows us to regard an emerging (pre)body[53] identity and treat its dynamic structure function as $\dot{k}_{body}(t_{observed}>\dot{t}_0)$.[54] Namely, the beginning of the individual human time is ascribed to the ephemeral transition $\dot{k}_{inherited}(t_{observed}=\dot{t}_0)\longrightarrow\dot{k}_{body}(t_{observed}>\dot{t}_0)$ at which time the CCF becomes a key element in the regulated formation of required anatomic and physiologic functions. Now, one may notice that in conjunction with the raising prominence of the CCF, the structure function of the nucleus $\dot{k}_{inherited}(\dot{t}_0)$ is marked with "individuality". In this regard, we can also relate the uniqueness of the functional expressions of the human zygotic nucleus to its genetically encoded[55] and labile bioorganic substance ingredients. Furthermore, it is important to reemphasize that despite a possible impression that the early developing human content is fully autonomous in conducting its self-assembling and maintenance

---

52 Among the different substrates taking part in these dynamics during the pregnancy, we highlight the secretion of growth hormones in the placenta. These are commonly known to regulate the metabolism of the mother and affect fetal growth. For example, H. A. Barrera-Saldaña, B. M. Contreras-Garza, and S. A. Barrera-Barrera, The Role of the Human Growth Hormone Gene Family in Pregnancy. In *Growth Disorders and Acromegaly*, edited by R. G. Ahmed, and A. Uçar (2019). IntechOpen. 10.5772/intechopen.89011.

53 Despite ascribing the developing content to the body, at this early stage it still contains no recognizable or functioning organs.

54 In Chapter 2 we will further distinguish physically and arithmetically between the body and the mind and use a general construction (GC) notation to better describe the individual's content regardless of the emergence and functioning of these DRSs.

55 It is known, for instance, that uniqueness due to rare mutations is also found in the chromosomes of genetically paired monozygotic twins. For example, J. Weber-Lehmann, E. Schilling, G. Gradl, D. C. Richter, J. Wiehler, et al., "Finding the Needle in the Haystack: Differentiating 'Identical' Twins in Paternity Testing and Forensics by Ultra-Deep Next Generation Sequencing". *Forensic Sci. Int. Genet.*, **9**, 42–46 (2014).

activities, it remains thermodynamically open and relies on substance/energy supply from the effective environment of the womb. We may thus assume that until the individual's birth his or her dynamic body orientation inside the womb and the individuality states (reflected by the IDs) of his or her carrying mother have a certain impact on his or her self-development. Expanding this to a lifelong perspective which continues with the death of the human at t_{death}, we may regard the individual's content and emerged functions at a given observation time as projecting on the incremental, circumstantial evolution of the initial life nucleus $\dot{k}_{inherited}(t_0)$, while considering persistent interactions between the evolved human products and their effective external environment $k_{st}^{eff}(t_{death} > t_{observed} > t_0)$.

So far, we have correlated the initial stages of the individual's development with CCF. In fact, some basic aspects of this functionality will remain active throughout the entire life of the human. During the first year of life, two meaningful events occur: First is the beginning of significant cognitive activity in the developing mind at an individual time corresponding to t_{0m}.[56] Considering the mind/brain correlation, the activity might be ascribed to a certain state of maturity of the nervous system. Second is the birth of the individual at t_{birth} and his or her physical disintegration from the carrying body of the mother. Such meaningful events are accompanied by a rapid expansion in the functionality of the human. Lacking self-survival skills at birth, the individual undergoes an impactful transfer from full and "stable" dependency in the mother's womb to a more dynamic and challenging EI environment k_{st}^{eff}, where guardians are watching him or her and mediating some of his or her energetic needs, while consequently becoming a key factor in the conservation processes for at least a critical initial phase of life. Parallel to that, the development of the mind and sensory abilities of the individual gradually improves his or her "half autonomous" potencies and skills to survive. These ideas lead us to the first and most fundamental genetic goal, the *individual's survival*. As with the other goals, we assume that certain designated parts of the genetic code are being expressed to structure the human systematicness and mechanisms towards incentivizing the fulfillment of the genetic objectives. Clearly, survival is a crucial prerequisite for

---

56 We relate this time to the formation of the most basic form of $k_f(t)$ (Figure 1.1) enabling emergence of cognitive functions, $k_f(t_{observed} = t_{0m})$.

the potential realization of the entire subsequent set of individual genetic assignments and the multifaceted life functionality of the human. One manifestation of the survival regards preservation in the continuity of internal body/mind CCF "background" processes. To sustain them, an effective macro-level human activity relying on GEAP-enabled sensing and motor functions is further required. In the book herein we decided to combine these functions and focus on the sequential human conversion path turning stimuli-triggered inputs into cognition-directed behavioral outputs. The physical progress along this functional path, which is often accompanied by time delays and apparent discontinuity, takes place in a multitude of reactions crossing the EM body and mind DRSs. Accordingly, connected by a presumably latent mind, the physiological tracts of the sensing and motoric activities will be treated here as a combined, integrated *sensomotoric* trajectory of contents-functions yielding human functionality through subsequent occurrences of sensing/reception (sensoreception) processes, sensation, cognition (including perception and decision), and body responses that can be identified as behavior. The latter are invested to a great extent in realization of the genetic goals, and we also note that the entire conversion is hypothetically reflected by a unique ID. Certainly, we are also interested in the *sensoperceptive* part of the process which may precede motor activity. Sensoperceptive responses involve sensation and allow humans to interpret spacetime and plan their motion and actions in it. With respect to that, we believe that a pivotal contribution to the functionality of the human, including to his or her life sustenance, is provided by *perception-based behavior* (*PbB*). Naturally, this functionality involves in part sensomotoric responses based on cognitive assessments of stimuli which yield motorically executed reactions.[57, 58] As implied, parts of the PbB aim to

---

57 PbB may also entail activity that appears to be disconnected from direct interactions with environmental stimuli. Moreover, it will be distinguished from other observed behaviors which do not necessarily require cognitive processing from the individual and his or her awareness and include different instincts and reflexes such as breathing. For simplifying reasons, we will often refer to PbB as "behavior" and qualify the generalization whenever needed.

58 Various systemic factors along the sensomotoric path often turn the analysis of the ongoing correlation between stimulation and behavioral response to a tough challenge. Physiological-based delays and the storage of sensoperceptive cognitive products in memories, may appear, for example, as disrupting the continuity of the responses (yet they may potentially contribute to belated behavioral responses). Despite the challenges, due to the importance of the PbB as a fundamental functionality, it will remain in the focus of the discussion to follow.

introduce changes to the EI spacetime as a means of self-intervention in favor of the individual's survival. We will later view the cognitive assessments of the sensory data leading to the PbB as weighing the potentials hidden in identified objects and situations to ameliorate, as well as preserve, own genetic achievements. These emphasize the *conservation/improvement* (*C/I*) facets of the PbB.

In conjunction with the gradually increasing interactions between the growing individual and his or her EI spacetime contents, the contribution of PbB to the total human functionality enables us to extend the discussion and describe additional genetic goals. While survival challenges already matter at the beginning of the individual time, we regard the potential realization of the rest of the genetic goals as delayed to certain phases of individual maturation and further dependant on circumstantial life events. Now, our attempts to explore the human behavior with respect to the assumed inherent targets will consider both genetic and environmental impacts on the PbB functionality. At first glance, GEAP-based structure-functionality relations may seem to imply that human behavior is strictly bound to hardwired "systemic" dictates and as such should be utterly "robotic". Nevertheless, in Chapter 3 we will intuitively assume that the mind-conversion processes are significantly affected by overarching influences related to emotions, feelings, urges, and others, which lead to perceive our own behavior patterns as far less predictable and "automated" than expected. With that said, we still believe that certain unbiased, "pristine" parts of human behavior are shaped by the genetic instructions accompanying the individual from the initial state of the zygotic nucleus.[59] Accordingly, it may be assumed that at least two kinds of human content distributions play a major role in the individual's behavior. These relate to "pristine"-genetic and "environmentally accrued" structures, where the latter also include the ever-changing organized arrays of the BES. With that in mind, we move on to the second postulated genetic goal, which is (b) *replication*. Replication and survival are clearly linked at the species level, but when it comes to the individual, implementing the former is not necessarily

---

59 The field of behavioral genetics is known to be studying direct genetic influences on human behavior. For example, M. McGue, I. I. Gottesman, Behavior Genetics. In *The Encyclopedia of Clinical Psychology*, edited by R. L. Cautin, and S. O. Lilienfeld, pp. 1–11. Hobooken, NJ: Wiley (2015); R. Plomin, J. C. DeFries, V. S. Knopik, and J. M. Neiderhiser, "Top 10 Replicated Findings from Behavioral Genetics". *Perspect. Psychol. Sci.*, **11(1)**, 3–23 (2016).

essential to the latter. In a similar way to the other goals, we do believe that the individual is genetically urged to act, in this case to reproduce, also from the pristine structural level. A further similarity between the goals relates to the investment of behavioral energy (work) and time of life towards their realization. In the case of the replication this investment typically concerns finding an appropriate partner and establishing necessary social/emotional/financial connections with, while employing different DRS-based resources for this matter. Depending on the circumstances, such preceding investments may be regarded as enabling the replication of the offspring but might not be fully accounting for the low entropy that is reflected from his or her amazingly ordered GEAP in spacetime. To explain some aspects of the feasibility and relative stability of the latter, we need to consider among other factors the energy being persistently transferred to the individual from the effective EI environment (k_{st}^{eff}), as well as to view his or her (humble) contributions to increasing the spatial entropy through metabolic and behavioral activities.[60] This and other thermodynamic considerations and incentives may also play a role in the expansion of the entire species and its replication tendencies.[61] We now continue to the third hypothesized genetic goal, (c) the *critical guardianship*. We have recently implied here that due to our restricted cognitive and motoric capabilities during the first years of life, we are forced to rely on human "donors" guarding and securing us, as well as providing us access to external resources needed for our survival. This behavioral pattern of *energetic support* by the guardians entails clear mediation aspects, and sustaining it over several years requires a considerable investment of resources and allocated time. Occasionally, the efforts are rewarding the guardian with "positive emotion" PCEs (see Chapter 3) associated with the infant. As we know, energetic support is also common when a guardian is not directly hereditarily related to the infant. Somewhat counterintuitively, we refrain here from perceiving such adoption instances as altruism. In fact, we further generalize that

---

60 Human-made entropic changes are discussed in C. Silva, and K. Annamalai, "Entropy Generation and Human Aging: Lifespan Entropy and Effect of Physical Activity Level". *Entropy*, **10(2)**, 100–123 (2008).

61 Plenty of studies and perspectives exist in regard to this topic. A few examples are: E. D. Schneider, and D. Sagan, *Into the Cool: Energy Flow Thermodynamics and Life*. Chicago: The University of Chicago Press (2005); J. L. England, "Statistical Physics of Self-Replication". *J. Chem. Phys.*, **139**, 121923 (2013).

"pure" human altruistic behavior in the sense of "spending without gaining" is merely an illusion whose acceptance is mostly shaped by social norms and standards. Beyond its marginal contribution to the evolution of the general spacetime, every human act of giving is a manifestation of PbB, which is accompanied by mind structure changes believed to be influenced, as was stated before, by urges, needs, and beliefs. Looking from a "cold", emotionless biophysical viewpoint, we believe that all decisions being taken by the individual, regardless of the net effects they exert and how these effects are perceived by him or her, or by an external observer, involve a certain phenomenological expression that is experienced as a reward.[62] Reward-focused PCEs are expected to be circumstantial, sometimes ephemeral, at times emerging following compromises between needs and/or consequent to the feeling of reaching a decision regardless of its implications. Despite not leading necessarily to a net gain for the individual, these PCEs allow us to negate any "pure" form of altruism which does not involve self-rewarding. It should be noted that from within the experienced illusion we still keep assessing altruistic-like degrees of our giving actions, and that such assessments are typically affected by interpretations biased by personal beliefs.[63]

These ideas lead us to the fourth elemental human goal, which is ascribed to (d) *enhancement*. Behind this propensity is the idea that the guardian individual keeps investing energy and time resources in the maturing or adult "benefiter" beyond the period of critical guardianship, thus ostensibly increasing the latter's *implementation potential* of their own genetic goals.[64] Now, depending on the extent and

---

62 In the adoption example, such a reward can be attributed, for instance, to enjoying the giving itself, a feedback from the infant or memory of such, reducing stress generated by the infant or by someone's expectations, self needs and urges, and so forth. From a physiological viewpoint, these are often accompanied by regulation of dopamine and serotonin levels which lead to experiencing rewarding PCEs.

63 Using the belief-based reference element to be presented in the third chapter as the energetic self, any individual transferring resources to others outside of his or her "hereditary ecosystem" may assess the relative changes this action will cause to his or her own state of resources. Accordingly, certain deliberate actions which are associated with resources-normalized low gained-spent expectancies might be (illusively) perceived as holding a potential for an altruistic behavior.

64 Following the maturation of the dependent individual during the critical guardianship period and the gaining of more autonomous skills to survive, we refer to him or her as a benefiter to the subsequent enhancement process. On the other hand, the term "guardian" will still be symbolically employed even at this stage where effective guarding and persistent securing stopped being an immediate necessity, as well as in cases where the dependence between the two has ceased or even energetically reversed.

fate of the resources transferred, they might have a long-lasting impact and become utilized for genetic purposes also by the descendants of the direct benefiter. This "dynasty" effect, along with its related social conventions, is also evident, for example, when a guardian gives away resources directly to his or her grandchildren. In view of these concepts, we treat the enhancement as potentially species-benefitting behavior and accordingly question possible correlations between its global characteristics and the evolution of the species. Looking at the different goals from a broad angle, the critical guardianship and the energetic enhancement may be viewed as activities in which the individual guardian serves as a "realization catalyst" to certain other individuals. Furthermore, unlike the first three goals whose main objective is conservation (of the self, the species, and the offspring, respectively), the enhancement is mainly oriented towards improvement (with conservation implications that might follow). These ideas draw our attention to the continuous *energetic struggle* over spacetime resources that is taking place amongst humans engaged in realization of genetic goals.[65] Whereas the struggle seems to occur more aggressively in local habitats where demands for resources are high while their availability might be changing fast, it fundamentally encompasses the entire race and is being reflected by a variety of human interactions and expressions. One prominent consequence of the struggle is an establishment of *polarization (inequality)* between individuals with respect to the resources they can potentially invest at a given moment on the genetic goals. This is occasionally evident through the difficulty or inability of the "weaker" human to realize the four genetic goals and especially to enhance his or her benefiters adequately as well as better than others in the local habitat. Such instances can be linked to evolutionary concepts along the lines of natural selection. With regard to that, uneven enhancement processes are expected to continuously increase the polarization at different locations and contribute to improving the quality of the species

---

65 Early ideas concerning the struggle for existence have been proposed by the Greek philosophers Heraclitus and Aristotle. In the 18th century some of these concepts were revived and further developed by prominent contributors such as Comte de Buffon, Benjamin Franklin, and others. Inspired by these, Thomas Robert Malthus and Charles Lyell published their interpretations which paved the way to later contributions by Charles Darwin, Thomas Henry Huxley, Alfred Russel Wallace, Peter Kropotkin, and others.

through the selection made.[66] As was implied, the enhancement is viewed as a direct continuation of the critical guardianship which follows the unrelated, natural gradual increase in the autonomy of the benefiter. Also highlighted is the common reversed pattern, according to which the matured benefiter supports his or her guardian who grew old. Such a situation does not necessarily terminate the original enhancement, except maybe in permanent, irreversible cases where the benefiter gives back considerably more energy than he or she has ever received. While we associate the enhancement with an active behavior, which might be in many aspects unique to humans in the living world, parts of it are often implemented through *inheritance* that follows the death of the guardians. Despite this custom leading to a situation in which the guardian is unable to witness a (typically significant) transfer of his or her own energy resources to the benefiter, due to nowadays relatively long life expectancy, he or she may still observe the benefiter exploiting his or her lifelong support and accomplishing the genetic goals while being alive. Among other factors, the "post-enhancement" inheritance relies on assimilated beliefs that reflect both genetic motivations and cultural traditions. Contrary to the genetic goals, we consider it an ameliorating custom which has no hereditary basis hardwiring it to our behavior.

Given the four postulated genetic goals and the intrinsic guidance towards their implementation, we ask, How come they are not always fulfilled? Why do individuals commit suicide, refrain from having children, abandon them or neglect their needs during various stages of life? Do these ostensibly *anti-genetic behaviors* contradict the hereditary assimilations in mind and body structures and mechanisms? Scrutinizing the questions, we believe that possible explanations for such anti-genetic behaviors need to consider at least three factors: (a) implications of interactions between the individual and his or her surroundings which are not bound themselves to species-favorable results; (b) projective mind assimilations left by such interactions

---

66 A question can be raised regarding the real strength in the struggle of well-enhanced humans. A lucky benefiter who has been well-enhanced by his or her guardians may sometimes fulfill the set of genetic goals more effortlessly in comparison to those who have not been similarly supported. While enhancement at different levels might have certain behavioral implications on the benefiters and as such also anthropologically distinguished, physics tends not to question the origins of the resources used in crossing energetic barriers and thus does not discriminate between benefiters and self-achievers when it comes to realization of the genetic goals (hence also allowing the former to be regarded as strong in the struggle).

which can turn into influences countering the genetic drive; and (c) certain body and/or mind pathologies, consequential to interactions with spacetime or inherent due to genetic expressions, that hinder or oppose the implementation of the goals. Let's return to our assumption that parts of the human content consist of pristine functional body and mind structures attempting to drive the individual into realizing genetic goals. Considering that, and assuming exposure to realization opportunities and awareness to them, it is reasonable to believe that the main factors that can sabotage this almost spontaneous genetic implementation are incompetence or unwillingness of the individual to act, and to some extent also prioritization of the goals. In its broad sense, incompetence can be regarded as a temporal or permanent state of obstruction. We generally associate it with external and/or internal physical events (or absence thereof), preventing the mind and/or body constructions from circumstantially executing certain genetic functionalities. Acknowledging that the physical processes participating in the evolution of nature are not necessarily "committed" to any localized biological progression, one may understand that anti-genetic (and genetic) behaviors are plain functional interpretations within the causal and circumstantial development of general spacetime. As such, they disharmonize with the biophysical plan embedded in the human "machine" and might look like a failure from the viewpoint of the species, yet they do not negate the plan's physical feasibility. Next to be mentioned is the unwillingness factor. We regard wills as awareness-crossing PCEs in which imagined changes in spacetime, often interaction-induced and occasionally related to one's self-goals, are assumed to yield rewarding experiences, and as such may motivate the individual to implement them. Therefore, wills are believed to have a strong impact on human resolutions and actions, while concurrently being influenced themselves by a broad spectrum of "psychoenergetic" PCE expressions, such as emotions, feelings, fears, and urges, discussed in Chapter 3. As was mentioned in the beginning of Section 1.2, our deterministic and physicalistic views lead us to accept that wills are also being contingently generated along nature's path of evolution and are thus affected by circumstantial physical events. Accordingly, we viewed the concept of free will, in the sense of the ability of the individual to unbiasedly experience wills and unbiasedly act in line with them, as an illusion.[67] In considering that the physical basis of the wills is taking a part in the universal evolution of general spacetime, we accept once again that the latter is not necessarily bound, but deterministically, to satisfying any genetic-favored scenarios. As physics determines heredity, cases of unwillingness to realize the genetic goals, driven, for example, by personal psychoenergetic considerations, are circumstantial to the progression of spacetime, and thus do not negate the local human constructions which might favor the goals in absence of these "environmentally imported" biases. As we stated, another factor which seems to play a role in anti-genetic behaviors is *prioritization of goals*. We regard the prioritization as a product of systematic cognitive activity relying on biased energy considerations. The possible mechanisms directing these as a part of the individual energy perception will be elaborated on in Chapter 3. One example of prioritization points out the intense multi-aspect investments needed in the second, third, and fourth goals as preventing some individuals from having (many) children. Instead, many of them prefer to channel their resources to own struggle for survival and/or to elevate the enhancement of their already-living offspring. One may observe that at the individual level the net effect of the prioritization in this case comes down to redirecting resources between different goals, but from the macro viewpoint of the species, this can lead to undesired consequences, such as when replication rates drop below the minimum requirement to replace the population. It should be noted that the prioritization of the goals can be affected by cultural,

---

67 It is interesting to think that the (illusive) intuition concerning the freedom of will goes hand in hand with the human's fundamental experience of responsibility for his or her decisions and actions, as well as for their results. These beliefs play a role in the self-commitment of the individual to his or her destiny and exerts a stress element in regard to the goals. The mental challenges taking part in the struggle for resources can help in comprehending the outstanding proliferation of religious beliefs (which are occasionally viewed by their followers as actually opposing the concept of free will). Religions allow the believers to share the responsibility for their actions and fate with one or more guiding entities. To a certain extent, such Gods resemble ideal guardians, yet to which typically different spacetime laws, frequently self-created and negating physicalism and physical restrictions, are believed to apply. In many cases the believers relate their fate, during their lifetime and beyond, to worshiping the Gods and complying with narratives that have been developed around them. Accordingly, the individual believer is urged to fulfill additional goals requiring a further investment, even if modest, of energy and time. In return, he or she is being rewarded with significant benefits, such as finding order patterns and guidance, belonging to a broad group of believers holding synergistic-catalytic amelioration potentials, escapist distraction, and so on. These assist in empowering the believer's perception of self-identity and moral standards, sooth the never-ending struggle, ease responsibility burdens, and help cope with fears of death and abandonment, to be later discussed herein.

age, gender, and other factors that extend beyond this discussion. Prioritizations also affect the time intervals spent by the individual on different activities in his or her life, including, for example, on recruiting resources and implementation of the goals. In this regard we will later suggest that the individual distributes his or her time between several "behavioral states" associated with different elementary interplays with spacetime in the light of the genetic realization. To summarize this part, the individual is believed to conduct a lifelong "energy dance" with his or her effective environment, a process which is made of subsequent interactive "steps" attempting to satisfy inherent genetic goals. Nevertheless, the general spacetime may obstruct this life functionality by physically biasing it, up to the level of its complete destruction. Using the analogy given, there are therefore no guaranties for the "dance" to succeed both from the viewpoints of the individual (dancer) and of the species (entire band/dance school), while a failed performance does not necessarily indicate insufficient skills or practicing by the dancer.

Before moving on, we wish to dedicate a few words to the genetic justification for the death of the individual. As we all know, different circumstances can lead to physiological failures that cease the living functionality observed from the human. A common convention to describe the state of *death* regards a stoppage in the interrelated physiological activity of the lungs, heart, and brain functions. This irreversible state[68] highlights the termination of the self-conservation processes and the end of the realization of the first genetic goal as it leads to the biochemical decomposition of the dead body. In absence of direct and strict genetic monitoring over the realization of the goals (especially the third and fourth goals in women and from the second and on in men), we believe that hereditary expressions promote the existence of rough "time frames" for their implementation by the humans, and which typically correlate with their age. These are normally accompanied by structural changes expressed in the body and the mind, and that can also be affected by certain environmental factors. Clearly, natural degradation eventually appears with aging

---

68 At least as is currently thought in regard to humans, as significant progress in the effective resuscitation of other dead organisms have been recently made. For example, Z. Vrselja, S. G. Daniele, J. Silbereis, F. Talpo, Y. M. Morozov et al., "Restoration of Brain Circulation and Cellular Functions Hours Post-Mortem". *Nature* **568**, 336–343 (2019).

and follows the typical decline in fertility that starts even years before. Hence, one may ask, Why does the survival-eager species not follow a better physical-structural plan to keep its individuals alive much longer while freeing them from time restrictions to realize the goals? As was stated, the heredity process and its replicating products are subjected to the physical dictates of nature. Similar to any conversion system exposed to internal and external reactions and interactions, a gradual decrease in the efficiency of the human conversion processes with time is inevitable. This has a direct destructive implication on the functionality produced that cannot be completely overcome by any alternative genetic plan or design (which at best could have delayed the consequences for a while). The natural death of elderly people connects to several interesting concepts and from which we will briefly mention two. First, it allows younger individuals supporting more vigorous metabolism and motoric capabilities to relatively ameliorate the entropic propensity of spacetime's evolution. Another concept views the death of elderly people from a "cold" and emotionless standpoint, suggesting that termination of their part in the consumption of the overall accessible resources increases the probabilities of genetic realization by younger people who may still reproduce and raise children. The dynamic (pseudo) balance between deaths and births and its general correlation with the extent of energetic implementable resources available to humanity at any observable moment are prominent factors in the evolution of the species, and we will return to discussing some aspects associated with them in Chapter 4.

Chapter 2

Functionality-Individuality Pathways

2.1 Individual human energy

Chapter 1 speculated several aspects of human behavior associated with attempts to realize inherent genetic goals. The laws of nature suggest that to achieve this essential functionality and conserve the achievements over time, the individual must rely on multiple content/ energy transfer processes from his or her external environment. Examining these ideas, one may notice that many organisms—humans being among them—share certain basic operational features with human-made *biofuel cells*, as devices which are designed to deliver electrical power on demand and supply it to sustain certain functional needs. In a similar manner to the biochemical reactions occurring in the artificial cells, for example, the living creatures biologically convert potential chemical energy stored in specific substances. As we know, the conversion in humans yields free energy which is then mainly invested in growing/sustaining their living structures and body/mind functions, as well as in enabling the work manifested by their activity in general spacetime. Naturally, besides these and other structural and operational analogies, there are also fundamental differences between the systems. Whereas for the artificial cells to generate power, a controlled supply of fuel and oxidizer substances must be externally delivered to the device, following the genetic plan the mature individual is responsible for obtaining appropriate reactants from the environment, including food and oxygen from air, for example, whose self-conversion will sustain his or her own life functionality. An effective recruitment of such essential resources requires the human in many cases to sense, among other spatial elements, their availability and at times also their absence. Combined with their subsequent perceptive interpretations, such sensing processes contribute to triggering the individual's perception-based behavior, PbB, which is referring to some of his or her most crucial responses to the EI world.[1]

Viewing the human as an open thermodynamic system which is analogous in various ways to an externally fed biofuel cell leads us to examine his or her energy exchange with the EI spacetime. Equation 2.1, the *equation of the dynamic balance* (*EDB*), suggests a transient ("pseudo-") balance in the energies transferred.

$$(2.1) \quad \dot{E}_{human}(t_{observed}=t_{present}) = \dot{E}_{inherited}(\dot{t}_0) + \int_{t_0}^{t_{present}} (dE_{st}^{in}/dt - dE_{st}^{out}/dt)\ dt$$

The equation, complying with the exchange of substance and energy between the human and the environment, alludes that, at any given moment in one's life, $t_{observed}=t_{present}\leq t_0$, it is possible to ascribe to a human an *individual human energy*, $\dot{E}_{human}$. The latter reflects an offset between the energy-projected content contributions (including of crucial resources) which have been transferred to him or her from the EI spacetime since the zygotic initiation at $\dot{t}_0$ and until the present observation time, namely $\dot{E}_{inherited}(\dot{t}_0)+E_{st}^{in}(t_{observed})$, and on the other hand the energetic profile of what he or she has transferred to the external environment during this duration, $E_{st}^{out}(t_{observed})$. In this regard, E_{st}^{in} and E_{st}^{out} respectively represent the time-integrated energy projections of the various input dE_{st}^{in} and output dE_{st}^{out} contributions transferred during the time limits under consideration.[2] The energy-projected contributions can be calculated by applying relevant, specific laws (included in the generalized Equation 1.2) with respect to the content exchanged between the human and the surroundings. Equation 2.1 implies a lifelong energy dependency of the individual on the external spacetime, and we accept that in its current EDB representation, which refers to person who is alive, the momentary balance formed should never turn negative. Evidently,

---

1 In accord with that, part of the recruited energy can be viewed as being invested in maintaining sensing and mind-processing functions which enable the spatial perception of the environment. These essential-to-life operations lay the foundation for all further recruitment processes aiming to advance the realization of the genetic goals, and it should be emphasized that they do so without violating the energy conservation in spacetime.

2 The notations "in" and "out" refer, respectively, to the arithmetic signs of the incoming and outgoing transitions and highlight the direction of the energy transfer with respect to the individual. We also note the use of the abbreviation "st" for the EI spacetime.

Equation 2.1 does not suggest any correlation between the genetic structure encoded in the human and the transitions, or between the latter and the evolution of the inherited nucleus. Further lacking is a possible linkage between the present energetic state and the human functions.[3] With that in mind, one may still intuitively assume a tight circumstantial correlation between the physical events affecting the individual's life and the changes they elicit in his or her structure, energy, and activity.

Next, we attempt to explore the effect of several meaningful events in the individual's life on $\dot{E}_{human}(t_{observed})$ and its formulation. We begin with the initiation of the individual time at $t_{observed}=\dot{t}_0$, Case I in Table 2.1. At this instant, $\dot{E}_{human}$ is identified as an *individual inherited energy* $\dot{E}_{inherited}(\dot{t}_0)$, which corresponds to the projection of the life nucleus $\dot{k}_{inherited}(\dot{t}_0)$, Equation 2.2. We recall that the latter is associated with a certain "proto-individuality" related to its unique composition of genetic code sequences holding immediate and future significances to the expressed life functionality.

$$(2.2) \quad \dot{E}_{human}(t_{observed}=\dot{t}_0) = H[\dot{k}_{inherited}(\dot{t}_0)] = \dot{E}_{inherited}(\dot{t}_0)$$

Moving slightly forward in time, internal activity in the activated nucleus correlated with respective interactions with the effective external environment in the womb facilitate the CCF-directed processes which also synthesize the individual's "general construction" (GC). This last term will be used as a generalized description of the human content at any stage of assembly and functioning throughout the individual's entire lifetime, and regardless of the specific DRSs which may be specifically ascribed to it at this time. We will associate the GC with the general structural distribution $\dot{k}_{human}\equiv\dot{k}_{GC}$. Now, during the earliest stages of human development, still in absence of a functioning mind and its contribution to the functionality of the individual (assuming basic mind functions emerging at $t_{observed}=\dot{t}_{0mind}$, see below), we will consider the GC as a "pure"[4] body DRS, $\dot{k}_{GC}=\dot{k}_{body}$ ($t_0<t_{observed}<\dot{t}_{0mind}$).

---

3 Including indications, for example, for body accumulation of potential resources that can be used for delayed conversion purposes, a common practice in many organisms.

4 Neglecting, at the moment, elementary mind activity which possibly precedes sensoperceptive functions and motoric responses to them.

Namely, at this time interval:

$$(2.3) \quad \dot{E}_{human}(t_0 < t_{observed} < t_{0mind}) = H[\dot{k}_{body}] = \dot{E}_{body}$$

Supported by transitions from the mother's body, the genetic code will direct the CCF in developing $\dot{k}_{body}$. It should be noted that whereas most of the efforts at this stage are directed towards the development of the embryo, some external transitions and inner $\dot{k}_{body}$ reactions might not directly or immediately contribute to this functionality. One can mention, for example, the absorption of incoming inert content or an external triggering of reorganization processes that have marginal or no effect on the present functionality. As such, we refrained from generally ascribing individuality dimensions to the transitions in Equation 1.2, despite acknowledging that every present change may possibly lead to a delayed impact, which can occasionally include disturbances to functionality. Scrutinizing the EDB, we also assume that despite the crucial structural-functional effects of the zygotic nucleus on the development of the human, throughout the individual time its initial $\dot{E}_{inherited}(t_0)$ projection becomes numerically minor in comparison to the energy associated with the evolved GC. Also to be acknowledged in this regard is that while the structure function $\dot{k}_{human}$ remains unique among individuals, the "reduced" projective value of $\dot{E}_{human}$ may occasionally show resemblance, within a certain level of accuracy, between different people.

The next significant event in the individual's life is ascribed to reaching a state of development in which his or her developing mind (see chap. 2, n. 4) starts to deliver cognitive activity that enables the generation of basic PbB, Case III in Table 2.1. The exact ephemeral individual time for the emergence of such an activity, recently referred to as t_{0mind}, is hard to determine, especially when considering the possible latency of the mind in the body. Hence, its limited estimations mostly rely on interpretations given to certain observed correlations between elementary behavior patterns of the embryo and the physiological maturation of his or her neural system.[5] Considering

---

5 While basic neural responses are typically detected approximately five weeks from fertilization in embryos who demonstrate certain autonomous movements, the cortical system further matures to support more advanced cognitive functions relatively closer to the time of birth: K. L. Moore, T. V. N. Persaud, and M. G. Torchia, *The Developing Human: Clinically Oriented Embryology*, Amsterdam: Elsevier (2020).

this, we employ our previous conceptual distinction between the EM body and the now operative latent mind to divide at this time the GC attribution into its DRS components of structural uncertainties.[6] Accordingly, at this lifetime interval:

$$(2.4a) \quad \dot{k}_{human}(\dot{t}_{0mind} \leq t_{observed} < \dot{t}_{death}) \equiv \dot{k}_{GC} = \dot{k}_{body} + \dot{k}_{mind}$$

Applying the energy transformations yields:

$$(2.4b) \quad \dot{E}_{human}(\dot{t}_{0mind} \leq t_{observed} < \dot{t}_{death}) = H[\dot{k}_{body}] + H[\dot{k}_{mind}] \sim \dot{E}_{body} + \dot{E}_{mind}$$

The solution, typically referring to the longest and most significant period in the lifetime of the maturing/mature individual, between $\dot{t}_{0mind}$ and his or her death at $\dot{t}_{death}$, demonstrates the complementary contributions of the functional DRSs to his or her human energy.[7] Looking at Equations 2.4a and 2.4b, we note that the abbreviated "body" notations refer to the "EM body" and point out the appearance of the "~" approximation sign in the latter formula. The latter expresses our wish to omit from the description any possible contributions from interactions between the body and mind contents (that could have appeared as a $\dot{E}_{interaction}$ term), and thus to emphasize the prominence of the functional DRSs in the calculation. It is also important to note that, like before, despite the elementary assumption that all structural distribution $\dot{k}_{human}$ states show individuality-based uniqueness, some of their energy projections might still occasionally coincide. Further acknowledged is that we refrain from applying Equations 2.4a and 2.4b to any potential mind structures whose formation could have preceded $\dot{t}_{0mind}$, yet they had no practical relevance to the PbB or to PbB-contributing mind arrays that might have been degenerated before

---

6 As our aim is to define, rather than to precisely solve, the contributions for the individual human energy with respect to his or her developmental stage, and since the veracity of the following equations is assumed to remain unviolated by the latency of the mind, we treat the DRS-based distributions (and their corresponding energies) as plain variables holding uncertainties in terms of their precise quantification.

7 In Chapter 3 we will assume that an energy-oriented perception triggers the human to believe that his or her energy also extends to the EI spacetime and corresponds to some of its perceived contents. Nevertheless, due to the belief-based subjective nature of the connections made, we naturally exclude them from the above objectivity-seeking formulation.

this time. As noted, the phase extending from the basic maturation of the mind to the death of the individual is typically significant in terms of its relative duration in life and the events being experienced throughout it (affecting the individual's accrued transitions E_{st}^{in} and E_{st}^{out} and functionality). One such event is the birth and separation from the nourishing womb of the mother, a transition that exposes the human at once to a "new", more varied and challenging external environment. Following the birth and during the critical guardianship and adolescence periods, further changes ensue to impact the individual's life and energy profile. These are reflected, for instance, in his or her increasing autonomous capabilities to self-recruit E_{st}^{in} for the realization of the genetic goals. Conforming to the EDB presentation of the individual as an open thermodynamic system conducting ongoing feedback with the EI spacetime, one may accept that internal human structural changes also correlate with the exchange, and as such are associated with certain variations in $\dot{E}_{human}$. These include genetic expressions taking part in the CCF, emergence of pathologies, and others. As expected, the interplay between this internal activity and the transitions with the EI world is crucial to sustaining the life of the individual. During old age, for instance, a typical decline in body and mind-conversion efficiencies due to different reasons frequently leads to increased difficulties in maintaining the E_{st}^{in} and E_{st}^{out} transitions needed for full sustained and independent functionality. Consequently, to prolong their lives, older people often energetically rely on others, in a manner somewhat resembling their years of infancy. Before moving on, it is also important to mention the emergence of comatose states characterized by only marginal cognitive activity for their bearers,[8] and which force them to fully depend on caretakers in prolonging their lives. We believe that Equations 2.4 still apply to these states, which support some degree of CCF.

The next case, IV in Table 2.1, deals with the individual human energy at death. Associating death with the impotency of several critical biophysical assemblies to continue functioning and maintaining both the transitions and conversion required for living functionality, we favor to define the individual human energy of the

---

8 For example, S. Laureys, F. Perrin, C. Schnakers, M. Boly, and S. Majerus, "Residual Cognitive Function in Comatose, Vegetative and Minimally Conscious States". *Curr. Opin. Neurol.*, **18(6)**, 726–733 (2005).

deceased (in contrast to the energy associated with the nonfunctional dead content, see below) as 0.

$$(2.5) \quad \dot{E}_{human}(t_{observed} \geq t_{death}) \equiv 0$$

This ascribed energetic state in which the individual energy has terminated may be regarded as the *collapse of the individuality dimension* at death. For example, ceasing of all cognitive and other mind activities revokes the fundamental contribution of this DRS to the living functionality and may be viewed as merging its content with the dead body, $\dot{E}_{mind} \longrightarrow E_{body}$. An interlinked collapse, $\dot{E}_{body} \longrightarrow E_{body}$, is similarly expected to occur, quenching the individuality of the body. Accompanying these is a stoppage[9] in the regulation of body activity, marking the beginning of the erosion of the corpse. The latter processes include irreversible chemical and biochemical transformations of the dead body, which can be perceived as contributing to a $E_{body} \longrightarrow E_{st}$ reaction, and which rely on, among other things, its remaining potential energy in the general spacetime, $E_{body}(t_{death}) > 0$. We further note that whereas a critical stoppage in dE_{st}^{in} transitions will quickly lead to the death of the individual, the general spacetime will asymmetrically continue to "function" long after the merging of the DRSs into the lifeless content form and the cease in the dE_{st}^{out} transitions. Taking these into account, we view the EDB as a fundamental energetic offset which alludes the existence of $\dot{E}_{human}$ as a projection of dynamic human changes shaped by interlinked internal CCF processes and external interactions with the EI space, including some associated with PbB. Accordingly, we attribute the life of the individual to a circumstantial deterministic progression in which hereditary and environmental factors play a major role in physically sustaining the dE_{st}^{in} and dE_{st}^{out} transitions that enable a "positive" $\dot{E}_{human}$ until collapsing. It is interesting to think that resembling perspectives are long held by humanity, and the view of the

---

9 Interestingly, there are evidences for post-mortal genetically dictated activities like transcription in body cells. For example: A. E. Pozhitkov, R. Neme, T. Domazet-Loso, B. G. Leroux, S. Soni, et. al., "Tracing the Dynamics of Gene Transcripts after Organismal Death". *Open Biol.*, **7(1)** (2017); P. G. Ferreira et al., "The Effects of Death and Post-Mortem Cold Ischemia on Human Tissue Transcriptomes". *Nat. Commun.*, 9(article 490), 1–15 (2018). Nevertheless, this activity cannot sustain a full living functionality and as such is not regarded as contributing to the human individuality.

individual as a temporal "entity" in spacetime is expressed, for example, in the Bible, "Till you return to the ground, for out of it you were taken; for you are dust, and to dust you shall return" (Genesis 3:19). We will soon return to the first part of this verse, which we believe is relevant to the energy-recruitment process.

Case	$t_{observed}$	State	Functioning body	Functioning mind	$\dot{E}_{human}$ ($t_{observed}$)	Main human functionality
I	t_0	Initial state of life (fertilization/ zygotic)	Nucleus	Absent	$= \dot{E}_{inherited}$	Prefunctional
II	$t_0 < t_{observed} < t_{0mind}$	Prior to a fully functioning mind	Present	Absent[#]	$\equiv \dot{E}_{GC} = \dot{E}_{body}$ ($> \dot{E}_{inherited}$)	CCF
III	$t_{0mind} \leq t_{observed}^{\#\#} < t_{death}$	Both body and mind are fully functional	Present	Present	$\equiv \dot{E}_{GC}$ $\sim \dot{E}_{body} + \dot{E}_{mind}$[###]	CCF, PbB
IV	$\geq t_{death}$	Death and collapse of $\dot{E}_{human}$	Collapsed	Collapsed	$\equiv 0$[####] $\dot{E}_{mind}, \dot{E}_{body} \longrightarrow E_{body}$ $E_{body} \longrightarrow E_{st}$	None

Table 2.1: The effect of several meaningful events between life and death on the individual human energy and its formulation. #, ignoring potentially degenerated mind structures/functions; ##, normally including the individual's birth at t_{birth}; ###, omitting further interactions between the EM body and mind contents; and ####, arbitrarily reflecting the collapse of the individuality.

From this point and on, we will focus our attention on the third case in Table 2.1, referring to contributions to the human functionality from both the mind and the body. So far, we have described the individual human energy from two complementary and interlinked perspectives. The "environmental" perspective, represented by the EDB in Equation 2.1, claimed that $\dot{E}_{human}$ reflects a continuous offset of energy-projected transitions between the individual and the external spacetime that defines his or her energetic state in every moment of life. On the other hand, Equation 2.4b explores $\dot{E}_{human}$ from an internal perspective as a projection of distributed content which is believed to facilitate the functionality of the living human. Combining these interlinked approaches alludes that the ongoing transitions needed for sustaining a positive balance facilitate the internal human constructions and the life functionality they elicit and vice versa. One may even contemplate the contingent dependencies of (certain elements in) $\dot{k}_{body}$ and $\dot{k}_{mind}$ on specific dE_{st}^{in} and dE_{st}^{out} inputs and outputs. This question is further linked to the concept of "broad individuality", presented in Section 2.3, revolving around our belief in internal-external feedback mechanisms that bias the transitions in an analogy to a system whose own dynamic states impact its inputs. One probable implication of this idea is that while Equation 2.4b is universal for all humans reaching an appropriate stage of development, their unique structural distributions at the present, following their specific environmental progression in accord with Equation 2.1, affect each individual's *dynamic interaction field* with spacetime, and from this discrete viewpoint turn certain aspects of the interaction field, including the implemented interactions in it, to be unique as well. Viewing the human as a medium for energy/ content transfer and simultaneously complying with his or her intrinsic separation to DRSs, we will now begin to discuss some potential internal transitions between the latter on the way to generate living functionality by responding to external triggers. Figure 2.1 suggests several possible transfer pathways between the EI spacetime, the EM body, and the mind. Two fundamental assumptions are depicted in the illustration. The first implies that incoming transitions from the EI spacetime to the mind always involve preliminary interactions with the EM body content. The second assumption, in contrast, claims that mind outputs are being released to the EI spacetime both through mediating interactions with the EM body, and also directly. It should be noted that these presumptions are bound to the premises regarding the latency of the mind in the body and its possible structural-functional correlation with the (neurology of the) brain. Accordingly, we rely on canonical anatomic and physiological observations depicting sensory and motoric conversion tracts in believing that EI spacetime→mind/brain and some of the mind/brain→EI spacetime transitions are indeed mediated by the EM body. Based on the same sources of knowledge, we are not aware of any non-mediated, direct reception of external spacetime content in the mind/brain, yet we are familiar with the emission of low-frequency synchronized neural oscillations, commonly known as brain waves, to spacetime in conjunction with different conscious mind responses coupled to cognitive activity. The correlations described[10] between this activity and the varying patterns of the output waves suggest that the mind/brain is capable of releasing energy to EI spacetime without conducting further interactions with the EM body.[11]

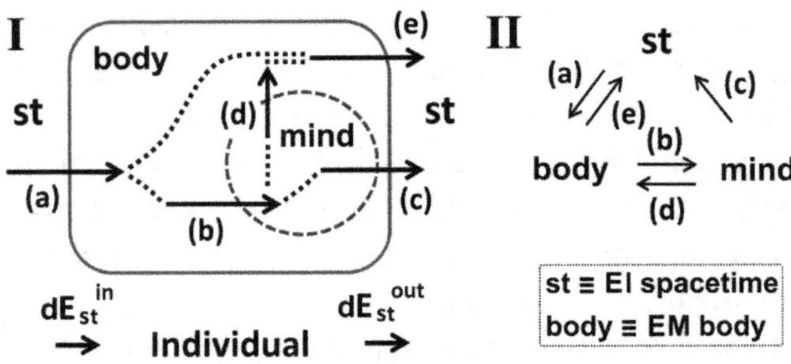

Figure 2.1: Illustrative (I) and equation-based (II) presentations of possible transitions between the distinct EI spacetime ("st"), EM body ("body"), and the human mind. The dashed lines connecting the arrows imply on potential continuation in the conversion processes. The energy projection of transitions (a) corresponds to dE_{st}^{in}, while the sum of the (c) and (e) projections correlates with dE_{st}^{out}. The dashed circle encompassing the mind symbolizes its possible latency in the individual's body.

---

10 Among the numerous studies in this field, we wish to mention K. Engel, and P. Fries, Neuronal Oscillations, Coherence, and Consciousness. In *The Neurology of Consciousness*, edited by S. Laureys, O. Gosseries, and G. Tononi, 49–60. Amsterdam: Elsevier (2016); A. L. Valencia, and T. Froese, "What Binds Us? Inter-Brain Neural Synchronization and its Implications for Theories of Human Consciousness". *Neurosci. Conscious.*, niaa010 (2020); A. M. Harris, P. E. Dux, and J. B. Mattingley, "Detecting Unattended Stimuli Depends on the Phase of Prestimulus Neural Oscillations". *J. Neurosci.*, **38(12)**, 3092–3101 (2018); E. Başar, C. Başar-Eroglu, S. Karakaş, and M. Schürmann, "Gamma, Alpha, Delta, and Theta Oscillations Govern Cognitive Processes". *Int. J. Psychophysiol.*, **39(2–3)**, 241–248 (2001); A. E. Symons, W. El-Deredy, M. Schwartze, and S. A. Kotz, "The Functional Role of Neural Oscillations in Non-Verbal Emotional Communication". *Front. Hum. Neurosci.*, **10**, 239 (2016); S. Huang, L. A. Holcomb, S. M. Cruz, and K. Marinkovic, "Altered Oscillatory Brain Dynamics of Emotional Processing in Young Binge Drinkers". *Cogn. Affect. Behav. Neurosci.*, **18(1)**, 43–57 (2018).

11 Due to the possible latency of the mind in the body, an unequivocal proof for such an assumption is absent and one may accordingly readjust the presentation in Figure 2.1, Panel I, and mark the beginning of transition "c" at the dashed circle attributed to the mind/EM body interface. Yet as this scenario cannot be excluded in view of the premises, and as we might be able to indicate its physical-evolutional incentive later by means of energetic considerations, we favor to adhere to it despite the uncertainties.

The incoming and outgoing transitions between the individual and his or her external environment relate to a broad range of conversion processes involving, for example, metabolic, sensory, motoric, and other activities. Additionally, the dE_{st}^{in} contributions can be distinguished in relation to the investment of energy by the individual in the transfer, where an absence of his or her efforts indicates "passively" receiving a contribution from an "actively" donating EI source. We acknowledge that passive contributions might also entail certain active human aspects due, for example, to the efforts made by the individual to be present at the location and time of their occurrence. Now, it is clear that not all body- and mind-conversion products ought to be emitted and/or form significant functionality, and that the internal processes facilitating the products do not necessarily follow constant paces or support continuity along their various tracts. As expected, the conversion facilitates the functions associated with the human assemblies from the micro- and all the way to the macroscopic anatomic scales. According to our physiological beliefs, this requires, among other processes, the oxidation of food in designated metabolic cycles. The biotransformations are further responsible for the generation of mechanical energy (motion and motoric responses to events), synthesis and growth (from single-cell regulation level and up in the structural hierarchy), body heat (also used to accelerate synthesis), and to preserve the biological constructions and their functions (as in homeostasis). Within these, conversion also allows regulation of processes that keep the mind active and further leads, for instance, to accumulation of body reserves which allow a delayed, on-demand channeling and utilization of the potential energy stored for variable needs. We regard all of these biophysical processes and their energetic and entropic incentives as establishing the life of the individual and providing him or her with potential capabilities to recruit resources in an attempt to realize the genetic goals. It should also be noted that despite appearing simple to be solved, an attempt to precisely calculate the "reaction kinetics"[12] solution for the time-evolved "cyclic" (triangular) array of transitions in Figure 2.1, Panel II,

---

12 Such time-integrated solutions are often applied in the dynamic analysis of chemical reactions and discussed, for example, in J. E. House, *Principles of Chemical Kinetics*. Amsterdam: Academic Press (2007); P. L. Huston, *Chemical Kinetics and Reaction Dynamics*. Mineola, NY: Dover Press (2006).

and correlate it with practical $\dot{E}_{human}(t_{observed})$ values is challenging both due to the latency restrictions and the physical/dynamic complexities associated with the interacting DRSs. Among these complexities, one may choose to highlight the large variety of heterogeneous stimuli arriving to the individual from the EI spacetime and his or her switching between several behavioral states, discussed in Section 3.3.

Based on the general road map of human energy transitions presented in Figure 2.1, we ask whether it is possible to correlate the origins of the individual's spacetime perception and PbB with physical events separately taking place in the different DRSs. Considering the conceptual distinction made between the latter, at first glance such correlation seems intuitively easy to achieve. Nevertheless, due to the persistent dynamic evolution of nature and the seamless transitions between the DRSs, ascriptions of "static" origins to absolute events might be harder than it seems. Let's explore three examples. In one instance, the individual uses his or her senses and recognizes a car parking nearby. The car is composed of different components that have been brought at a given point in time to a specific location and assembled to form the product holding the potential functionality it is believed to possess. Prior to their gathering, the components themselves had a history of changes and, quite similarly, ever since it was constructed and until its observation by the individual, the whole assembly of the car has been exposed to structural changes. One may notice that all of these structural changes have occurred externally to the observing human and that parts of this evolution happened, at times preceding his or her own existence as a living functionality. A second example refers to a tooth which is growing in a baby's mouth and evoking pain sensations for him or her. Undoubtedly, during its sensation, the tooth constitutes a part of the baby's body and its growth is being regulated by GEAP processes. Nonetheless, in order to practically grow the tooth, the baby's body relies, as insinuated by the EDB, on incoming EI content. The third example deals with human body symptoms that appear following a mosquito bite. Whereas the bite is carried out by an external object, its triggered reaction products become a part of the individual's body and can only be sensed after a short while.

We return now to the question regarding the DRS origins of such sensed/perceived events and emphasize first the differences between our reasoning- and objectivity-seeking perspectives of them, as compared to their direct experiences in the examples given. As with all interpretations, we assume that this relativistic difference can intensify with increased dissimilarities in BES arrays and the distinct subjective beliefs between the viewers/observers. These further accompany the observers' specific awareness to (and ability to process) details concerning the events. In contrast to the way we perceive it, for example, we clearly do not expect a baby who is sensing pain, such as from a growing tooth, to be able to indicate its physical triggers or even associate it with a bodily event. As one can expect, estimation of the DRS origins of each referred event relies on different subjective factors that bias perception and might turn the assessments to "fluid" or inconsistent. Physically speaking, this assumption does not contradict the idea, also reflected from the EDB, that global dynamics connect any internal human occurrence to the EI spacetime. Examining the case of the parking car, we refer to an object whose physical projection is circumstantially arriving to the observer's mind from the external environment. As the source of the projection is believed to remain EI throughout the entire observation time, we intuitively associate the origin of the experience with this DRS. Furthermore, we assume that as long as the patterned recognition of the car as a functional object remains sufficient for the observer's present assessments, typically no further attention is given, and awareness is raised to the past circumstances which have led to its current state of construction. Compared to the car, the baby's tooth and the mosquito bite clearly involve body-related events that extend beyond the systematicness needed for their sensations and interpretations. Being mostly unaware of the intake of minerals required for the growth of teeth, we tend to relate the origin of the event to the EM body DRS. This is also logically supported by the idea that the GEAP processes in the body trigger and regulate the growth of this functional content. In contrast, even if we have not noticed the biting event by the mosquito in real time, we tend to assume that our observed body symptomatic responses have been triggered by its presence and actions in the EI spacetime. The perceptual shifting of the origin of the event in this case to the EI world alludes that our spacetime assessments strongly rely on repetitive experiences which consolidate our beliefs in causality and circumstantiality as well as on an intensive personal use of the cognitive function of imagination in processing sensory information (also see Chapter 3). In the case of the question discussed and the dynamic shifting of the origins, these ID-reflected factors can also be associated with some sort of a *time qualia* among humans.

Within the possible personal interpretations, Table 2.2 attempts to standardize for us, the outside observers, the ascriptions of sensed and perceived events to their DRSs of origin. Whereas the possible guidelines still rely on subjective interpretations, they attempt to adopt a more objectivity-seeking, stricter nature which is based on physiological considerations. The first (I) type of incidents, *EI spacetime events*, is ascribed to the activation of the individual's body sensory units by external EI stimuli. The triggers consist of living or lifeless content elements capable of forming significant stimulation which can subsequently induce sensation and perception. Interestingly, a special case of living stimuli entails *communication events* with other humans.

Case	DRS-based event	Incident (immediate cause)	Stimulus
I	EI spacetime event	Activation of frontal sensory units by external stimuli (and conduction of the resulting structural changes to the mind for processing and transmission). Special case: communication event.	Sources/carriers of EI content capable of stimulating the sensory units with or without the individual's active intervention. Direct/indirect forms of physical communication transferred through EI spacetime medium.
II	EM body event	Activation of (mainly) internal sensory units (and conduction of the resulting structural changes to the mind for processing and transmission).	Changes in the EM body in the absence of clearly noticeable and immediate external stimuli causing them.
III	Mind event	"Non-sensory" changes in the ongoing mind activity.	Circumstantial reorganization in mind structures in the absence of clearly noticeable and immediate external stimuli causing them.

Table 2.2: DRS-based differentiation between physical events triggering perception and possibly PbB.

The second (II) type of incidents, *EM body events*, refers to physical triggers for perception that are recognized as occurring within the individual's body while activating its mostly internal[13] sensory systems and subsequent neural responses in the absence of clear and direct preceding stimuli from the other DRSs. It should be noted that the definitions of "clear" and "direct" remain dependent on our subjective interpretations, even as objectivity-seeking outside observers. Adhering to these guidelines, we regard both the experiences related to the baby's aching tooth and the symptoms of the unnoticed mosquito bite as EM events and ignore their causal past connections to the EI spacetime. The third (III) category of incidents refers to *mind events*. These relate to activity entailing circumstantial reorganization of mind structures which appear to occur separately from immediate EM stimuli,[14, 15] yet leading to an internal perception with possible impacts on the individual and his or her behavior. For convenience, the triggering in this case will be referred to as "non-sensory". We further believe that the mind events, which accompany the ongoing systematicness of the mind and affect its processes, rely on the activity of several cognitive functions related to memories, associations, and imagination, as well as on beliefs and other PCE transmissions. Clearly, we accept that all these processes hold a solid physical foundation in the general spacetime, complying with its global energy conservation dictates while externally depending on the EM body-mediated supply to function.

2.2 Sensoresponsive conversion: From external events to perceptions and behavior

The conversion tracts that supposedly lead to perceptions and PbB in the human are explored by science and we accept the present beliefs in them despite all the theoretical challenges and obstacles involved. From what we know and assume, the fundamental physiology behind many

---

13 One mentionable exception is the self-sensing of the individual's own body by means of his or her frontal sensory units. While the stimulus in this situation originates in the EM body, it is being received by the frontal units just as any other external EI event, and hence we may view it as a hybrid event amid Cases I and II in Table 2.2.

14 The occurrences may still involve memories of previously assimilated EM stimuli.

15 To be discerned from top-down processing of sensory inputs (see later in this chapter).

PbB processes entails consecutive sensory, processing, and motoric reactions distributed over GEAP-designated body and mind tracts. As we briefly mentioned in Chapter 1, we favor here to combine these reactive routes into a unified "sensomotoric response" corresponding to the trajectory of transitions a→b(→c)→d→e in Figure 2.1, and whose initial "sensoperceptive" part, given by transitions a→b(→c), involves mind activities related to sensation and perception of the EI world, decision making, and others. For simplicity, we will generally refer to such sensory-triggered human reactions as *sensoresponsive*. Examining the PbB elicited by the activity in these tracts, and especially its functional contribution to *recruitment* of EI resources, one may easily find the sensoresponses essential to the realization of the individual's genetic goals.[16] Namely, to sustain a positive $\dot{E}_{human}$ balance and preserve his or her own state of life, the human has to interpret the sensory signals from the EI spacetime and respond to them in a way which enables transferring some of the identified resources as E_{st}^{in}. Concurrently with that, realization of other goals requires allocation of parts of the converted recruited energy towards working on these matters in the sensory-interpreted EI spacetime.[17] With that in mind, we wish to emphasize that not all recruitment activities rely on cognitive processing and spatial decryption. For example, breathing air containing oxygen, which is required for our life-dependant "biofuel cell"-like operation is normally an unconscious behavior with different aspects of a reflex, and as such, it is not regarded as a PbB. Accordingly, we may distinguish between aware and unaware recruitment behaviors and focus our discussion on the former. Next, we return to Figure 2.1 and aim to identify the aware recruitment within the overall transitions taking place between the DRSs. We start with transition (a), which corresponds to the incoming dE_{st}^{in} transfer. Ignoring previous recruitment activities and their current implications on the human, we regard the relevant contributions at present to the upcoming successful recruitment processes as only

---

16 Unsurprisingly, the causality between the need to recruit energetic resources and life sustenance has been clear to humankind throughout the ages and is historically documented, for example, in the Bible verse Genesis 3:19 (whose other part was found relevant to the EDB): "By the sweat of your face you shall eat bread till you return to the ground".

17 When presenting the energy perception principles in Chapter 3, we will come across an intuitive belief that the recruitment also enriches us with some EI potential energy reserves.

certain[18] projections of sensory stimuli which are being contingently received by the human from the EI spacetime. We name these specific energy-directed vectors $a_{sensory}(recruit.)\equiv dE_{st}^{in}(sensory)$, bearing in mind that they occur in parallel to other incoming transitions, namely $dE_{st}^{in}(sensory)\in dE_{st}^{in}$, including, for example, some which fuel the metabolic cycles and as such are energetically vital also to the sustenance of the sensoresponses themselves. Physiology alludes that following the stimulation of the body's external (frontal) receptor units, the received sensory information is being neurally conducted to the brain(/mind) in an "inwards" afferent direction. Adhering to these concepts, we mark our next specific transition as $b_{afferent}(recruit.)$. The arrival of the neural projection of the EI stimuli to the mind is believed to be followed by its sensation and interpretation via cognitive processing. The systematicness involved in the latter frequently yields higher hierarchy-level operational decisions regarding possible interactions with the objects identified in the experienced situations. All these constitute a crucial initial stage in the execution of the PbB and the postulations regarding the mind mechanisms which facilitate it and lie at the heart of this book (as will be elaborated in Chapter 3). Following the processing stage, the neurally coded operational instructions are further being conducted, as indicated by the $d_{efferent}(recruit.)$ transition, to peripheral body effectors (mainly muscles) in order to trigger their motoric execution with respect to the decisions made regarding the recruitment. Following the activation of the effectors, we mark the resulting (senso)motoric response directed to the EI spacetime as $e_{recruit}$ and ascribe to it an output energy $dE_{st}^{out}(recruit.)$. This transfer is participating in the overall human emission processes, namely $dE_{st}^{out}(recruit.)\in dE_{st}^{out}$. Understandably, we assume that under the global, restricted-contingent causal deterministic dictates, $e_{recruit}$ is invested in "fruitful" interactions with the perceived objects that will genetically ameliorate the individual. Accordingly, we may describe the successful implementation of a given recruitment action by the consecutive chain of vectorial transitions $a_{sensory}(recruit.)\longrightarrow b_{afferent}(recruit.)\longrightarrow d_{efferent}(recruit.)\longrightarrow e_{recruit}$, accompanying the respectively tuned PCE emissions to spacetime.

---

18 Not all sensory inputs necessarily yield a fertile recruitment, as some will only lead to unimplemented or dormant perceptions and memories, whereas others may generate motoric responses lacking a significant genetic gain.

Whereas Figure 2.1 can serve as a valuable source for numerous energy-related hypothetical ideas,[19] it overlooks the practical and mechanistic complexities associated with the generation of human functionality. Among these complexities, one should highlight the *nonlinear conversion* characteristics of the body and especially of the mind functions, where, in the case of the latter, they are also ascribed to the cognitive activity establishing the spatial assessments. The nonlinear characteristics are associated here with an ongoing bias caused by a wide range of overarching physiological and mechanistic-systematic influences as well as by often-interlinked EM body and mind events. One exemplary complex factor relates to the formation of nonuniform delays between the sensory stimulation and the perceptive/motoric responses also due to the varying time constants of the specific physical processes operating along the biased pathways of the conversion. Further acknowledged is the complexity entailed in the integration of the heterogeneous multi-sensory stimulation inputs and their cognitive interpretations into coherent experiences and perceptive projections of spacetime. Considering all these, we expect that no simple, accurate, and practically reproducible way to estimate the direct linkage between E_{st}^{in}(sensory), E_{st}^{out}(recruit), and the consequent genetic gain exists. Nevertheless, we still regard the physical projections as milestones on the way to forming sensoresponsive PbB functionality and view the progressing trajectories that they form as some sort of a "contingent continuum" of energy transfers and structural changes. These cross the different DRSs (while forming a cyclic-like path, Panel II in Figure 2.1), are trajectory-specific in terms of structure and progression pace, and can be hypothetically linked to respective ID measures. As seamless transitions are persistently required in executing the inherited life functionality plan, it is not surprising that the GEAP has evolved into structural diversity and functional flexibility of sensory units and conduction/processing tracts which can occasionally overcome the impact of sporadic "failures" by providing certain conversion alternatives.

---

19 For example, that direct emission of the mind to EI spacetime accounts for a possible discharge of excessive sensory energy otherwise to be accumulated (or partly dissipated through additional routes) in the human via the incoming dE_{st}^{in}(sensory) transition.

We begin now to focus our discussion on the transitions participating in the formation of the spatial perceptions and their consequential sensoresponsive PbB. To aid the descriptions, we will refer to the illustration depicted in Figure 2.2. As we previously mentioned, we adhere to elementary physiology concepts encompassing sensory reception, neural conduction, mind/brain processing, and motoric implementation directed towards the external world. Our descriptions start with the EI spacetime, and more specifically the effective environment from which the individual is being contingently stimulated from and interacting with. We accept that at any given moment this "local region" in nature: (a) is bound to the universal physical laws of general spacetime; (b) some of its content circumstantially triggers the sensory systems of the individual human, initiating specific conversion processes which are congruent with our focus here; (c) provides a medium for the realization of different human genetic goals; and (d) contains other human individuals who uniquely experience more or less similar triggers and reactions, and under certain conditions interact with each other. Now, in regard to the first statement, we accept, for example, that spacetime is constantly changing, partly in attempt to reduce local accumulations of potential energy excesses and to increase the dispersion of energy states.[20] This is also reflected by many spontaneous consecutive reactions in nature, following specific paths dictated by energetic "downhill" and/ or entropy-increasing tendencies. Looking at the second statement above, one may accordingly parallel the EI spacetime to a dynamic "donor" from which the individual receives, spontaneously or normally by means of his or her own actions, crucial sensory signals. The *reception* process in this case, or in regard to any referred unit along the conversion pathways, causally follows a preceding *arrival* of stimulus content to trigger and activate its systemic functionalities.

Among different factors that determine the exposure of the human to EI stimuli and sensoreception of the latter, we wish to highlight the dispersion characteristics of content in spacetime. This can be exemplified by a few examples indicating various exposure-arrival patterns. The arrival of sun radiation to Earth affects every living

---

20 We acknowledge that some energy/entropy tradeoffs involving in some situations an investment of external energy (work) also exist and may at times lead to formation of metastable states in spacetime.

individual. Examining, for example, the ceaseless influx of thermal radiation, mainly as infrared/visible photon carriers, from our closest star to the atmosphere and the surface of our planet, we notice its continuous thermal contribution to all humans[21] regardless of variations and time-dependent fluctuations in its intensity.[22] Accordingly, we may regard the sun's thermal effect as exhibiting a dispersion pattern of "non-contingent background (persistent) stimuli" arriving to the individual from a continuously donating EI source. The persistent influence of the thermal radiation can be compared to the emission reaching the human from a far more distant star which is occasionally observed in the night sky. Like our sun, the distant star also emits radiation to its surroundings, yet due to its immense distance from Earth, the flux of photons arriving from it is insufficient for causing any noticeable thermal (but visual) effect. While the distant source is constantly emitting photons, due to external (such as cloudiness, light pollution, etc.) and individual (willingness to watch, ability to perform the observation, etc.) reasons, its visibility stays intermittent and discontinuous. We accordingly claim that in regard to the observing human, this case exemplifies a pattern of "contingent stimuli from a persistently dispersing source". Another light-concerning example describes a lamp installed in a room. Based on our experiences and beliefs, the light from the lamp may reach the individual as long as he or she is present in the room, the electricity switch is turned on and delivers power, and the instrument is functioning. As the lamp is occasionally switched off, the light bulb burns out, and the individual does leave the room, we associate case with a "contingent stimuli from a noncontinuously dispersing source" pattern. It should be noted that some EI sources also demonstrate periodically recurring dispersal characteristics that consequently yield cyclic stimulation patterns to humans.

---

21 Assisted by the thermal equilibrium formed between the photonic flux and the content of the atmosphere as well as its regulation via heat conduction and reflection of photons back to the outer space.

22 Numerous physical factors play a role in the sun's thermal effect experienced by every individual. These include the current position of Earth in its planetary revolution around the sun, Earth's rotation around its own axis, the thermal conductance characteristics of the environment the individual is present in, weather conditions, and so on.

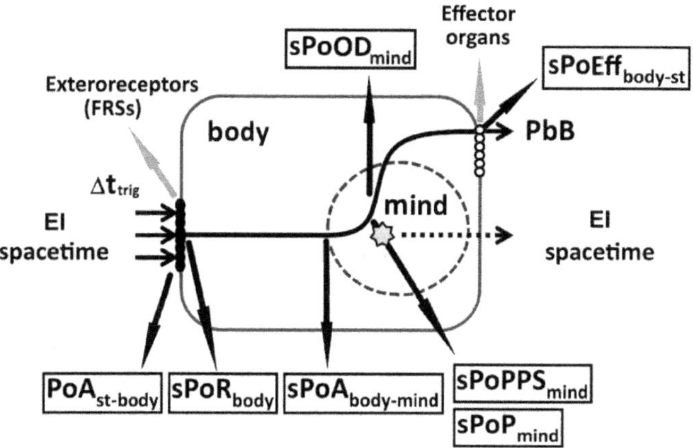

Figure 2.2: Selected milestones in the externally stimulated generation of several human perceptions and sensoresponsive PbB: Projection of EI spacetime content arriving to the frontal sensory units of the individual ($PoA_{st\text{-}body}$); body projection of sensory reception ($sPoR_{body}$); projection of the respective impactful body responses arriving to the mind ($sPoA_{body\text{-}mind}$); mind projection of pre-perceptive sensations ($sPoPPS_{mind}$); mind projections of generated perception layers ($sPoP_{mind}$); mind projection of operational decisions directed to the body ($sPoOD_{mind}$); and projection of activated effectors ($sPoEff_{body\text{-}st}$). All projections refer to DRSs-localized, dynamic structure/energy distributions emerging from the stimulation of the sensory units for the limited time interval Δt_{trig}. To simplify the presentation, anatomically inconsistent spatial separations were made between the afferent/efferent conduction tracts as well as between the sensory/effector units. The systematicness involved relies on E_{st}^{in} transitions, including contributions to $PoA_{st\text{-}body}$, which are not sensory.

Due to the restricted-contingent nature of the physical transitions and other reasons, not all the heterogeneous EI content arriving at a given moment to the individual can be received by his or her frontal sensory units and trigger sensoresponses. Needless to say, a similar fate is expected for content arriving to body regions which are uncovered by (their matching) sensory units. The frontal units are known to consist of different *exteroreceptors* which are deployed, in accord with the GEAP plan, at and near the individual's body interface with the EI world (Figure 2.2). Clearly, the componential functionality of these is to respond to the arriving content and transduce its presence and some of its arrival characteristics. As physiology alludes, the stimulation-reception process requires an initial potent physical interaction between the external stimuli and the receptors in order to trigger them and start converting the activated structural imprints formed into neural signals (followed by their transduction towards the mind/brain). Throughout the evolution of life on Earth, different exteroreceptors have been adjusted to match specific characteristics of environmental stimuli and as such require structural and energetic compatibilities with the arriving contents. We also acknowledge that some exteroreceptors are preceded anatomically by frontal body units or certain body-content interactions whose function is to improve accessibility to the incoming stimuli or to focus, amplify, or attenuate them prior to reception. These functional units are actively involved in most sensory arrays, including the crystalline eye lenses and the cornea, which help in focusing the arriving rays of light on the retina's photoreceptors, the outer and middle ear organs which respectively assist in collecting and channeling sound waves and in deducting acoustic energy losses before their conversion to neural signals, the saliva which dissolves orally consumed substances before their molecular binding to the taste buds, the nasal hairs that filter the breathed content, and so on. Due to their influence on the arrival characteristics of the EI stimuli to the exteroreceptors, these units and systemic actions are viewed here as integral[23] *pre-reception elements* which are also significant, as will be suggested later, to shaping the "broad individuality" dimension. Attempting to follow the sensoreception of EI events, and at a later stage correlate respective products of perception and behavior with the received inputs, we favor to restrict the exposure time of the individual to the stimuli. Accordingly, we introduce to our energetic description a theoretical limitation to be referred to as a *triggering time interval*, Δt_{trig}, and whose boundaries will be discussed. Through our choice of

---

23 One can also mention different artificial constructions in the EI spacetime which are analogous to the pre-perception elements. Products of human-made manipulations on external contents including spectacles, telescopes, microscopes, and others are widely employed these days, where some of the work (energy) invested in their assembly can be viewed as enhancing observations and promoting access to new observations via altering the arrival characteristics of the stimuli involved. The physical changes induced by these devices are subsequently transferred to the core perceptions of their human users and hold a potential to affect their PbB.

dynamic distribution function of structure or energy (or frequency), the triggering interval allows us to refer to the total EI content arriving to the exteroreceptors of a given individual within this duration as *projection of arriving EI spacetime content (PoA*st-body*)*.[24] As we let the exposure prolong to Δt_{trig}, we acknowledge that, at least on the absolute microscopic level, EI spacetime is changing during this time as well. The connection between the structural-organizational states of the externally dispersing sources and PoAst-body is often complex. It is easy to see, for example, that before reaching the individual, carriers which are travelling from the sources in the EI medium may circumstantially interact with other contents, and become reflected, scattered, transmitted through matter, and so on. Such processes will impact the arriving projection and our perceptive interpretation of the externally dispersing order. Adhering to the restricted nature of physical effects in general spacetime, we also assume that only an insignificant fraction from the latter is being effectively projected in PoAst-body, yet the information held by this projection seems to suffice for the human to decrypt his or her effective environment to produce functionality in. Quite often (yet not always, as will be explained in Chapter 3), our spacetime perceptions and beliefs align with the restricted-contingent principles of the universal construction and progression, in this case regarding the organization of the dispersing environment. For instance, while staying in an isolated room, it is intuitive for us to assume that our relatively meager and dull sensory projection of arrival does not insinuate an absence of a far richer external spacetime behind the walls.

We move on to focus on the sensory reception as the initial stage in the human conversion processes of interest. Examining the EI stimuli arriving to the individual, we find them to be diverse and associated with different complexity levels. Upon reaching the exteroreceptors in compositions, energies, and intensities/quantities that match their capabilities to interact and dynamic states, the stimuli trigger them, producing activated systemic impacts to be referred to as "body sensory inputs". The restricted-contingent progression principles of the process, which are manifested through the compatibility required

---

24 Besides its representation by a projective distribution function, we also regard PoAst-body as projecting the effective structural organization of the EI surroundings dispersing its contents on the individual.

for the interaction, raise the question whether the receptors are ready to become activated at all times. Similar to any physical system whose components are repeatedly/cyclically changing between certain transitional states during sustained activity, we expect the receptors to intrinsically possess periodical micro-level structures which we call *dynamic operational states* (*DOS*). One may ascribe to these states in this case some functional meanings, such as "standby", "activated", or "transduction", which allow referring to a *reorganization* process in the receptors. As expected, the process enables the receptor to revert to its standby state at the end of the consecutive operational transitions, thus allowing the continuity of the sensing process. We also accept that the lifetimes of the DOS and their transition times depend on the physical-structural characteristics of the respective receptors. The limited durations associated with these suggest an existence of synchronization limitations due to the inevitable presence of, even ephemeral, time intervals during which the receptors' interactions with the incoming stimuli are physically impossible.[25] With that in mind, we still acknowledge that the lifetimes of the DOS and the durations of their transition intervals are typically far shorter than the prolongation of many of the external stimuli effectively contributing to our perception and PbB. Under these circumstances, we assume that the mind has evolved to coherently decipher spacetime regardless of any possible "quantization" (see chap. 2, n. 25) disturbances to continuous sensing. Nevertheless, as we view the DOS as an integral feature of the conversion process and which is also reflected in the human ID, their contribution to the compatibility restrictions is highlighted. The time-related considerations lead us back to the triggering interval Δt_{trig}. With respect to the DOS, we choose the interval to extend beyond the time required for activating a single exteroreceptor, and ideally to prolong enough (in order to imitate a more realistic life scenario) for the system to be able to potentially interact with multiple stimuli, namely with some sort of Δt_{trig}-limited *stimuli cluster*.[26] At the end of the exposure interval any reception will theoretically be blocked, and an attempt to estimate the implications

---

25 These limitations may appear as imposing some sort of a quantization on the sensory reception.

26 In this context, the term "cluster" intends to visualize that several stimuli are dispersed within a limited time interval rather than that triggering is sequential and continuous.

of the reorganization caused by the stimulation cluster in the human will be performed. We note that while limiting the exposure time is expected to simplify the analysis and the descriptions, identifying the precise fate of each triggering-reception event in the perception/ motoric outputs remains a major challenge. Considering the multiple stimulations and outputs, nonlinear complex nature of the conversion, the time delays entailed in its processes, as well as our subjective interpretations, similar challenges are also expected upon shifting the focus in reverse to the individual's specific output and retrospectively assessing the exact specific sensory contributions that yielded it. Such difficulties suggest the individuality dimension as a theoretical link between all causal and circumstantial occurrences along the human conversion trajectories leading to functionality.

The physical processes behind the stimulation of the exteroreceptors have been intensively studied and different scientific methods allowed their verification and canonization. Regardless of any particular receptor or stimulus examined, the observations persistently reflect the restricted-contingent progression principles associated with the need to overcome activation barriers while maintaining structural/ frequency and intensity compatibilities, as well as matching the time synchronization with the sensing units. Given that, we return to the biophysical characteristics of the receptors. Several conventions are broadly used to classify these key units, including their anatomic deployment in the body (frontal exteroreceptors as opposed to internal interoreceptors), morphology (such as free nerve endings versus encapsulated forms), the type of stimulus they respond to (chemical, mechanical, photonic, thermal, etc.), their adequate stimulus (referring to the specific physical trigger which enables activation at the lowest threshold), adaptation rate (phasic or tonic), and so on. Naturally, we are also familiar with the different sensory modalities related to light/vision, sound/hearing, pressure/touch, taste, smell, temperature, and others, which are formed by triggering the respective receptors. Various observations demonstrate that specific exteroreceptors can be activated by different stimuli to yield modality sensations. One example is the visual responses obtained by stimulation of the photoreceptors at the eye's retina by either photons, pressure (forming "phosphenes"), artificial electrical trigger, or via other means. In other cases, activation of a specific receptor by same-source stimuli, yet differing in physical characteristics, will affect the outcome of the experienced sensation. For instance, applying different degrees of pressure on our skin leads to sensations of touch, pain, and others. We also ascribe a great importance to the adequate stimulus that is natural to the experience of each sensory modality,[27] and which probably correlates with the long-term preferential evolution of the receptors. For example, the activation of retinal photoreceptors by photons from the visible range is known as the natural trigger for human sight. Evidently, this light stimulus triggers a visual response of a far higher sensitivity as compared to the rest of the aforementioned alternative stimuli and provides the only option that can naturally generate the full and rich experience of sight. Further observations suggest that arrays of multiple receptors are often required to distinguish between sensations triggered by the same adequate stimulus possessing different physical/chemical characteristics.[28] One basic reason for this necessity stems from the GEAP-dictated physical unity of the action potential which is undistinguishably produced by all receptors to trigger the neural responses to the sensing event.

Next, we attempt to describe the reception process and initiation of sensoresponsive conversion with respect to the most anterior body point relative to the EI trigger. As a part of that, we notice that in every receptor exists a *frontal reception unit* (*FRU*) whose stimulation activates an unfolding systematic reaction to the sensing event.[29] FRUs

---

27 One notable exception is the pain-sensing polymodal nociceptors which react to more than one type of threshold stimulus (such as mechanical triggers, irregular temperatures, or chemicals which are expressed during tissue damage). This capability is supported by the free nerve ending structure of the nociceptors which are staying dormant until the damages appear.

28 For example, specific excitation patterns in arrays of olfactory chemoreceptors are essential in discriminating smells of odorants from mixtures. For example, D. Zwicker, A. and Murugan, M. P. Brenner, "Receptor Arrays Optimized for Natural Odor Statistics". *PNAS*, **113(20)**, 5570–5575 (2016). Another known example is that color perception relies on comparisons between excited arrays of cone photoreceptors, in accord with the univariance principle. See R. L. De Valois, and G. H. Jacobs, Neural Mechanisms of Color Vision. In *Comprehensive Physiology*, edited by R. Terjung (2011).

29 As most descriptions often focus on the bigger picture of physiological systematicness, they tend to pay less attention to the FRUs and regard them only as integral assemblies (organelles) important to the overall operation of the exteroreceptor cells. Nevertheless, it is commonly accepted that the stimulation of these units triggers an influx of cations into their respective receptor cells. As a result of the consequential depolarization in the electric charge across the cell's membrane (correlating with the intensity of the stimulation), graded receptor potentials are formed and can locally contribute to the buildup of the voltage required to fire the action potential (as the core signal for neural transduction).

can be associated with the optically active proteins of the retina's cone and rod photoreceptor cells (sense of sight); with G-proteins[30] which bind certain odorant molecules and compounds found in food (taste and smell modalities); with stereocilia as a hair cell organelle bending by the acoustic waves that reach the fluid within the cochlea of the inner ear (hearing); with a variety of mechanoreceptors, including Pacinian or Meissner's corpuscles, Ruffini endings, and Merkel's disks, which are activated by different extents of either pressure, cutaneous tension, vibration, etc. (also participating in the sense of touch); and with stretch-activated ionic channels. Within this diversity, Equation 2.6 describes in general the stimulation of a single FRU, associated with a given receptor and represented through the structure function k'_{FRU}, by a compatible external trigger, $k'_{stimulus}$, to yield the activated k'^{*}_{FRU} DOS which marks the initial response of the receptor to the sensing event.

$$(2.6) \quad k'_{FRU} + k'_{stimulus} \longrightarrow k'^{*}_{FRU} + k''_{stimulus} \text{ (single activation)}$$

It should be noted that the $k''_{stimulus}$ product is often quenched or consumed by the body. Next, we estimate the respective energy change in the FRU due to its stimulation:

$$(2.7) \quad \Delta E'^{*}_{FRU} = H(k'^{*}_{FRU}) - H(k'_{FRU}) \text{ (single activation)}$$

Interestingly, the precise E'_{FRU} rest state value may vary between similar receptors and is somewhat susceptible to the environment the receptor is exposed to (for instance, how deep it is located within a sensory ephithelium tissue) and physical changes in it. Adhering to these ideas, we define the *body projection of sensory reception (sPoR_{body})* as the dynamic distribution of all activated FRUs during the Δt_{trig}-limited exposure to the sensory cluster, and ascribe to it a respective energy distribution function which encompasses the entire

---

30 As well as other elements which are specifically involved in the activation of the proton entry channel and epithelial sodium ions channel. One may also associate the FRUs in these cases with the "rest levels" of the interior ion concentrations in the cells and correlate the reception states with the increase in the latter due to the direct influx of the H^+ or Na^+ from the stimuli.

$\Delta E'^{*}_{FRU}$ time-dependent contributions.[31] As shown, in attempt to mark the causal correlation between $sPoR_{body}$ as well as the subsequent projections and their sensory stimulation origins, we add the prefix "s" to their names. While some EI triggers can circumstantially lead to formation of sensations and perceptive/PbB responses, others may fail to do so and dissipate through biophysical and biochemical reorganization and other processes (some leaving an impact on future conversions). Further acknowledged is that in accord with the universal conservation laws, the overall energy changes represented by the $sPoR_{body}$ cannot exceed the energy donated from its source arrival projection. We should also emphasize that $sPoR_{body}$ may also reflect activation events which are not necessarily originating from the adequate stimuli of the receptors involved, and that with respect to the varying composition of the incoming flux of stimuli, the exact same FRUs can be reactivated multiple times during the exposure.

The sensory reception of EI contents arriving to the individual imparts to them a human projective dimension. Namely, $sPoR_{body}$ reflects a set of local body changes which start to relate at this point to the human individuality while they can also be causally and circumstantially associated with the greater organization of the dispersing environment from which the stimuli have been effectively arriving and received.[32] One may notice that the human systematicness involved in the generation of sensation, perception, and sensoresponsive PbB relies both on the intrinsic physical properties of the stimuli arriving and also on their occasionally interlinked, specific *arrival characteristics*. The different intrinsic properties (such as composition, structure, mass, frequency, etc.) of the incoming content will not only contribute to determining which modality-related units become activated in the sensing process but will also govern the

---

31 From now on we will similarly elaborate several significant activated states along the senso-responsive body and mind-conversion tracts and view them as time-expanded projections systematically evolving from the initial, limitedly triggered state of the system $sPoR_{body}$. In a similar manner to their $sPoR_{body}$ nucleus, the subsequently evolved projections to be described in this chapter will correspond to specific structure changes and energy functions, yet we believe that the accrued complexity they generate along the sensoresponsive tracts also increases due to the nonlinear nature of the conversion processes entailed.

32 These are naturally expected to fall within the receptive fields of the exteroreceptors, referring in this case to the EI regions from which the body-sensing units can be activated. Receptive fields are explained, for example, in A. Das, Receptive Fields. In *Encyclopedia of Cognitive Science*, edited by L. Nadel. Hoboken, NJ: Wiley (2006).

specific GEAP-designated regions in the mind/brain towards which the transduced information will be channeled. In this context, we further reconnect with our assumptions from the first chapter and suggest that different intrinsic properties of spatial contents might be scientifically correlated with their respective distribution functions which are based on reduced combinations of finite numbers (n) of fundamental frequencies ($v^0(n)$). Unlike the intrinsic properties, some prominent arrival characteristics that ought to be considered are the magnitude/intensity of the stimulation (I), which is occasionally expressed as a dynamic flux; the arrival direction of the stimulus, which under common conventions can be linked to a certain spatial angle (θ); and the continuity/frequency of its arrival, which are further related to the aforementioned exposure patterns. As we know, neurophysiology suggests that upon a proper activation of the FRUs, they trigger processes which translate the magnitude of the stimuli to proportional influxes of ions, and these subsequently form graded membrane potentials in the respective receptor cells. Compared to the magnitude, the direction of arrival of the stimuli is typically encoded through the asymmetric distribution of the activated exteroreceptors within the anatomically ordered sensory arrays.[33] The prolongation of the stimulus flux is marked in the body through the response patterns of the receptors, respective to their ability to react to continuous or segmented/intermittent stimulations and transduce them. It should be noted that physical dependencies between the different arrival characteristics of the incoming stimuli, as well as between them and the intrinsic characteristics, occasionally exist and thus can be accordingly formulated. Some of them are even intuitive to our direct spatial perception.

The physical compatibility needed during the sensoreception of EI stimuli leads to some questions regarding identicalness in experiencing and perceiving spacetime events. Let's assume that an ideal technology has been developed and it can produce an identical body reception projection sPoR$_{body}$ from two fully controlled arrival

---

33 In some cases, the human is taking an active part in the encoding. We tend to unawarely tilt our heads slightly sidewise, for example, while estimating if a source of sound is located exactly in front or behind us, thus forcing an asymmetric reception of the pressure wave in our ears' receptors. In other cases, involving, for example, the senses of smell or taste, the direction of arrival of the stimuli often coincides with the preceding motion and/or movements of the human, allowing access to it and enabling its sensing.

projections, $PoA_{st\text{-}body}(1)$ and $PoA_{st\text{-}body}(2)$, supporting differences in the properties of their stimuli clusters.[34] A second example compares two hypothetical EI spacetime dispersion (organization) states that under ideal conditions lead to identical arrival projections $PoA_{st\text{-}body}$ and thus to the same $sPoR_{body}$ (in this case we may also rely on adequate stimuli). Now, as each of these two scenarios begins with different spacetime content distributions and supposedly ends up with one,[35] we wonder if this has any implications on the human systematicness attempting to elicit functionality, and whether it challenges the concept of causally progressing correlated states, which we regard as pivotal for the entire sensoresponsive process. In regard to the first question asked, it is reasonable to believe that from physical and mechanistic standpoints of the sensory conversion it makes no difference to the human body what is the external stimulus behind the activation of its receptors. Under such circumstances, the individual is nearly incapable of distinguishing between the scenarios.[36] Unlike the individual who is unawarely experiencing the different scenarios as similar, we, the side observers, have the privilege to notice their distinct reactions. Depending on the cases compared, these reactions differ in the stimulation mechanisms, compositions and configurations of the contents involved, as well as other related physical characteristics such as energy barriers and efficiencies. These allow us to further scrutinize the entire "cyclic" sensoresponsive process described in Figure 2.2 and view its *correlated evolution* along

---

34 Such hypothetical situation relies on the aforementioned idea that some receptors can be stimulated by more than one trigger. Nevertheless, in this case we deliberately attempt to refrain from considering the adequate stimuli, whose sensitivity cannot be matched by any alternative trigger.

35 The physical identity of the projections stays purely at the hypothetical level, as we leave the question of its feasibility to external discussions dealing with physical restrictions over identity in nature.

36 Contrary to our choice here to strictly limit the triggering interval and mainly focus on processing present time-like information associated with relatively short Δt_{trig}, in real life the sensoperceptive process keeps being updated over possibly longer durations. Given enough time, broad sensory exposure, and attention, the probability of the individual to become aware of the artificial manipulations involved in the exemplified scenarios increases. Nevertheless, in absence of such an awareness it is fairly expected that the identical body projections would be processed in a similar manner. Consequently, it can be argued that such hypothetical events defy or at least weaken the probability for an ultimate veridicality to always exist, and contrarily enhance the probability, as small as it may be, that our perceivable world consists of artificial illusions in which our sensoresponses are externally manipulated and tuned by living others. It should be noted that in order to fully experience perfect replications of sensations and their perceptions, it is not only necessary for the body reception projections to entirely overlap, but also for all subsequent relevant conversion paths to demonstrate unity.

the heterogeneous and convoluted trajectory of changes entailed. This causal and circumstantial physical correlation encompasses all progression stages and elements, including, for example, the structural arrangement of the EI dispersing contents, the arrival of the stimuli to the FRUs, the reception with respect to the specific intrinsic and arrival characteristics, as well as all subsequent (biased) sensoresponsive projections and among them the back reactions and emissions towards the EI environment. Unsurprisingly, we believe that this correlation, contingently connecting one step to another, follows the causal determinism dictates governing the evolution of the general spacetime, to which we will briefly return in Chapter 4.

The reception of the EI stimuli in the exteroreceptors marks the beginning of the *conduction* of the freshly formed body structural impacts to the mind. By adhering to the mind/brain assumption and relying on standard physiological beliefs, we accept that the conduction sets out basic tracts of the sensoresponsive processes. Considering that, our choice to distinguish between the EM body and the mind leads to an unorthodox distinction between "body conduction" and "mind conduction" that should not defy the physiological continuity of the process. Despite the minor complications evoked by the distinction, we may view it as an aid to the description of the conversion systematicness and as a tribute to the fundamental role of the mind in it. Next, we accept that the heterogeneously distributed exteroreceptors transduce their stimulated responses to the mind through a network of neural connections crossing various sensory-sensation pathways.[37] Here, we aim to examine these biological processes from a broader, yet "simplified", physical dimension, perspective, and view them as a set of consecutively changing human microstructures bound to overcome restricted-contingent progression thresholds. At the most basic functional level, the changes are manifested as transitions between GEAP-dictated DOS that are further regulated, and thus biased to a certain extent, by other processes. In other words, we view the sensory conduction as emerging from an immense yet finite number

---

37 This utterly succinct description has intentionally left out many systemic factors and processes. In their most elementary form, for example, the electrochemical transitions between the peripheral and the central nervous systems involve activation of FRSs, regulation of cation flows generating graded membrane potentials, buildup and firing of action potentials, and mediated (synaptic) cell communication. The study of these and other related factors lies at the heart of neurobiology whose observations and interpretations are readily available to those seeking further knowledge in the field.

of subsequent restricted-contingent microscopic transitions between interacting physical units. With respect to that, we regard the net effective structural/energetic changes which are locally progressing in the human due to the reception of the external stimuli cluster as *travelling disturbances* (*TDs*), a term which is often used in describing wave motion and energy propagation in physical medium. Such TDs might be directly or indirectly affected by other TDs preceding or overlapping their existence in the conversion system, as well as by the non-sensoresponsive human processes. We further note that due to the restricted-contingent nature of the transitions, any transduction incompatibilities are expected to quench contributions of TDs to the functional responses while causing reorganization in the system. All these allow us to assume that the physical footprints of the TDs are being pronouncedly reflected in the human individuality dimension.

The body conduction of the sensory-triggered reactions eventually leads to the generation of a *projection of impactful body responses arriving to the mind* ($sPoA_{body\text{-}mind}$). From a physiological perspective, yet considering the uncertainty imposed by the latency of the mind, this projection can be hypothetically associated with a time-dependant distribution of action potentials and other cell/chemical potentials which are about to trigger the subsequential mind-conversion events (as a part of the entire respective distribution of activated and dormant nerve cells and their effective biochemical environments). While believing that each body content change reflected in the projection $sPoR_{body}$ originates "linearly" and "forthrightly" from a $PoA_{st\text{-}body}$ contribution, the physical correlation between $sPoA_{body\text{-}mind}$ and $sPoR_{body}$, as a part of the correlated evolution of the sensoresponsive process, already turns to be more complex and somewhat less intuitive. We believe that some of the reasons for that relate to: (a) the mechanistic transition to neural conductance and its physiological principles of operation; (b) the incremental and accrued impact of several influences during the conduction;[38] and (c) as a modular

---

38 We wonder if EM body events, shown in Table 2.2 (Case II), also have any effect at this stage over $sPoA_{body\text{-}mind}$, considering that later-stage correlations between interoceptive and exteroreceptive processing have been reported; for example, C. J. Koeppel, P. Ruser, H. Kitzler, T. Hummel, and I. Croy, "Interoceptive Accuracy and Its Impact on Neuronal Responses to Olfactory Stimulation in the Insular Cortex". *Hum. Brain Mapp.*, **41(11)**, 2898–2908 (2020); A. C. Marshall, A. Gentsch, V. Jelin čić, and S. Schütz-Bosbach, "Exteroceptive Expectations Modulate Interoceptive Processing: Repetition-Suppression Effects for Visual and Heartbeat Evoked Potentials". *Sci. Rep.*, **7**, 16525 (2017).

physical process, the conduction is prone to efficiency losses which might gradually increase the diversion between the projections. These include, for example, circumstantial losses of functional contributions below the thresholds required for firing the action potentials to obtain neural signal transfer. It is interesting to think that the nonlinear drifts can have an effect on the sensations and further challenge the already questionable veridicality. Nevertheless, as we lack the self-ability to recognize the inherent existence of the drifts, it may well be that we are used, and even hardwired, to sense and perceive the environment without awareness to them. In fact, we believe that experiencing the EI spacetime alongside distortions of the kind is nature's lesser energy-consuming evolutionary alternative to equipping us, for example, with individual nonlinear "keys" in order to compensate for their existence and for the specific qualia they may introduce into the experiences. Further complexities regarding the conduction relate to the space-over-time (dynamic location) distributions of the evolving projections. Contrary to viewing the activation of the FRUs as the beginning point of the sensoresponsive tract in the body, its exact intersecting location with the mind remains uncertain due to the hypothesized latency of the latter.[39] Embracing physiological concepts, we still believe, however, that the sensing-sensation pathways terminate at well-mapped specific brain regions, forming "wired" modality connections with their external world stimuli. The activity in these regions is believed to be based on similar fundamental principles of neural conduction as in the body, yet the progression at this stage demonstrates increased complexity partly due to the greater density of connected and activated cell units involved, and in accord with their specific wiring patterns. As implied, the complexity of the conduction is also enhanced by time-related factors. If we focus, for example, on the summation processes generating the action potentials to be fired along the conversion tracts, we notice that the absolute time required for the (biased) buildup of each significant transfer imposes an uneven

---

39 One may notice that we deliberately refrain from associating the body-mind interface with any specific region of the nervous system, including, for example, the Redlich-Obersteiner's zone, anatomically referring to the region which borders the peripheral and central systems. Additionally, we avoid referring to an exact number of neural cell junctions (nodes) participating in the conduction to the mind, and consequently refrain from employing notations such as "primary", "secondary", "tertiary", and so on, in regard to neural connections along the periphery-to-cortex trajectories.

progression pace for the TDs across the system. This effect does not only lead to a time-based dispersion of sPoA$_{body\text{-}mind}$ over the body/ mind but also contributes to such "expansion" (broadening) in the spatial distributions of all subsequent projections to be specified.[40] Following the conceptual-functional distinction between the DRSs, we view the transition of the TDs between the body and the mind as an *injection* of the gradually arriving sPoA$_{body\text{-}mind}$ projection to an ever-active[41] mind-processing "reactor" site. The injections of the TDs associated with the time-distributed sPoA$_{body\text{-}mind}$ projection trigger different reactions at the destination mind regions determined by the specific conduction pathways.

The anatomy and physiology of the human brain and their suspected connections to cognitive functions are at the heart of the multidisciplinary field of brain sciences. As a complex genetically expressed construction, the brain's tissue is composed of various ingredients such as cells of different kinds, blood vessels, organic and inorganic compounds, and others. Different structural and functional aspects of these have been unveiled and are still being relentlessly explored from different standpoints employing a variety of analytical techniques which enable, among other results, the mapping of neurally wired and communicating brain regions and units. The broad knowledge collected so far suggests, for example, that respective to the physical properties of the stimuli at their initial reception stage, the sensory signals (TDs) are being conducted to designated processing regions in the cerebral cortex lobes where modality-dependant sensory awareness is formed. From there, the neuro-response tracts proceed to the association areas in the frontal cortex lobes and then to the multimodal integration regions which are responsible for combining the sensory contributions into a "unified" experience. Upon monitoring and modelling the contingent neural transduction in the trajectories in conjunction with the PCEs formed and/or the behavior observed from the individual, and by occasionally correlating the discoveries with the existence of certain pathologies,

---

40 Highlighting, for example, the "binding problem", referring also to the necessity to harmonically integrate sensory contributions arriving to the mind (combined with other internal processes) in order to persistently generate coherent perceptions (for instance of spatial objects and dynamics).

41 Considering that mind activity is also sustained during times of sparse sensory injections and possesses an adaptive base-level operational energy.

scientists learn a lot about the plasticity of the brain and on the way that cognitive functions shape the human responses to the external stimuli. One important finding is that the neural networks encode high-resolution electrochemical projections of the sensed stimuli, and thus of the sensory-compatible EI "dispersing" environment (as a part of the individual's overall dynamic interaction field). An example of that is given by the retinotopic maps in the visual cortex (in visual area V1 as well as in other regions where they appear with enhanced complexity) showing excitation responses that are directly correlated with the light-stimulation of the photoreceptors at the retina. The encoding also relates to the principle of *neural tuning* which highlights a fundamental correlation between certain characteristics of the stimuli situated in the EI environment and their electrochemically induced activation of specific brain constructs. We may further speculate that the systematicness behind such correlations demonstrates a certain *trajectory encoding* which corresponds to the path-specific conduction of each TD following its external stimulation event. We also acknowledge the existence of GEAP-based splitting in the neural channels, such as in the case of the "ventral/dorsal" streams relevant to the sight and the hearing modalities. The specific conduction of the TDs through these channels seems to also relate to the type of cognitive assessments performed during the generation of the core spacetime perceptions for the sensory information they carry. Such examples are naturally just a tip of the iceberg regarding the global knowledge that has been acquired over the years in neurobiology and brain sciences. Also worth mentioning are the remarkable efforts invested in simulations and modelling of brain activity, and particularly the use of machine learning techniques, such as the brain-inspired "artificial neural networks". Many believe that these directions hold a promise for a better understanding of mind assessments and in predicting perceptive and behavioral responses to given stimuli.

Next, we wish to succinctly acknowledge the two well-known fundamental processing approaches accepted as "bottom-up" and "top-down". Bottom-up processing accounts in our context for a systemic attempt to interpret EI sensory inputs, which is solely confined to the "afferent" TDs information being conducted to the mind and is independent of previous knowledge, experiences, or expectations. Contrarily, all these are employed, while substantially relying on existing mind arrays including memories of encoded beliefs, for example, in top-down processes attempting to interpret the sensory inputs[42] and predict their changes and implications. The processing activity is believed to rely on a seamless operation of *cognitive functions*, also involving utilization of memory and imagination. The use of memory functions is often physiologically associated with the existence of synaptic plasticity along certain neural transduction tracts, and from a macro-level mechanistic viewpoint we stress the *comparisons* it conducts between incoming or awareness-evoked information and BES or other mind-stored data. These assist the top-down patterned recognition of objects and predictions of their changes. Commonly distinguished are the sensory, short-term (working) and long-term memory arrays, to which different brain regions, operational storage timescales, and, most importantly, type of stored information and functions are ascribed. Numerous factors affect the fate of the information encoded and stored in the memories. In addition to different biological regulation processes and pathologies, human behaviors such as experiencing, rehearsing, and others, are known to shift the "unequilibrated" offset between consolidation and forgetting of memories. As we mentioned, crucial to the processing is also the imagination. Among its different functions, we believe that this cognitive tool helps "flexing" (compromising) the above-mentioned "strict" comparisons while exposing the collated elements to fluid associative patterns. Such activity is particularly important during attempts to interpret abstract or newly experienced patterns, despite the further compromises made on the reliability/veridicality of the assessments.[43] Also acknowledged is the concentration function as a tool which aids the individual focusing his or her cognitive processing on specific mind distributions and which often brings, for the time being, to his or her attention the respective PCE transmissions of these operations. Accordingly, we view the concentration as a *mind lens* whose application may correlate with intensified localized conversion showing expedited action potential firing in specific parts of the

---

42 We also recognize an involvement of top-down processing in mind events as well as in higher cognitive activity preceding, for example, behavioral decisions (see Chapter 3).

43 We wonder if any analogies can be drawn between the imagination function and machine-learning operations which potentially self-readjust the program's own hidden layer functions to fit a certain input pattern.

neural network.[44] Consequently, we may regard the concentration as prioritizing some processing objectives while restricting others.

Functions like memory, imagination, and concentration will be regarded herein as emerging from the *physiological toolbox of the mind/brain* and we assume that their role in shaping the cognitive processes yielding the core perceptions and human decisions is prominent. Having said that, we deliberately leave the physiological exploration of these functions to the ongoing research in brain sciences and for its experts. Now, the lack of consensual and conclusive answers to theoretical issues such as the "hard problem of consciousness", regarding the phenomenological aspects of sensations and perceptions and their interlinked qualia, brings us back to the speculated mechanisms of mind processes. Examining the mind contribution part to the sensomotoric conversion process, we wish to mention three systemic projections whose generation is assumed to rely on its specified physiological "toolbox". The first in the suspected order of occurrence is the *mind projection of pre-perceptive sensations* (*sPoPPS*$_{mind}$). This hypothesized dynamic distribution refers to the body-channeled sPoA$_{body-mind}$ TD contributions selectively received by (injected into) the mind, and whose footprints are being transmitted as "pristine" PCE sensations that lack any perceptive interpretations at this stage. Such footprints are further assumed to relate to the aforementioned neural projection maps of the received external stimuli. Still devoid of spatial recognition and subjective energetic significance to the individual, the transmission of the incremental TD contributions of sPoPPS$_{mind}$ therefore corresponds to the direct sensation of the dynamic interaction field with the external environment. Partially siding with this idea are our intuitive observations that the sensation is "richer" in details as compared to the cognitively assessed interpretations which we provide to (only some of) them,[45] and that a certain processing time, even if short and mostly unnoticed, is required for the spatial recognition processes to

---

44 From a phenomenological standpoint, the concentration can be hypothetically linked to focusing the awareness for a given time (a process that we associated with "attention") on a specific region of an inner mind "screen" projecting the overall PCEs, or alternatively on one specific mind "screen" out of many which are simultaneously projecting different PCEs.

45 This systematicness seems reasonable considering the energy and time resources ostensibly being saved by avoiding excessive interpretations and through reliance on patterned recognition.

follow the sensation. The next set of mind arrays is ascribed to *mind projections of generated perceptions (sPoP*mind*)*.[46] These are viewed as cognitively processed products of sPoA*body-mind*, whose essence, differentiation, generation mechanisms, and influences, will all become the main focus of the next chapter and, as such, will be discussed in depth. We also note the enhanced complexity and subjectivity of the conversion at these stages, which contribute considerably to the uniqueness of the human individuality dimension.

The next dynamic array to be defined along the sensomotoric pathways is the *mind projection of operational decisions directed to the body (sPoOD*mind*)*. The projection corresponds to the mind products of the cognitive processing of sPoP*mind*, and reflects the decisions taken regarding the execution of motoric responses following the (spatial and energetic) interpretations of the TDs input components. Accordingly, we may physiologically associate sPoOD*mind* with the distribution of electrochemical and chemical potentials accompanying the neural responses that start being conducted efferently towards the body on the way to activate its selected arrays of *effector organs*.[47] Adhering to the mind/brain assumption, we might also anatomically localize the sPoOD*mind* projection within different motoric areas in the cortex which are responsible for motion planning. It should be further noted that the subsequential conduction pathways, including the lateral/anterior-divided corticospinal tracts extending from the upper motoric neurons in the cortex to the activation regions of the skeletal muscles at the lower part of the spinal cord, are well-known to science, and a considerable amount of information regarding them is readily available for further reading. The last human array we refer to and which marks the final stage of the sensomotoric conversion is the *projection of activated effectors (sPoEff*body-st*)*, which corresponds to the dynamic distribution of the effector organs activated by the conversion intermediate TDs associated with sPoOD*mind*. With respect to that, we may causally correlate the projection with subsequential, immediate physical interactions formed between the individual and

---

46 We further relate these projections to high-cognition processes, such as thinking and de-cision making, which extend beyond the core spatial perceptions and are believed here to be crucial to the generation of the sensoresponses.

47 In view of our interest in sensoresponsive PbB, our attention is naturally focused on the voluntary activation of the body's skeletal muscles.

his or her targeted external surroundings, as well as with the effective kinetic energy that was invested to enable them (and was "released" as dE_{st}^{out} from his or her $\dot{E}_{human}$). The resulting human intervention in the external spacetime is viewed as forming localized physical-structural reorganization, leading to some sort of "contingently progressing EI TDs". Occasionally, such sensoresponsive PbB contributions hold direct implications on recruiting resources and the realization of their executor's genetic goals.

Figure 2.2 depicts the sequence of suggested projections along the sensomotoric trajectory. These can be viewed as fundamental milestones on the way to elicit sensation, perception, and sensoresponsive PbB functionalities in every living individual. As implied, each successful transition between the projections requires compatibility and is susceptible to various systemic and other circumstantial biasing factors. We believe that the fate of the responses is dictated by the causal determinism governing the general spacetime and will refer to this idea in Chapter 4. Before moving on, we wish to briefly reacknowledge the complexity arising from the time-dispersion of the projections. From the triggering interval to the intrinsic prolongation of the conduction and the processing (and particularly regarding delays related to memory utilization), many factors increase the time-dependent localized dispersion of the TDs-based projections in the human and make it hard to follow the exact dynamics of their structural distributions. To assist our analysis somewhat we restricted the stimulating conditions and blocked sensory triggering right after and possibly also for some time before the exposure of the individual to the activation cluster. Additionally, we may rely on physiological and real-life observations and experiences to crudely approximate the times required to effectively generate functional outputs and consequently confine the analysis of the evolution of the projections to these limits.[48]

---

48 Upon a controlled triggering of the system, one may aim to analyze the dynamic distributions of the projections for a duration that can be possibly expressed as a multiplicity of Δt_{trig} by an expectancy factor (related to the nature of the trigger and other variables), and that would be typically suffice for the entire sensomotoric response to complete. Despite constituting only rough estimates which do not reliably address the complexity associated with the time dispersion of the projections, such semi-empiric time intervals for analysis may still apply to our practical needs. It almost goes without saying that, contrary, to that, we expect the hypothetical, ideal ID detector to accurately monitor and report the exact dynamics occurring in all relevant localities of the human conversion system.

So far, we have emphasized the critical processing contributions of the mind/brain to the human sensoresponsive products and conformed to their (bio)physical grounds. As with the EDB, at any given observation time which coincides with the individual's present we may ascribe to the content of his or her latent mind, represented by the hypothetical structure function $\dot{k}_{mind}(t_{observ})$, an energy value that relates to its progressive evolution:

$$(2.8) \quad \dot{E}_{mind}(t_{observ} \equiv t_{present}) = H[\dot{k}_{mind}(t_{observ})] =$$

$$\dot{E}_{mind}(\dot{t}_{0mind}) + \int_{t_{0mind}}^{t_{present}} (d\dot{E}_{body}{}^{in}/dt - d\dot{E}_{st}{}^{out}/dt - d\dot{E}_{body}{}^{out}/dt)\ dt$$

Looking at Equation 2.8, one may recognize the aforementioned assumption suggesting a single inlet versus two possible DRS outlets from the mind. As expected, we believe that, besides the sensory TDs, other $\dot{E}_{body}{}^{in}$ transitions from the body to the mind exist and correspond, for instance, to resources allocated to sustain the latter's activities and further support its conduction, synthesis, and conservation processes.[49] On the other hand, we regard the release of content/energy from the mind to the EM body (marked in the equation as $\dot{E}_{body}{}^{out}$) or to the EI space (marked as $\dot{E}_{st}{}^{out}$) as including, for example, efferent neural signals which are targeted to activate muscle effectors and the low-frequency waves caused by neural oscillations (that appear to correlate with the mind activity), respectively.[50] Similar to the EDB from Equation 2.1, Equation 2.8 also portrays a dynamic balance which reflects a positive individual mind energy, $\dot{E}_{mind}$, throughout its existence as a functioning DRS over the course of the human's life. Upon the death of the human and collapse of his or her ID, the ceased-functioning mind "merges" with the dead body as they turn into a lifeless content with a certain potential energy in the general spacetime. Scrutinizing the equation, one can also notice that the energy balance was time-adjusted to the

---

49 Also including the synthesis of ATP molecules in the brain cells' mitochondria through cellular respiration reactions. As biochemistry suggests, the energy released upon the ad hoc hydrolysis of the ATP enables the sustenance of the essential brain (mind) activities.

50 We refrain from treating PCE expressions like sensations, feelings, emotions, and so on as emissions per se and favor to view them as phenomenological reflections that stay within the structural-physical boundaries of the mind. Also see chap. 2, n. 10 and 11.

emergence, at t_{0mind}, of elementary cognitive functionality supporting basic sensoperception and sensoresponsive PbB. We note that prior to this instant, the mind's energy can be ascribed to its respective GEAP/CCF-shaped content which has been developing from the primordial zygotic core, while similarly depending on various EI transformations. Further acknowledged is that, as with the EDB, due to the use of energy as a projective measure, different structural states of the mind may coincide with the same $\dot{E}_{mind}(t_{observ})$ values. It is also interesting to assume that an analogous balance to Equation 2.8, adjusted to the relevant transitions in Figure 2.1, can also be formulated for the EM body.

2.3 Human individuality dimension

We return now to the hypothetical property of "individuality" suggested in Chapter 1 and examine its potential applicability to the individual human's core perceptions and sensoresponsive PbB. In this regard, we believe that the ID also reflects a circumstantial, structural- and energetic-based linkage between the states of the sensory-triggered body and mind projections described herein. We have previously assumed that the conversion is being gradually carried out by means of ongoing micro-level interactions-reactions, as opposed to viewing it as coarsely relayed between discrete physiological/functional projections. We suggested that such transformations maintain nonlinear input-to-output physical correlations whose complexity is presumably peaking at the mind-processing stage. Upon viewing the ID as correlating the—often hard to be exactly pinpointed—sequential dynamic human distributions, we approach the sensoresponsive conversion processes they reflect as a "black box", which is complying with the universal causal determinism dictates and locally contributing to the physical evolution of the general spacetime.[51] Now, it is known that the human body serves as a host for other organisms. While these guests convert and generate their own functionalities, they often play a certain role in the individual's life and thus we may consider their functional content

---

51 This generalized view enables us to leave out precise physiological as well as mechanistic descriptions and disregard, for instance, the circumstantial interactions between TDs, discontinuation in the conversion process due to different considerations, the cognitive comparison processes and their implications, and so on. As we stated, the exploration of these is deliberately left to brain sciences and relevant other fields of research.

distributions and even their own nonhuman IDs as contributing to his or her physical integrity and individuality. Another complexity relates to the multiple internal human influences acting on the sensoresponsive process and which impact the ID. Metabolic and homeostatic activities, pathologies defying genetically favored equilibria states, non-sensory mind events, and products of external interventions[52] are a few example for such influences. Despite the added complexity, we presume that the "ideal ID detector" is flawlessly sensing these impacts, and that their effect on the conversion is expressed from within the GEAP-limited divergence of the DOS among all humans.

We move on now to discussing some individuality-related aspects of the interactive interface between the human and his or her EI environment. It is quite natural to assume a correlation between the structural-operational state of the individual's frontal sensory arrays and his or her direct interactions with the external environment. Two critical factors to note in this regard are the contingent readiness of the sensory units to receive the stimuli and their momentary orientation with respect to the externally "dispersing" spacetime (which is partly determined by the individual's own motion). Considering these, we can define a dynamic interaction field for the sensory reception and refer to it as an *individual sensory field*. The latter corresponds, at any given moment of observation, to the distribution of EI content potentially holding an effective compatibility to activate ready-to-receive sensory units in the individual.[53] One may also "symmetrically" define an *individual motoric emission field* at the other terminal of the sensomotoric tract. The latter corresponds to the spatial distribution of the EI environment which is compatible to "receive" the physical responses projected by sPoEff$_{body\text{-}st}$ (the states of the ready-to-act effector organs upon their activation by the sensoresponsive TDs). The connections between the reception/emission fields to the readiness states of the frontal sensoresponsive body units as well as to the spatial

---

52 And among them intake of food or drugs. For example, M. Briguglio, B. Dell'Osso, G. Panzica, A. Malgaroli, G. Banfi, C. Zanaboni Dina, R. Galentino, and M. Porta, "Dietary Neurotransmitters: A Narrative Review on Current Knowledge". *Nutrients*, **10(5)**, 591 (2018); E. J. Nestler, S. E. Hyman, and R. C. Malenka, *Molecular Neuropharmacology: A Foundation for Clinical Neuroscience.* New York: McGraw-Hill (2001).

53 Somewhat analogous to the general receptive fields of the frontal receptors (or FRUs) yet referring now to specific stimuli elements that hold a genuine capability to activate the conversion and yield functionality.

orientation of the units towards the EI world, imply that the fields are also[54] impacted by the mind-body responsive feedback.[55] Elementary examples for this include orientation changes due to planned motion in spacetime or implications on visual reception by intentionally closing the eyes. Assuming that on the way to elicit functionality, certain inner systemic processes affect the frontal EM body units and impact the individual's interactions with his or her EI spacetime, we find these dynamics resembling a general case of system whose inner conversion processes affect its own inputs and thus actively influence its future IDs. This situation will be referred to as *broad individuality*.

As we continue to focus on the individual's responses to the EI spacetime, the concept of broad individuality leads us back to the uniqueness of the ID. In realizing the importance of human uniqueness to the discussion, the term "individuality" will be occasionally associated with the unique aspects of the conversion processes. Looking from an absolute level perspective, the organization of the frontal body constructions of every individual relative to his or her momentary orientation in spacetime is always distinctive. Nevertheless, general spacetime dynamics can still summon situations in which differences in reception by different individuals are small. One exemplary case describes two individuals standing in close proximity and watching a distant star in the night sky. We assume a relative resemblance in the readiness of the observers' visual systems to receive the starlight and minimal interferences around, allowing it to be the main contributor to their present sensations. Under these conditions, the remarkable distance between the participants and the star irradiating the photons leads to high similarity in the arrival projections of the incoming light at their photoreceptor arrays. Such a situation may consequently yield, depending on the inevitable extent of structural divergence in their overall conversion paths, close sensations and (patterned) perceptions of the EI event. Now, contrary to the case of the star, the great majority of external objects which we are used to sensing and experiencing in daily life are located far

---

54 It should be noted that the functional state and orientation of the frontal units can also change or be determined by circumstances which do not necessarily involve direct cognitive processing and awareness, such as in the cases of reflexes, pathologies, or externally forced events.

55 In Chapter 3 we will assume that this feedback may be biased by spatial estimations participating in the energy perception.

closer to us. The relative vicinity of the objects combined with their frequently inhomogeneous structural-topographical characteristics enhance the apparent differences in their (often mediated) arrival and reception projections, increase the probabilities to sense and perceive them dissimilarly. Unsurprisingly, when the observed object is indeed close-by, the spatial separation between the observers may indeed substantially contribute to these differences. Such situations are common when, for example, two adjacent individuals watch a certain object and only one of them can notice from his or her specific location a feature which is visually hidden from the other.[56] In accord with that, it is interesting to think that exposure differences could have been hypothetically avoided if only humans were able to condense into a volume allowing their sensory units to overlap. Needless to say, this situation is impossible due to, among other things, the anatomic and physiological restrictions.[57]

The inability of humans and their sensory systems to spatially overlap (to overcome reception differences) might remind us of the physical limitations occurring in nature on the *condensation of fermions*, as a class of subatomic particles—among them electrons, protons, and neutrons—that are commonly regarded as the building blocks of spacetime's matter. Based on renowned quantum mechanical considerations, Pauli's exclusion principle alludes that two fermions of the same species cannot share the same quantum state. Since the latter is theoretically required for the condensation, under regular conditions[58] fermions do not condensate to overlap in spacetime.

---

56 Frequently taking part in our daily experiences, we find such instances to be utterly intuitive. It should also be noted that the asymmetry in the sensory data received by humans, as in the case of the hidden feature, might have at times a substantial impact on the interpretations they give to the observations.

57 Cases where the same receptors are seemingly serving more than one conscious mind (or self, see Chapter 3) may be ascribed to Siamese twins sharing different body organs yet possessing two brains, for example, C. D. Murray, "The Experience of Body Boundaries by Siamese Twins". *New Ideas Psychol.*, **19(2)**, 117–130 (2001), including cases of a shared body with separate heads. Nevertheless, from a viewpoint that considers experiences produced by entire body constructions, we believe that an asymmetric reception also prevails in these special cases. Worth mentioning in the context is also the reversed situation in craniopagus twins who share certain brain parts while processing sensory data from different receptors distributed over separate body organs of similar functions.

58 Except for special cases, such as entailing the formation of "Cooper couples". One exemplary source of information addressing these matters is L. P. Pitaevskii, and S. Stringari, *Bose-Einstein Condensation*. Oxford: Oxford (Clarendon) Press (2003).

It should be noted that the quantum limitations in the suggested analogy are paralleled to the anatomic-physiologic restrictions and that different connections can be further drawn between the human individuality and the fermions' quantum states (upon viewing the particles as functionally contributing, for example, to the global construction/dynamics of spacetime).[59] Considering these ideas, the implications on the individual sensory fields by the physical restrictions forcing the separation of humans in spacetime will be referred to here as *fermionic-like limitations*, and their contributions to distinct experiences of individuals, possibly as a source of "fermionic qualia", will be acknowledged. Adhering to the fermionic-like limitations, we argue that even if two completely identical individuals were about to appear at the same moment on Earth, the asymmetric distribution of the EI content around them and thus their sensory fields would begin to diverge with time. Under these conditions, the gradually accruing changes in each individual's mind structures will impact to a certain degree his or her own interpretations of spacetime and subsequently leave a mark on his or her sensoresponsive PbB. In summarizing the concept of "broad individuality", we reemphasize that the unique states of the body and the mind arrays and their dynamic feedback mechanisms affect the specific frontal organization and orientation of the individual with respect to his or her external environment. As these impact the human interactions with the EI world, we regard the interlinked internal systematicness and external conditions involved as holding a fair potential to affect the individual's life and functional gains.

Examining the concept of "uniqueness", one can ascribe this property in general to an object with some observed/perceived characteristics (which in principle can be also correlated with structures) believed to be different from those of all other objects being compared to it. As such, uniqueness may support an identity in major parts of the compared objects, yet it still requires an overall difference between them as a whole. Now, due to the remarkable structural as well as dynamic complexities associated with the human conversion processes, including the exceptional distribution of

---

59 Regardless of the analogies made, we accept that human IDs remain unique even in the somewhat "bosonic states" of an embryo in his or her mother's womb, or of Siamese twins who share certain body organs yet differ in their overall conversion pathways.

branching conduction pathways, multiple active units and their DOS promoting the advance of the TDs along these tracts, and numerous microscopic-level factors and external influences, we expect that at any given moment the overall IDs reflecting the conversion processes in every individual will remain unique. The ascription of this structural "fingerprint" dynamic state to the human allows us to ask whether his or her functionality in terms of responding to EI stimuli is also unique. In order to address this topic, we need to first understand whether exposing individuals to similar events under similar conditions will necessarily lead them to different perceptions and responses. For this purpose, we describe herein several experiments, attempting to simulate real-life scenarios that test the question. In the first experiment, several individuals are asked to identify an object reflecting—as generally agreed on by us, the outside observers— certain physical properties of a "red ball". During its course, the experiment is preferably performed under conditions which attempt to fixate the external exhibit as well as to unify the orientations of all participants with respect to it. In addition to minimizing the potential effect of the fermionic qualia, an effort to eliminate the presence of possibly interfering stimuli will also take place. While these attempts do not withhold the structures of the individual, the observed object, and the EI medium between them, from changing at least on the micro level, we still expect that the majority of answers given to the question will yield similar descriptions of observing a "red ball". These can be further validated by us, the outside observers who analyze the situation and might even possess more information regarding the exhibit, and who naturally share the same body and mind systematicness with the participants.

Let's scrutinize the observations from a broad perspective. Considering the complex processes entailed in interpreting the exhibit and communicating its lingual description, it seems that the simplicity of the nearly identical, repetitive answers is somewhat deceiving. In fact, despite their similarity, we insist that the answers given do not challenge the uniqueness of the IDs during the observation and response. One may expect, for example, that the results of the experiment would only apply to a limited group of individuals among the entire population. The participants must show, for example, some resemblance in their memory-embedded BES[60] and related other mind structures which are required for the top-down processing of the sensory information received and for assembling the verbal descriptions (in a language that could be deciphered by the examiners), must have unimpaired body organs that can potently sensorespond, should abstain from consumption of different substances which can bias or fail the experiment (see chap. 2, n. 52), and so forth. To further assess the apparent discrepancy between the similarity of the given answers and the suspected variance in the IDs among the participants, we wish to refer both to the systematicness behind the "normalization" of the answers and potential ways to counteract it.

Despite the multiple differences between the humans participating in the "red ball" experiment, we believe that common to them all is the ability to recognize and interpret external objects and their properties using patterned perception. This type of "accelerated" systematicness is often carried out at the cost of losing a massive amount of unprocessed information which we suspect can still be directly experienced via the sensation of sPoPPS$_{mind}$. A further acceleration, this time from the communication standpoint, is obtained by the use of language to succinctly categorize identified objects, such as the red ball in our case, and dynamic situations. The lingual descriptions ascribed to many observations are bound to complex influences that concern the individual's verbal abilities and other personal factors such as knowledge, experience, wish to satisfy an examiner, and others. Despite occasionally leading to discrepancies between the descriptions given, these are often normalized by the systematic assembly of the language and its expressive limitations. Indeed, many recognized objects, such as the red ball in our case, fall within conventional patterns which are shared by many as categorized descriptions. As expected, we suspect that these processes occur without violating the unique IDs of the communicators, and that they fit well in expressing real-life situations from the perspective of the practical human needs. It should be noted that it is also possible to reduce the impact of the patterned lingual descriptions in the experiment by monitoring brain

---

60 One extreme example to support this claim involves a similar experiment, yet with participants who have hypothetically just come out of a "Plato's cave" (Plato, *The Allegory of the Cave*, P & L Publication. (2010)). Such a group of humans is likely to interpret the exhibit in entirely different ways, implying the great importance of accrued personal experiences to the perception of EI events.

activity (mind emission) responses instead of verbal reports. Whereas sensoperceptive physical responses are being commonly transmitted by all humans, upon analyzing their exact features, personal differences that can also be attributed to every participant's individuality may become evident. Clearly, such analyses can be hard to interpret.

In fact, one does not necessarily need any additional methods or specific instrumentation to notice variations in perceptions of "fixed" objects among humans. Increasing the number of the participants in the aforementioned experiment would enhance, for instance, the probability to find dissimilar responses. An akin tendency is also expected upon asking a group of participants to increase the level of detailing and report their estimated impressions regarding, for instance, the exhibit's composition, dimensions, weight, texture, hue, and so on. While these assessments are naturally still bound to different patterns associated with the top-down processing, their increased diversity projects on the structural differences between the individuals.[61] An alternative way to modify the original experiment into accentuating individual differences is by increasing the abstraction of the exhibit. Following the exposure of the participants to objects whose characteristics are not easily recognized via "conventional" patterns, an increased activity of the imagination functions prevails. The latter enhances the associations-based fluidity of the top-down comparisons with BES arrays, thus enabling further, "less patterned" channels of the individuality to become expressed within the responses. Accordingly, replacing the "red ball" item with an abstract exhibit is expected to diversify the descriptions given to it by participants of the experiment, indirectly reflecting their unique structural differences.

Whereas variations in the perception and behavior of humans

---

61 The different lingual expressions obtained in the experiments can also reflect variations related to qualia. We assume a strong correlation between language and qualia as we view many of the words and expressions used to be unified reflections of "qualia blends". The term "red color" expresses, for example, a sensation which, according to scientific conventions, is mainly triggered by photons of a certain wavelength range. A major contribution to the definition of this range, however, can be attributed to a collection of experienced hues reflecting personal qualia from different observations made by numerous observers. These helped standardize the commonly accepted convention regarding the color "red", which enables, for example, different individuals to agree that they observe a red object (and decide if someone is impaired to see it and as such remains outside the norm), even if each of these humans is experiencing the same stimulus slightly differently or upon sensing photons of different wavelengths in the acceptable range. Such examples highlight the power of the language in communicating patterned descriptions of sensations and interpretations of the environment.

might appear minor behind different patterns, each individual remains unique throughout his or her life. We believe that this uniqueness emerges hand in hand with an ongoing interplay between the human and his or her environment, and it coincides with the feedback which allows the sustenance of the living functionalities. Despite the inevitable differences between people, we may still discuss the similarities in their GEAP-dictated conversion systematicness and focus on the common mechanistic aspects of their core perceptions and PbB. Quite frequently, these shared traits enable humanity to establish efficient communication transfer while describing spacetime and to share beliefs that narrow down relative mind dissimilarities while uniting perfectly unique humans around them.[62] Our next stage aims to use these evolutional tools in exploring the mind systematicness behind the conversion processes of interest.

---

62 In Chapter 4 we will also mention cases in which communication catalyzes the abandonment of present beliefs and dissociation from social structures gathered around them.

Chapter 3

Individual Energy Perception and its Contribution to Human Behavior

3.1 Precursory mind activity: From direct sensation to the "classical" spacetime perception

In contrast to Chapter 2, which emphasized several physical aspects of the human sensoresponsive process, we want the current chapter to further focus on the mechanistic side of the individual's core perceptions and their behavioral implications. We start by noting that we are fully aware that some of the assumptions to be presented herein might not entirely harmonize with certain observations or beliefs by others and, as such, call for further debate, exploration, or adjustments, and yet we still believe that they can contribute to the present understanding of the human response mechanisms and/ or trigger further hypotheses in their regard. One such assumption suggests the existence of an *individual energy perception* (*EP*), to which we will give major focus in this book and try to associate with several elements in the evolution of nature. We start by postulating that the experience of sensations and then perception-based PCEs is systematically following a *layered-like pattern*. The outcome is somewhat similar to experiencing an augmented reality, where its basal roots in this case correspond to direct pre-perceptive sensations of the EI stimuli, and the layered parts added gradually contain, among potentially other PCEs, the chronological transmissions of the mind projections of the incrementally generated perceptions, $sPoP_{mind}$. Now, due to their status that is not entirely consensual, we approach the "transmission processes" forming the different PCEs involved in the whole layered pattern with a considerable carefulness. Irrespective of any possible physical explanation for these occurrences, we acknowledge their potential analogy to modern practices employing "projection" of data on displays (which, in our case, correspond to mind structures supporting the individual's consciousness). Driven by external energy supply to sustain their continuous operation, these functional processes require three main components: information to be projected, a projector, and a screen. Throughout this chapter, we will regard the projector and the screen as some sort of "black box" mind/brain components and, as we previously implied, leave the debate regarding their physical functioning to external research. Nevertheless, our efforts will mainly focus on the projected information and the systematic structural transformations it is exposed to while being converted into the mind products projected to the screen. In accord with our assumption of a layered-like experience, we believe that the gradual buildup of the perceptions, as precursory mind projections to potential PbB, is based on several generally sequential, but at the same time co-dependent and in this sense alternating, steps. Each of these, except the nonperceptive basal, relies on cognitive processing and transmission of the converted information encoded in specific mind structures. We further assume that these processes do not necessarily require the awareness of the individual to all the PCEs generated throughout their progression.

As mentioned, the first (basal) mind array believed to begin the layered experiences relates to the sensory projection encoding the "pristine" pre-perceptive sensations. With respect to the mind/brain assumption, we suspect that the mind arrays relevant in this case correlate with the aforementioned "projection maps" reflecting the imprints of the EI stimuli in the neutrally wired cortex regions. These were associated in Chapter 2 with the direct pre-perceptive projection $sPoPPS_{mind}$, whose structural distribution can be referred to at any given time as $\dot{k}_{mind}(sPoPPS_{mind})$.[1] It should be noted that from now on we will refer to the transmission of the pre-perceptive projection using the abbreviated notation $\dot{k}_{mind}(sPoPPS_{mind})\{sPoPPS_{mind}\}$, where $\{sPoPPS_{mind}\}$ corresponds to the transmitted PCE of the mind distribution function $\dot{k}_{mind}(sPoPPS_{mind})$. Starting from Chapter 2, we have assumed that the transmission of the pre-perceptive projection precedes the PCEs of the core perceptions. As we stated in that chapter, this might be

---

1 We recall that this distribution is dynamic and considered to be time-expanded throughout the Δt_{trig}-long exposure to the triggering cluster (while allowing the systematic processes involved to take place).

noticed by occasionally experiencing delays between perceptions and sensations and by the absence of many spatial details from the perception in contrast to experiencing them through direct sensation. While these impressions do not rule out the possibility that cognitive processing can occur in parallel or even before sensation (while we experience sets of delayed PCEs, for instance), they intuitively lead us to assume that the direct {sPoPPS$_{mind}$} functions as a precursor PCE in the sensoresponsive chronology. Following the experience of the sensation, we assume that its dynamic $\dot{k}_{mind}$(sPoPPS$_{mind}$)-based[2] mind arrays start being cognitively processed to yield a sensoperceptive product which contributes to the "classical" spacetime perception (CP), {$\dot{P}^0_{CP}$}. It should be noted that the "^{0}" sign assigned to the PCE is used to indicate the involvement of cognitive processing at this stage and its reflection through a subjective perception "layer", which is not necessarily veridical in regard to spacetime. Among its broad capabilities, the CP is believed to decipher identities and interpret physical properties, relations, dynamic situations, and other features in the mind projection of the direct sensation (projecting by its own on the EI interaction field and thus on the dispensing environment). All these still lack at this stage any energetic-genetic meaning to the observing individual. To perform the spatial assessments and convert the pre-perceptive sensations to effective perception schemes and PCE, the processing significantly relies on top-down processes employing memorized BES arrays (Equation 3.1).

$$(3.1) \quad O^0_{CP}[\dot{k}_{mind}(sPoPPS_{mind}), \dot{k}_{mind}(BES)] = \dot{k}'_{mind}(CP)\{\dot{P}^0_{CP}\}$$

Thus, in accord with the descriptions above, which expand the elementary observation mechanism suggested in Chapter 1 (related to Figure 1.1), certain parts of the structural distribution $\dot{k}_{mind}$(sPoPPS$_{mind}$) are being converted to the respective mind products $\dot{k}'_{mind}$(CP). The

---

2 For simplicity reasons, we will keep referring throughout our descriptions to plain distribution functions in the mind, such as $\dot{k}_{mind}$(sPoPPS$_{mind}$). Nevertheless, we assume that some basic characteristics of these are being systematically assimilated in memories of various degrees of temporariness. Such intrinsic operations might allow us to reevaluate the cognitive interpretations at later stages, when the initial distribution function has already collapsed (as a result, for example, of the conversion process), at the cost of a compromise in the accuracy of the duplicated structures.

latter are then transmitted as transient contributions to the CP,[3] forming the $\{\dot{P}^0{}_{CP}\}$ layer on top of the $\{sPoPPS_{mind}\}$ phenomenological conscious experience. The assessments carried out in conjunction with the structural transformations are attributed to systematic mind processes whose "macro" mechanism of operation is represented by the operator $O^0{}_{CP}$. We believe that $O^0{}_{CP}$ and other assessment operators we will soon elaborate on are genetically expressed to include various sets of rules regarding targeted methodological interpretations and that their operation is implemented through the functional cognitive toolbox of the mind. In doing so, these operators correlate certain relevant mind distributions with phenomenological experiences. As shown, Equation 3.1 suggests that the cognitive processing conducted by $O^0{}_{CP}$ relies on both the incoming sensory information and the BES arrays, $\dot{k}_{mind}(BES)$,[4] with the latter corresponding to the accrued assimilation of the individual's experiences of EI spacetime, EM body, and mind events in the designated memories. From the physiological standpoint, the cognitive operations are likely to be carried out through the neurobiological conversion systematicness, which we associate here with the operational mind functions emerging from the dynamic distribution $k_f(CP)$. Due to our belief that assessment operators such as $O^0{}_{CP}$ are fundamentally shared among humans, we refrain from assigning them individuality notations.

At this stage we may ask: What is the function of the PCEs themselves? Or, alternatively, Why were we not evolved in a simpler way to respond to external events without the formation of consciousness intermediates?[5] Despite these interrelated questions not being trivial, we can speculate several possible answers for them

---

3 The prime sign (') assigned to the distribution function $\dot{k}'_{mind}(CP)$ is used to indicate that the generated products provide a specific contribution to the entire perception, namely $\dot{k}'_{mind}(CP) \in \dot{k}_{mind}(CP)$. A similar notation will follow in subsequent perception layers.

4 As suggested, we believe that the top-down processes participating in the cognitive interpretations involve imagination-driven, fluid associative comparisons with the key arrays of $\dot{k}_{mind}(BES)$ stored in memories. Despite deliberately omitting it from the formulation, we further assume that respective to the systemic transformation $\dot{k}_{mind}(sPoPPS_{mind}) \rightarrow \dot{k}'_{mind}(CP)$, the BES arrays also change, as in $\dot{k}_{mind}(BES) \rightarrow \dot{k}'_{mind}(BES)$. These relative changes may nevertheless be subtle and occasionally become indirectly noticed through drifts in our memories with time. The modified $\dot{k}'_{mind}(BES)$ contributions are assumed to be belatedly updated in the long-term memory during the behavioral state of sleeping (see Section 3.3).

5 In an analogy, for example, to an autonomous car which is designed to navigate and drive also via assessments of environmental inputs, yet supposedly without generating consciousness.

The first (a) suggests that some of the generated PCEs are themselves mechanistically involved in promoting or restraining the PbB of the individual. Besides its various impacts to be discussed later in this chapter, this "regulation" mechanism is also assumed to be responsible for creating several illusions regarding, for example, freedom and altruism, which help in "lubricating" the persistently working human mind "machine" towards achieving, ameliorating, and conserving the inherent genetic goals. Another speculation (b) is that through their transmission processes, either onto a single or multiple yet linked consciousness "screen(s)", the PCEs integrate converted contributions that might not have otherwise been able to gather and connect efficiently due to the physical limitations posed by their deployment in the mind or from a parallel physiological perspective, to the restricted-contingent synchronization and wiring limitations in the brain. In this sense, the PCEs act as a tool which promotes integration and, as such, they have remarkable implications on the responsive outcome. It should be noted that in none of the stages of these projective processes (which might to a certain degree resemble a communicative exchange of data regarding physical events) appears any violation to the restricted-contingent physical progression dictates of the general spacetime, and the physicalistic-materialistic nature of the latter is well conserved. A third potential reason (c) to justify their occurrence associates the PCEs with their proceeding emission processes. While confining the transmissions to the mind DRS, we recall their correlation with the emission of (distinct patterns of) neural oscillation-triggered, low-frequency waves to the EI world, holding functions that have been speculated by many.[6] Despite the neural conduction which possibly facilitates the mind/brain processing being regulated by $\dot{E}_{st}^{in}$ metabolic-based energies, it might be that the specific emission processes coupled to the PCEs inherently function in reducing—even marginally and in parallel to other dissipation pathways—a potentially excessive energy buildup

---

6 Including, for example, improving the propagation of the neural signal and carrying information about diverse modalities from the early stages of the sensory pathways. For example, K. Koepsell, X. Wang, J. A. Hirsch, and F. T. Sommer, "Exploring the Function of Neural Oscillations in Early Sensory Systems". *Front. Neurosci.*, **4(1)**, 53 (2010); E. Başar, "Brain Oscillations in Neuropsychiatric Disease". *Dialogues Clin. Neurosci.*, **15(3)**, 291–300 (2013).

in the individual caused by his or her persistent[7] sensory excitation dE_{st}^{in}(sensory).

We continue now to describing several factors which are assumed to play a role in the generation of the CP and its transmitted PCE layer $\{\dot{P}^0{}_{CP}\}$. Ahead of the discussion, we reemphasize the basic desire to shift our focus away from the technical aspects of the spatial perception. One main reason for that lies at the rapid scientific and technological advances during the last few decades which have driven current high-level research and the collection of immense knowledge in brain sciences and related disciplines.[8] Accordingly, we choose to deposit the technical elements of the CP in the expert hands of the scholars researching it. Another incentive in doing so relates to the prime importance we ascribe here to an assumed existence of a complimentary core spacetime perception, which refers to the individual EP. The energy perception receives the main focus of this book due to its postulated critical role in directing the PbB towards the realization of the human genetic targets. With this in mind, we still wish to add several of our own notions and interpretations regarding the CP: (a) we reemphasize that experiences of EI events are always separated in space and time from their source occurrences. Examining the observations carried out by a certain human over an extended time period, it appears that he or she is repeatedly switching under certain circumstances between different observing states. In accord with this view, spacetime perception can be analogously compared

---

7 Demonstrating fluctuations that possibly also depend on switching between behavioral states (described at the end of this chapter).

8 As a drop in an ocean of discoveries, we highlight, for example, the specific connections found between the characteristics of received external stimuli and different neural structures and dynamics in the human brain. Research has indicated, for instance, a correlation between recognized places and activation of specific neural arrays ("place cells"). Also worth mentioning is the Gestalt psychology which is mostly known for pointing out the human propensities to preferably assess and perceive the spatial properties of entire patterns contrary to their discrete components. Some relevant findings and opinions regarding these and other CP-related topics can be found here: J. J. Gibson, *The Ecological Approach to Visual Perception: Classic Edition*. New York: Psychology Press (2014); M. S. Castelhano, and K. Krzyś, "Rethinking Space: A Review of Perception, Attention, and Memory in Scene Processing". *Annu. Rev. Vis. Sci.*, **6**, 563–586 (2020); F. L. Dolins, and R. W. Mitchell, Eds., *Spatial Cognition, Spatial Perception: Mapping the Self and Space*. Cambridge: Cambridge University Press (2010); D. D. Hoffman, M. Singh, and C. Parkash, "The Interface Theory of Perception". *Psychon. Bull. Rev.*, **22(6)**, 1480–1506 (2015); A. D. Ekstrom, and C. Ranganath, "Space, Time, and Episodic Memory: The Hippocampus is All Over the Cognitive Map". *Hippocampus*, **28(9)**, 680–687 (2018); G. Vallar, and A. Maravita, Personal and Extrapersonal Spatial Perception. In *Handbook of Neuroscience for the Behavioral Sciences*, edited by G. G. Berntson, and J. T. Cacioppo. Hoboken, NJ: John Wiley & Sons Inc. (2009).

to an interpretation of a "film", made of sensory-triggered sensations $\{sPoPPS_{mind}\}$, whose filming, directing, script-writing, and playing are conducted in part by the individual who is intermittently watching it. It should be noted that whereas some fundamental aspects of such a "film" are shared amongst humans, its specific "plot" and experience remain personal, and that the "film" is mostly documenting the projection, contrarily to the absolute physical states, of the dispensing spacetime. Furthermore, we believe that the interpretations given by different humans to their individual "film" experiences rely on the same perceptive mechanisms yet are susceptible to different influences and biases. The impact of the latter is assumed to increase even further at the subsequent stages, where energy evaluations and genetic considerations become dominant factors in the processing. Now, to complement our descriptions, we may also use an additional analogy, and view the $O^0{}_{CP}$ operator processing and interpreting our "film" as "software". The latter is globally coded for humans through the hereditarily expressed mind dynamics of $k_f(CP)$, and during its operation it is running designated modules which systematically trigger—even if ad hoc to the presence of the TDs crossing the system under specific conditions—the activation of cognitive functions related to imagination, concentration, memory, and so on. While running, the "software" assesses some of the $\dot{k}_{mind}(sPoPPS_{mind})$ "script" inputs in attempt to decipher their contents, with the output interpretations being consequently transmitted as the $\{\dot{P}^0{}_{CP}\}$ layer on top of the basal $\{sPoPPS_{mind}\}$ "pristine film".

Continuing these ideas, we also suggest that (b) the ongoing sensory contributions to the CP rely on processing of cognitively focused fractions from the $\dot{k}_{mind}(sPoPPS_{mind})$ projection of the dynamic interaction field. In fact, we suggest that the human is being constantly "pushed" to focus on certain parts of the pre-perceptive projection. Let's refer to a situation in which an individual enters a room containing heterogeneous contents which can be generally perceived as distinct objects or elements in the environment. At the instant of his or her entrance, several factors, such as the spatial orientation of the individual relative to the observed objects and his or her state of self-organization (also regarding the sensing units and the momentary activity which is crossing his or her mind), will determine a specific set of *basic consciousness foci* (*BCF*), of which he or she is not necessarily aware. This type of *preliminary event focusing* allows us to differentiate between "focused" and "background" parts in the mind projection of the EI event, and we regard it as an important precondition for the spatial assessment. We note that the BCF continue being frequently updated throughout the sensory scanning of the environment, in our case the content of room, by the individual. Under these conditions, their quick "replacement" of one with another is often prompted by sensitive detection of sudden motion, unusual intensity of arriving stimuli, as well as by recognition of certain objects and/or the expectancy to sense them there (already relying on some feedback with ongoing spatial perceptions). Considering these, we view the BCF as momentary "nuclei" for potential assessments from which the dynamic core perceptions develop.[9] Equation 3.2 exemplifies a contribution of a certain set of BCF to the CP.

$$(3.2) \quad O^{0}{}_{CP}[\dot{k}'_{mind}(\text{focused part of } \dot{k}_{mind}(sPoPPS_{mind})), \dot{k}_{mind}(BES)]$$
$$= \dot{k}'_{mind}(CP\text{-}BCF)\{\dot{P}^{0}{}_{CP}(BCF)\}$$

Our next assumption (c) suggests that the CP not only utilizes the cognitive "toolbox" of the mind in identifying discrete BCF and their characteristics but also assists unveiling and predicting some of their properties in relation to other objects or to the entire situation experienced. Among other possibilities, this applies to detecting relative orientations and dynamics, as well as to certain spatial interplays and interactions between objects. Such interpretations naturally rely on top-down processing that involves comparisons with memory-stored BES arrays, as well as on the OCAs that employ experience-acquired beliefs in causality, repetitiveness, stability, relativity, and the like. In this regard, we choose to view the $\{\dot{P}^{0}{}_{CP}\}$ experience layer as expressing an extended set of beliefs. These lead

---

9 In fact, we postulate that a cognitive feedback can even merge the assessment nuclei into *assessment clusters* corresponding to perceptively connected, focused parts of the sensory projection $\dot{k}_{mind}(sPoPPS_{mind})$. One example in this regard is of a goalkeeper who, during a soccer game, keeps processing different assessment clusters corresponding to EI events sensed from several visual and/or auditory focal planes in the soccer field. We further note that due to the structure function collapses during the conversion processes, the assessment of the clusters is expected to occur only at the sensory update stages (while also relying on a bottom-up decryption of the BCF), or alternatively, upon processing a temporal duplicate of the sensory projection (see chap. 3, n. 2).

us further to suggesting that (d) the formation of the CP intersects with other cognitive pathways which yield other perceptions, and that towards the generation of PbB, this "overarching" activity elicits several different componential functionalities. It should be noted that we regard some of the perceptions formed as contributing to the overall perceptive projection sPoP$_{mind}$. From an analogous mechanistic viewpoint, we may accordingly suggest the existence of "interplays" between $O^0{}_{CP}$ and several other operators and their perceptive rules, including some to be later associated with individual energy assessments.

We continue postulating that (e) the cognitive interpretations of the BCF do not depend on back-decoding of the neurally wired tracts in which the received sensory information was channeled, and consequently no pinpointing of the specific receptors that have been activated by the arriving stimuli is carried out. In this regard we believe that the extended individuality state of the human and its reflections on this "one-way physiology" reduce the probability for a hypothetical scenario of a "genetic key" held by $O^0{}_{CP}$ or other mind operators, allowing them to back-decode the accurate activation-conduction paths and (bottom-up-)interpret spacetime accordingly. This clearly does not contradict the significance of the "injection" location of the sensory TDs to the mind, which possibly encodes part of its "bottom-up information" itself. We find it also important to reemphasize that (f) even if the perception is causally, circumstantially, and physically correlated to its EI contributing sources, it lacks a solid ground to objectively and reliably reflect the latter physically. Aside from our skeptical approach towards veridicality and the persistent experience of the previously mentioned "illusions", we argue that contributing to this limitation is also the nonlinear sensoperceptive conversion and its susceptibility to a complex set of influences, some acting from within the system.[10] The complexity of the transformations is also accompanied by numerous operative challenges. These include sensory adaptation in the receptors, occasional interferences and crosstalk by stimuli leading to the masking of some, imperfect conversion efficiencies and information losses, inevitable impacts from traversing mind

---

10 Nevertheless, and regardless of the possible limitations, the high coherence which is normally experienced for the CP interpretations suggests that the body and mind DRSs act harmonically in generating perceptive outputs through converting countless heterogeneous inputs.

activity related to other internal events and PCEs including feelings and emotions, and switching between human behavioral states, to mention a few. Some of these will be further elaborated on later in this chapter. One basic veridical/reliability concern relates to the "complete" or "deficient" appearance of perceived EI objects and to the possible attribution of unreliable physical properties, including energy, to their directly recognizable patterns. Staring at a "red ball" exhibit, for example, we tend to perceive its "complete" presence regardless of the fact that our mind is only processing the neurally coded map of the photons reflected from parts of its surface. To the list of complexities affecting the reliability of the spacetime perception we wish to add the influence of the (integral to spatial) perception of time and its apparent correlation with the individual time of the observer. This is exemplified by the widespread feeling experienced by aging people that their life is passing faster than it did when they were younger.[11]

We next speculate (g) a correlation between specific mind dynamics and a *reference point for spatial assessments* to be referred to as the *spatial self* of the individual. In absence of certain pathologies, our own intuitive impressions allude that our sensations and "layered" interpretations revolve around an altering "singularity" towards which our interactions with the EI environment and its stimuli are perceived to be "converging" into or relative to. Using the CP, we build our *spatial self perception* around the experience of this "singularity" and then reemploy it as a reference point for assessing the environment and creating our individual spatial narrative.[12] As expected, the persistent reliance of the individual on past and present interpretations from the "singularity" reference point of the spatial perception and its respective narrative requires processing and transmission of specific mind content distributions. Such mind activities are common to all

---

11 Possible explanations for this kind of illusion are suggested in A. Bejan, "Why the Days Seem Shorter as We Get Older". *Eur. Rev.*, **27(2)**, 187–194 (2019).

12 A coherent spatial narrative that is correlated with our time perception allows us, for example, to believe that the local surroundings which we presently observe will continue to exist, even in a modified state, after the location of our self has shifted from it, and, from another point of view, that there are general spacetime localities which our spatial self does not, has not, or will never observe or observe from. We also believe that the cognitive tools of the CP allow the individual to project from his or her reference self viewpoint and assess different properties of spacetime events without observing them directly. Accordingly, we may view the spatial self as a systemic element which also links between TCAs and OCAs through their cognitive functions.

humans yet can be addressed individually regarding their unique variations in the individuality dimensions throughout the generation of the functionality. We also wish to emphasize that the "spatial self" is deliberately distinguished here from the overall "self" concept, to which it is still believed to belong. Accordingly, we regard the self as a combined reflection of the spatial and genetic-energetic (see Subsection 3.2.1) selves of the individual, and hence as a unified "singularity". The interpretation of this *self perception* (perception of self) experience may be compared to known works by others and their later influences regarding the essence of the self.[13]

We return to the BCF and assume that (h) occasionally and under the circumstances which allow it, their interpretations are accompanied by verbal descriptions. Most of these lack vocal expressions and remain uncommunicated. As such, the verbal descriptions often participate in, or even assist in promoting, *high cognition processes* such as *thinking* and *decision making* that precede the emergence of PbB. Unsurprisingly, these functional contributions are believed to occur in parallel with the natural role of the language in relaying human communication. In this regard, we further assume that the mind/brain's decoding and interpretation of language-modulated communication show a certain mechanistic similarity, extending beyond the one entailed in the physiology, to the systematic decryption of incoming sensory stimuli lacking the patterned verbal coding.[14] Finally, we assume that (i) the CP does not impart any *meaning* (significance) to the spacetime objects it identifies. In fact, we believe that a "meaning layer" is being derived and incorporated to the total perception experience only in the subsequent systemic stage, which mainly aims to assess the potential contribution of

---

13 Such as by John Locke, who viewed the self as overlapping (continuous) chains of psychological connections involving memories and beliefs: P. R. Anstey, *John Locke and Natural Philosophy*. Oxford: Oxford University Press (2011); by Tomas Reid, who perceived it as a spiritual immaterial substance containing unique mental states that, in this case, lack continuity: R. Copenhaver, Reid on Memory and Personal Identity. In *The Stanford Encyclopedia of Philosophy*, edited by N. Zalta (2018), https://plato.stanford.edu/archives/win2018/entries/reid-memory-identity; as well as by other contributors: Personal Identity. *Internet Encyclopaedia of Philosophy*, https://iep.utm.edu/person-i/#2.

14 Whereas such traits are believed to be common to humans, we view the vocabulary of every individual and to some extent also his or her articulation skills, as a rough reflection of accrued experiences regarding certain interactions with the external spacetime. This perspective is somewhat analogous to accepting the assimilation of experiences in memory-stored BES (under ever-changing extended individuality dimensions).

the recognized objects to the realization of the individual's genetic goals. Namely, while the CP employs cognitive tools to recognize some of the characteristics of the spatial content/dynamics sensed by the human and to orient him or her in order to interact with it in certain ways, it does not provide the incentive or motivation for the individual to execute these interactions. As will be next assumed, among other factors, the significance of sensed EI events to the individual and his or her motivation to interact with them are determined via specific assessments regarding the worthwhileness of responding to their presence in different possible ways. We believe that these assessments, and their connection to considerations such as the feasibility of interacting in a profitable manner as well as the expected "energetic" cost to do so lie at the heart of a complementary spacetime perception, which is the individual energy perception.

3.2 Individual energy perception

As we continue postulating the mind mechanisms involved in the formation of the PbB functionality, we reach a major point of interest concerning the EP. The energy perception, assumed to appear in all humans yet to be generated and experienced individually and uniquely, relies on a series of estimations performed for the CP interpretations of certain BCF and "assessment clusters". Based on the spatial characteristics recognized and previous observations/interactions assimilated in the mind arrays, the perception is grading the potential *individual energetic benefit (IEB)* of the CP-interpreted elements in the experienced event with respect to their possible contribution to the self-realization of the fundamental genetic targets. We should also keep in mind that some of these estimations are also projected from the "energetic self" standpoint onto other humans, holding different significances in the individual's life. Considering these ideas, we may view the EP as a systemic, cognitively regulated channel in the sensoresponsive process, which is designated to tailoring PbB responses with genetic incentives to spatially interpreted events. As we will later suggest, the relative weight of the EP in the human behavior correlates with different fundamental behavioral states which the individual is circumstantially switching between during his or her life. Among these we find the "genetic-focused" states, entailing recruitment and conservation activities, which are of prime importance to the discussion at this stage. Looking from a general viewpoint, one behavioral emergent implication of the EP among living humans which will often be mentioned here is the *struggle over energy resources*. Unsurprisingly, this persistent struggle also greatly affects the individual's further decisions and behavior. With respect to that, it is tempting to think that the mechanisms behind the individual EP constitute an evolutionary product of multiple energy "struggles" which have started prior to appearance of life on Earth and both causally and circumstantially led to its formation.[15] Despite scientific indications for evolutionary changes in the human brain since the dawn of humanity and appearance of our first ancestors,[16] we doubt the occurrence of dramatic changes to the EP mechanisms during this relatively brief period in terms of global life evolution time.[17] Accordingly, we refrained from ascribing any form of time dependency to O^0_{CP} in Equation 3.1, and we will apply this convention to all assessment operators throughout the chapter.

We continue to suggest that EP can also occur in other living creatures which are genetically equipped with the necessary cognitive abilities to support it. With that said, we assume that its pronunciation in humankind should be outstanding, partly due to our developed mind structure which promotes, along with other salient macro expressions,[18] an intensive use of the versatile imagination function. Examining the spacetime perceptions, it is possible to

---

15 By adopting a functional perspective which sees the energetic struggles between potential reactions as aimed to locally evolve general spacetime, such a long and complicated evolutionary process can be hypothetically viewed as deterministically linking, mostly nonhuman, individuality dimensions of multiple components.

16 For example: A. Verendeev, and C. C. Sherwood, "Human Brain Evolution". *Curr. Opin. Behav. Sci.*, **16**, 41–45 (2017); J. DeFelipe, "The Evolution of the Brain, the Human Nature of Cortical Circuits, and Intellectual Creativity". *Front. Neuroanat.*, **5(article 29)**, 1 (2011); S. Neubauer, and J. J. Hublin, "The Evolution of Human Brain Development". *Evol. Biol.*, **39(4)**, 568–586 (2012).

17 While the mechanisms behind the core perceptions might have remained unchanged, we still believe that throughout the energetic struggles and side by side with the historical revolutions and evolution of humankind's beliefs and capabilities, continuous drifts kept appearing in assimilated human BES. Such drifts can be therefore associated with as an indirect evolutionary-based impact of external environmental processes on our perceptive interpretations.

18 Among these we find, for example, the pragmatic abilities to adapt PbBs to varying situations, the competence to study, develop, gain access to, and improve the energetic utilization of resources, habitat regions, and communication means, as well as attempts to socially moderate the energetic struggle within the species.

find basic similarities between the "classical" and energetic core functions. As expected, both spacetime perceptions rely on, and are further engaged in producing, self-reference points ("selves"). The two of them also employ TCAs and OCAs, which are based on, among other cognitive processes, top-down comparisons with memory-stored experiences. Naturally, there are also differences between the perceptions. As we noted, in contrast to the CP interpreting the content of the observed environment and its features, the EP is focused on assessing the potential IEB or harm for the individual observer by, or in interacting with, the interpreted objects and dynamic events experienced. EP estimations are believed here to rely on a dynamic reference point which is based on a mind distribution to be referred to as the *energetic self*. As expected, we relate the latter to, yet differentiate it from, the individual's spatial self. The additional dependency of the EP on the subjective perception of the energetic self[19] and its high susceptibility to overarching subjective influences by emotions, fears, and other PCEs, may decrease the reliability of its assessments below those of the CP. Regardless of the possible similarities and differences between the core perceptions, we believe that their integrated operation requires a sustained feedback between them. Speculating the systematicness involved and its causes provides an opportunity to highlight the concept of *psychoenergetics*. Psychoenergetics will be associated with environmental influences over these inner-mind processes by certain external events which relate to the energetic challenges faced by the individual throughout his or her life and the struggle over the fulfillment of his or her human goals.[20] The psychoenergetic approach will also support the hypothesis that, combined with the previously mentioned illusions, some of the PCEs accompanying the EP are designated to function as consciousness distractors to a possible realization that we are intrinsically "enslaved" to the genetic goals as a part of the global deterministic evolution of spacetime (see further details in Section 3.3).

---

19 Requiring, for example, additional cognitive operations that contribute to the nonlinearity of the conversion.

20 Also considered in this regard is the more comprehensive viewpoint of the species, as the primary benefiter from the individual EP.

The next several subsections will be dedicated to an introduction of the simplified *detection-reaction model*, attempting to postulate some basic macro mechanistic elements behind the operation of the EP. Presumably lacking a direct, empirical validation at present, the model remains hypothetical, and as such it calls for further discussion, criticism, and extension, which may include conceptual and/or algebraic refinements and improvements. Nevertheless, we believe that the importance of the detection-reaction model does not stem from its necessarily precise descriptions of the cognitive considerations behind the EP and PbB but rather due to two main reasons in particular. The first highlights the fundamental integration of the distinct individual EP into the interpretation of spacetime. The second reason regards our will to introduce a further related assumption, later presented as the "perceptive physical dimension", suggesting that the macro-level operational mechanisms behind the EP reflect fundamental patterns that follow the principles (and thus to some degree the plain formulation) of physical laws of general spacetime. We will assume that this functionality has been directed by the restricted-contingent evolution of nature, which abides by the same laws itself.

3.2.1 Perception of the energetic self

Our recent discussion made a conceptual distinction between spatial and energetic human selves based on their human perceptive functions. As we suggested, both selves refer to distribution states of mind arrays associated with "singularity"-experienced points of self-reference used by the individual's core perceptions. Now, whereas the spatial self perception relies significantly on the direct sensation and interpretation of stimuli arriving from spacetime, a pivotal factor in the *energetic self perception* (*EPself*) are self-assessments concerning "multi-DRSs" energetic aspects of the individual which include, for example, evaluation of his or her potential possessions. These promote the formation of an "energetic narrative" that enables the human, as a crucial part of the EP, to estimate, while projecting from this unique reference a "singularity" standpoint, the potential IEB of CP-recognized objects and situations. It is important to emphasize that in contrast to the straightforward "organic"[21] nature ascribed so far to the term "energy", from now on we will mainly refer to it in the context of the EP and from a broader perspective. While we keep always referring to energy as a universal property of spatial content (see Chapter 1), when it comes to dealing with the individual EP, the term also represents beliefs regarding resources/potentials which have previously been, are presently being, or can be exploited to implement/empower the inherent genetic goals. Despite assuming that some of the perceived resources and potentials indeed hold "organic" tangible fundaments in the materialistic physical world, due to the enhanced subjectivity involved in their perceptions (see chap. 3, n.19), we will not regard the EPself (and EP in general) interpretations as physically reliable or veridical. The "multi-DRSs" cognitive assessments of the EPself which are assumed to yield the mind distribution $\dot{k}_{mind}$(EPself) and its transmitted $\{\dot{P}^0{}_{EPself}\}$ PCEs are described in general in Equation 3.3.

$$(3.3) \quad \sum_{\substack{DRS \\ \text{(El spacetime, EM body, Mind)}}} O^0{}_{EPself}(DRS)[\dot{k}'{}_{mind}(impact),\ \dot{k}'{}_{mind}(BES)] = \dot{k}_{mind}(EPself)\{\dot{P}^0{}_{EPself}\}$$

The equation suggests that during the time of assessment, certain mind-distributed arrays, generally indicated as $\dot{k}'{}_{mind}$(impact), refer to past and present assimilations holding a relevance to the energetic self function (examples are given below). This dynamic memory element keeps being updated with respect to the events experienced by the individual and his or her EP processing and interpretations. Assisted by BES "keys" such as $\dot{k}'{}_{mind}$(BES), a series of EPself operators,[22] $O^0{}_{EPself}$(body), $O^0{}_{EPself}$(mind), and $O^0{}_{EPself}$(st), harness the mind's cognitive functions to compare, interpret, and estimate the different DRS contributions to the "energy self" coded in

---

21 We use the term "organic" to highlight a tangible attribution of physical properties to a certain spacetime element in the pure scientific sense, believing that this element can be measured and/or theoretically derived (or predicted) through objectivity-seeking principles.

22 The distinction between the DRS contributions was intended to increase the coherence of the description and one may alternatively use a general formulation employing a combined operator instead. Furthermore, Equation 3.3 was deliberately simplified as other mind distribution "keys" may apply to it as well. It should be noted that at this stage the process is subjected to overarching subjective influences, including contributions from non-sensory mind events (referring to Case III in Table 2.2), as well as to direct feedback from immediate CP processing, in accord with Comment (d) in Section 3.1.

the impact projection. Consequently, the EPself is expected to reflect the entire set of $\{\dot{P}^0_{body}(\text{EPself})\}$, $\{\dot{P}^0_{mind}(\text{EPself})\}$, and $\{\dot{P}^0_{st}(\text{EPself})\}$ contributions. These are majorly perceived as the self-potency to pursue, improve, complete, or preserve the genetic goals as well as solid accomplishments in this regard (or on other projected matters). The EPself is also believed to occur in every human regardless of his or her momentary aspirations or resentment to realize the goals and independently of his or her "objective" capability to fulfill them. As we stated, combined with the spatial self perception, the energetic self interpretations determine the unified narrative of the individual's self.

Scrutinizing the different "DRS contributions" to the EPself, we believe that some of the EM body-related experiences which effectively leave a mark on $\dot{k}'_{mind}(\text{impact})$ include interoreception signals correlated with wellness and functional integrity, as well as self-experienced and externally communicated observations over one's own body functions. Among these, one may indicate, for instance, sensations of pain signaled by activated nociceptors (or lack thereof), experiencing fatigue and/or different symptoms of diseases (in contrast to feeling sound), awareness to motoric abilities (or disabilities), strength and stamina, and so on. Mind-related contributions projecting on $\dot{k}'_{mind}(\text{impact})$, and thus on EPself, relate to the degree of experienced motivation to advance and implement the inherent goals in conjunction with the predicted self-competence to do so. We also associate the determination of these with experiencing a complex set of PCEs that includes a wide range of emotions[23] It is also interesting to speculate that in an analogy to the EM body, the systematicness of the mind entails self-sensing (neural?) functions which detect and signal random flaws in its "macro" operation, and these are being consequentially weighed in the $\{\dot{P}^0_{mind}(\text{EPself})\}$ assessments.

Besides assessing one's own body- and mind-related potencies, we believe that the individual is also persistently evaluating his or

---

23 Such emotions, originating also from mind events and occasionally reaching the awareness of the individual, can be viewed as possessing a positive or negative polarity which can be rationalized through adopting a psychoenergetic viewpoint. Experiences leading to negative emotions include repeated failures to increase IEB, social rejection, neglection accompanied by poor external support, and others. We assume that traumatic events and/or repeated exposure to events which consistently lead to negative or positive emotions are specifically expected to influence the assessments of the energetic self.

her own "achievements" in the EI world and cognitively associates/ projects them on his or her energetic self $\{\dot{P}^0{}_{st}(self)\}$ component. From an intuitive standpoint, our EI word constitutes the part of general spacetime where some of our goals are, or can be, realized, and it contains energetic resources which we collect and receive in doing so.[24] Assessing EI self-resources and potentials relies on broad beliefs, among which we wish to highlight those concerning the "ownership" of spatial contents and their distribution between the living. Beliefs of this kind are known to form a basis for *social laws and conventions* which are shared between humans in an attempt to regulate the ongoing energetic struggle. With respect to that, one can view the *ascription of ownership and possession* as contributing to the hypothetical (and illusive from an "organic" perspective) idea behind the "individuality of energy" in general spacetime. While the topic of social interactions will be addressed more specifically in the first section of Chapter 4 presenting a short introduction to energy-directed group behavior, for now we will generalize and ideally assume that in order to avoid potential conflicts and/or penalties accompanied by "EPself losses", most individuals are inclined, at least habitually, to align with some social laws and take possession over resources while abiding by them.[25] Upon complying with social laws and conventions, an individual may tend to recruit energetic resources upon realizing that others do not "own" them, following an explicit consent from an "owner" to transfer from his or her possession, and so forth. Such impactful beliefs start developing during early childhood stages when the child learns how to project from his or her energetic self-reference "singularity" and use the core perceptions in ascribing ownership

---

24 We emphasize the distinction made between active recruiting and passive reception, in which the latter requires no significant investment of energy from the individual. Active recruitment is occasionally also facilitated via interactions between the individual and other human mediators and requires an investment of efforts on behalf of the individual in triggering the chain of events. In other common situations, showing more passivity from the individual, the mediators transfer to him or her resources without a direct preliminary persuasion effort on his or her part. Such events take place when the mediators are motivated to act accordingly due to their own energetic assessments and psychoenergetics.

25 Clearly, we still accept that an inevitable part of the energetic struggle involves cases of confiscation, theft, exploitation and taking over, which can all be subjectively justified from the energetic standpoints of their executors. One may even further postulate that these "unmoral" behaviors also act as perturbations which are essential to the evolution of the struggle, the advances that follow it, and the human race as a whole.

and possession of EI contents to others.[26] We should also emphasize that social conventions, which normally play an important role in regulating the human struggle, can occasionally miss their aim and even locally aggravate it.

We now return to discussing the assessments of the $\{\dot{P}^0{}_{st}(self)\}$ component. Looking at the PCE's notation, we see that in contrast to the individuality-absent $dE_{st}{}^{in}/dt$ and $dE_{st}{}^{out}/dt$ "organic" transitions (see the discussion in the former chapter regarding the EDB), it is marked now with individuality dimensions. Unsurprisingly, the individuality of the $\{\dot{P}^0{}_{st}(self)\}$ is associated with the highly subjective and biased assessments derived at this stage. A further examination of the estimated EI component of the energetic self allows us to conceptually divide it between resources which are already being genuinely implemented in the realization of the individual's genetic goals, $\{\dot{P}^0{}_{st}(impl.)\}$, and possession which holds a future potential to be channeled towards these directions, $\{\dot{P}^0{}_{st}(p)\}$. In light of our physical views of spacetime and yet behind the inextricability restrictions, we suggest that in every moment of the individual's life, a certain part of the general spacetime's energy, for example $E'_{st}(t_{observ}=t)$, can be considered as "organically" projecting on his or her effectively implemented goals with respect to the different DRSs. This energy can thus be divided to $E_{body}(impl.)$, $E_{mind}(impl.)$, and $E_{st}(impl.)$ components. Whereas the intrinsic realization of the survival, corresponding to the balanced $\dot{E}_{human}$ from the EDB, is reflected by the $E_{body}(impl.)$ and $E_{mind}(impl.)$ contributions, $E_{st}(impl.)$ can be correlated with external contents related to the actual implementation of the replication, critical guardianship, and enhancement targets. It should be emphasized that some of the external content behind these can be perceived as belonging to more than one person (such as in the case of an offspring of two parents).[27] Next, we can also describe a different "organic"

---

26 As is also indicated by the acquired lingual distinction between "mine", "yours", "his or hers", and so on.

27 From an "organic" point of view, the ascription of ownership and possession to content is a fictious mind interpretation. The "belonging", for example, of a baby to his or her parents sounds natural to our ears as we believe in social norms which dictate energetic dependencies and responsibilities with respect to the hereditary process. Yet from an emotionless "organic" perspective, the baby is a unique content which "belongs", if at all, to the general spacetime and not to any of its locally distributed content elements. Accordingly, we may argue that no physical law in spacetime defines ownership of resources, and these only represent mind product-based interpretations.

part of general spacetime, with an energy projection corresponding to $E''_{st}(t_{observ.}=\dot{t})$ at a given individual present time, containing content which is believed by this specific human to belong to him or her. Now, although this content is perceived as holding a tangible potential to become converted and used, and as such is considered as a part of $\{\dot{P}^{0}_{st}(self)\}$, at this time it is not being directly utilized for any of the individual's genetic goals.[28] The possibility to associate such objects in our life with $E'_{st}(t_{observ.}=\dot{t})$ and $E''_{st}(t_{observ.}=\dot{t})$, insinuates that certain parts of the EI spacetime pointed at by the EPself, potential and implemented from its reference viewpoint, hold an "organic" tangible basis. We refer to these specific content distributions as *individual external genetic possession (IEGP)* (again, "genetic" in the sense of related to hereditary-focused goals) and embrace their compliance with the physical, materialistic, and causal deterministic nature of the universe. As the IEGP extends beyond the body of the individual, and considering the physical restrictions prevailing in spacetime, he or she is expected to have a limited influence over it. One way to exemplify it is through an individual whose growing child has become independent enough to spend significant time (and, consequently, self-change) beyond his or her effective conservation/amelioration reach. In accord with these concepts, the IEGP is viewed as the "organic" fundament in spacetime for the genetically based *individual ecosystem*, encompassing the person and his or her achievements, including the alleged energetic resources in possession. It should be noted that we regard the interactions of the individual with the $E_{st}(p)$ inside the IEGP as often reorganizing the latter, redistributing the states of these EI resources or leading to their implementation and conversion to $E(impl.)$.[29]

Considering the apparent differences between the EPself and its related "organic" IEGP, we wish to reemphasize that even if the

---

28 Accordingly, we may regard E''_{st} as $E_{st}(p)$. One should note that even if $E_{st}(p)$ is not implemented eventually to fulfill its self-perceived potential, awareness to it can still impact the assessments of EPself.

29 A few related ideas in this regard are: (a) conversion of $E_{st}(p)$ to $E(impl.)$ can be occasionally reversible; (b) assessments of (genetic) potentials can also be carried out in situ during the implementation of their objectives; (c) side implications of converting or refraining from conversion of the EI-based $E_{st}(p)$ can also affect the self-assessments of the body and mind components; and (d) also to be considered are body- and mind-related contributions to $E_{st}(p)$; for example, the translation of motoric and mind activities to work producing EI reserves.

perception is bound to the unfolding physical transformations across the sensoperceptive process, due to its highly biased nature, we cannot correlate the two reliably or simply project one on the other.[30] Additional differences between these projections relate to the human inability to observe and interpret the vast majority of physical modifications occurring in the IEGP, determining its ongoing sequential ΔE_{IEGP} changes, for example. In view of the discrepancies between the "organic" and purely perceptive interpretations, our discussion may be regarded as confined to predicting probabilities for circumstances that support coherent and consensual correlations between them. With that in mind, we can approach the energy recruitment processes from a broader angle which extends beyond considering solely the individual and is focusing on changes to his or her ecosystem as a whole. Accordingly, we may refer to the interactions carried out between the latter and an "external-to-individual ecosystem" spacetime.[31] We generally assume that the individual's attention to such interactions as well as to their consequences increases the probability for him or her to assess the respective changes, biased as they are, in $\{\dot{P}^0_{self}\}$. It should be noted that changes in such EPself assessments can also arise due to conversion, reorganization, and transfer reactions of self-resources which require no further recruitment. Before going further, we wish to succinctly refer to what can be intuitively viewed as an asymmetry in the contributions of the different DRS assessments to the EPself. One major reason for that lies in our tendency to prioritize the contributions in accord with the accrued life experiences and needs. Basic similarities in these push us, for example, to attribute high importance to $E_{st}(p)$ possessions, as we believe that recruiting and converting them extend our survival and, whenever applicable, increase the chances to realize the other goals. Among other factors, the prioritizations are also likely to be biased by beliefs concerning the limited time and potency frames for

---

30 Unless we hypothetically had an absolute practical knowledge of the entire physical conditions and causality entailed in the process. This unrealistic demand is one of the reasons for the absence of an energetic analog to $\{\dot{P}^0_{st}(self)\}$ and its $E_{st}(p)$ in Equation 2.4b describing the individual human energy $\dot{E}_{human}$.

31 Namely, interactions of the individual ecosystem with interactable parts of the general spacetime that are excluded from the content distributions k'_{st} or k''_{st} (with respect to the energies E'_{st} and E''_{st} associated with the examples given in this context) at a given individual present time.

implementing the replication, critical caretaking, and enhancement targets.

To summarize this part, we assumed that a dynamic mind reference element identified as the energetic self is being systematically employed in assessing some sort of a (pseudo-quantitative) "index" of self-genetic achievements and potencies. The multi-DRS-focused perception, EPself, of this mind element was suggested as serving as a reference point for certain cognitive processes which play a critical role in human sensoresponses. Combined with its "classical" spatial analog, the perception of the energetic self contributes to the formation of a unified self perception which establishes the ideally coherent spacetime/energy self-narrative of the individual. It is possible to assume that the awareness to the EPself is intermittent, and that the mind arrays involved in the processing and transmissions employ different BES-stored memories. We also suggested that overarching effects reduce the objective and "organic" reliabilities of the EPself's assessment and predictions and increase their apparent complexity. One type of an essential influence to which we attribute a special mechanistic importance relates to emotions and other associated PCEs.

3.2.2 Psychoenergetics of emotions and urges

With the exception of the direct sensation experience, we have so far mainly focused on PCEs associated with perceptions and beliefs. As the title suggests, another type of human experience relates to *emotions*. Whereas emotions can also originate from "standalone" mind events, in attempt to rationalize the human perceptive and behavioral responses to EI sensory events, our discussion will mainly focus on those which are being triggered by them. During exposure to EI events, the individual's experience of specific emotions of varied intensities is believed to be partly[32] related to his or her EPself reference state with its broad range of respective present beliefs, memories, and expectations regarding the perceived goals and potentials to fulfill them. In an attempt to highlight one possible

---

32 We also acknowledge that experiencing emotions is further linked to different cognitive and macro-level psychological or anthropological expressions. These include association with others, projecting on them, identifying with them, morality-related issues, and more.

connection between emotions and the individual's psychoenergetics, we examine the life course of a human who grew up to become an adult and then lived until passing away. Looking at the life timeline of this person (see Figure 1 in the Appendix), we identify the major events of his or her formation at t_0, birth at t_{birth}, and death at t_{death}. The early stage mind development to support basic sensoresponsive activity, by itself a highly important event, allows the individual to experience an extreme environmental change during his or her birth. The sudden separation from the intimate surroundings of the mother's womb is accompanied by an abrupt discontinuation of the energetic provision and requires the baby's fast adaptation to a new habitat and assimilation of survival practices. To this overwhelming experience adds up the rough physical detachment transition, exposing the baby during the delivery to friction and pressure levels unexperienced by him or her until this moment. Taking all these into account, we suggest that even if the birth appeared from an outside perspective to last shortly, to be relatively "easy" and complication-free (as in most cases of caesarean sections, for example), and even if it is quite hard to recognize its emotive impact on the newborn immediately after the birth, the transition from the "half-bosonic" configuration in the mother's womb to the external "fermionic-like state" is expected to dramatically trigger the infant's sensory and mind systems. In accord with that, we assume that the birth experience and the difficulties accompanying it leave a significant mark[33] on/at the individual's mind as they induce a strong emotion identified here with an *elementary fear*, the *fear of absolute abandonment (FoAA)*.[34]

---

33 It might be possible that the harsh response produces shockwaves which pass through the mind and change (contrarily to its anatomy) some of its systemic equilibria. Reorganization at such levels is not only accompanied by drastic ID changes at and around t_{birth}, but speculatively can also alter certain fundamental traits (extending beyond reversible plasticity levels) in the systematicness of the developing DRS.

34 The term "abandonment" refers in this case to losing the "bosonic" state associated with the confinement and energetic dependency in the host mother, whereas it is obvious that beyond sensing the steep changes the offspring is not aware at this stage of the biophysical or other aspects of the process. As the individual matures, he or she is believed to project from this as-similated state of loss and distress to situations involving potential social abandonment and/or self-energetic changes (one straightforward example is a possible divorce of the parents). These impactful events lead humans to seek and follow pathways of enhanced social attention which become reflected in their needs for acceptance, understanding, and being loved (in resemblance to regaining the attention and protection normally given to babies in their early times of life).

As all born humans have experienced their own birth events and assuming that the experiences left impacts on their mind structures and/or systematicness, we further speculate that the combination of external conditions and intrinsic organization during birth leads to certain structural differences among humankind that contribute at later stages, also emotively, to individual differences affecting "high cognition" processes and PbB. Now, one common impact of the birth experience which is assumed here to exist in all humans concerns emergence of primordial, BES-assimilated, basic beliefs associated with the transition between the two energetic states prior to and after the delivery. Adopting an open-minded perspective from our scientifically oriented adult viewpoint, we believe, for example, that experiencing the entire transformation is somewhat analogous to sensing some fundamental aspects of the energy barrier needed to overcome the biophysical transition. Accordingly, we assume that at a very early stage of life, all humans observe certain elementary facets of the general spacetime's laws, and commonly assimilate their individually impactful impressions in their mind structures. We will come back to this idea later in this chapter while discussing the "perceptive physical dimension" assumption. Another fundamental fear experienced by all humans is the *fear of death* (*FoD*). The FoD follows a set of beliefs suggesting that the experience of life as we know it terminates for us at the end of our individual time without us being eventually able to resist it.[35, 36] Comparing the FoAA and FoD core fears, one can see some resemblance and even a sort of causality between them. Having witnessed his or her own birth transition, it might well be that the human fears experiencing "resembling" harsh sensations which might also shift him or her, again, to an unknown state. Yet, unlike the FoAA, which seemingly begins at birth, the individual becomes aware of the concept of death only at later stages of his or her life. The acknowledgement is typically carried out

---

35 This realization does not contradict the previously mentioned beliefs that we can extend the duration of our survival by acting or refraining to act in certain manners and does not defy beliefs in afterlife scenarios. We regard the FoD as involuntary intuitive emotion which is common to all humans, including those who are holding beliefs that seem to defy it.

36 Many individuals experience anxieties from the discomfort expected before dying. These might be even associated with some manifestations of traumatic birth events. Nevertheless, in the context of the book the FoD strictly refers to emotions aroused by imagining the implications of the cease of consciousness and experience of life (including the loss of genetic achievements).

through directly witnessing mortality of others or via communication-mediated learning which triggers imagination-driven processes. As with the experience of the birth, the exposure patterns in both these cases are individual, and their unique assimilation impacts humans differently. We further note that the FoD intersects with the FoAA whenever the individual projects the former on others who are being perceived as close to him or her and thus fears his or her own abandonment by them. Given the fundamental core fears, we believe that their combinations become reflected in all incidental fears encountered by the individual throughout his or her life (see Appendix for more details).

As we suggested, the dramatic environmental changes experienced by the individual during his or her own birth as well as the infancy's early development stages possibly leave an impact on his or her assimilated mind structures and spatial beliefs. A simple example related to such events and which can further assist us in visualizing the energetic-emotive connection is the frequently observed calming effect of a pacifier being suckled by an emotionally flooded toddler. One way to address the effect is by attributing it to the chemical responses triggered at the baby's brain by the suckling activity. These include, for example, secretion of hormones like cholecystokinin and cortisol, with the latter participating in the regulation of the parasympathetic nervous system in response to the experience of emotional stress. An additional factor assisting the relaxation stems from the distraction evoked by the suckling activity regarding the stress factors. In fact, the practice itself might even bring out more pleasant emotions, as the baby can associate it, for instance, with rewarding experiences like breastfeeding. Once such dependencies and contingent mind connections have been established, we know that it can be challenging to wean the baby off the pacifier. Inspecting the example, we recognize that some spatial events and their energetic "significances" are often projectively expressed, instead or in addition to perceptions, by emotions. Now, in contrast to the pacifier, which is given to the toddler by a mediating guardian, upon maturing, the individual starts searching himself or herself for *order patterns* in an attempt to relieve his or her own expressions of stress and fears, and ameliorate his or her energetic narrative.[37, 38, 39] Interestingly, by ignoring energetic barriers and believing that long-range interactions control their own as well as others' lives, many humans adopt order patterns which defy the restricted-contingent "organic" progression principles of spacetime. Later in this chapter we will discuss the possible causes for such "counter physical" beliefs.

In view of the calming effects of the pacifier, it is hardly surprising that taking it away from an infant frequently brings about an emotive response to which we will refer as "negative" and which in this specific context is typically accompanied by a physical expression of crying. It should be noted that regardless of definitions proposed by others, we chose to semantically distinguish emotions such as sadness, frustration, or loneliness, from *feelings*, like pain or warmth. Feelings are associated here with the emergence of typical PCE sensations in response to internal and/or external triggering of the individual's body sensing units (independently of the current state of the EPself). Emotions and feelings may circumstantially interlink and stimulate one another, as we all know from the example of pain which can stimulate sadness. Both types of PCEs are occasionally followed up by body

---

37 It is tempting to relate the need for finding order patterns to the necessity of processing the vast amount of multi-DRS information under the influence of many different biases—and among them contradicting urges.

38 Finding order patterns to believe in is not necessarily ameliorating the genetic-energetic condition of the individual even if, by itself, the discovery often rewards the human with positive emotions which can temporarily divert his or her attention from fundamental and incidental fears. We also intuitively accept that a given human may find patterns that sharply contradict his or her current expectations and basic beliefs, or which are overly structured and exact, and as such may raise a suspicion of experiencing some sort of manipulation or illusion.

39 It is known that large parts of humanity find clear order patterns in religion and theological beliefs (see also chap. 1, n. 67). Among the reasons for the massive compliance to these, one can highlight the relatively high reward-to-investment ratio which is unawarely motivating the followers. We suspect that some of the principal rewards relate to the powerful order patterns provided by such beliefs and to the ability of the believers to share responsibilities over their past, present, and future, with supreme deity(ies) (for the sake of practicality and convenience, part of these responsibilities are often handed over to religious officials believed to interpret and mediate the deities' wills). Clearly, the unification of the believers can also ameliorate them in the overall energetic struggle (see Chapter 4). In most cases the deities are believed to be capable of creating, controlling, and defying the restricted-contingent progression principles of the physical world (and thus, from this perspective Gods should not be equated with science). Moreover, Gods are being often imagined as guardians who accompany their believers at all times (early mentioning of such dependencies also exists in the Bible; for example, "Even though I walk through the valley of the shadow of death... for you are with me" [Psalm 23:4]). With respect to that, we assume that abiding by religious beliefs and following their narratives and traditions assists the followers in coping with some aspects of their fundamental fears of abandonment and death.

expressions such as the crying of the baby in the example above. As the baby grows up, the rapid increase in his or her volume of interactions with spacetime contents combined with the gradual buildup of one's own complex self-identity, expose him or her to experiencing a broad spectrum of emotions. We believe that each of these can be regarded as a vector, holding specific magnitude (in terms of the intensity of the experience) and direction. The direction is intuitively chosen to correlate with our general experiences of pleasure ("positive" direction) and suffering ("negative" direction). Given that, we can relate certain negative emotions to failures in conserving or improving genetic goals, and conversely positive emotions to successfully executing C/I interactions with spacetime. Similar outcomes also apply to predicting the potential success or failure of the processes and will also correlate with the self-investments expected in them, where large efforts normally evoke negative, even if occasionally low-magnitude, emotions. The different vectorial combinations of emotive directions and magnitudes are often given lingual expressions which are bound to vocabulary limitations and their connections to human perceptions, narratives, and memory capacities. This allows "normalization" of the emotions in lingual patterns that are being communicatively shared and then interpreted by others. Based on these concepts, we argue that: First, emotions are PCEs which emerge upon exposure to certain mind, EM body, and EI spacetime events. We speculate that one of their basic functions is to serve as coarse systemic indicators for immediate energetic assessments of different elements in these or future events spatially associated with them. With respect to that, we believe that in a somewhat similar manner to the spatial recognition of objects by the CP, the emotion-based indications rely on memory-assisted comparative processes. These require previous mind assimilation of expressed emotions, in the form of *emotions-encoded structures* (*EMES*), accompanying directly observed and/or communicated consequences of different, successful and failed, genetic (C/I) interactions. One may assume that the EMES are stored in a designated *emotive memory*, to be associated with the dynamic structural distribution function $\overset{.}{k}_{mind}(EMES)$, whose assimilation and storage characteristics also depend on the vectorial distribution of the emotions expressed. In a similar manner to BES-memorized beliefs, we believe that the stored EMES array and their recalled emotions will change with new experiences, and will be susceptible to consolidation and reconsolidation processes, forgetting, and so forth. Another resemblance between beliefs and emotions concerns the paramount role they play in the generation of the core perceptions. Beyond the assumed functionality of the emotions as crude indicators for energetic assessments, we identify in them some basic properties of catalysts or inhibitors for the systemic cognitive processes interpreting spacetime observations.

Second, experiencing a certain event can evoke different emotion vectors. The specific emotive combinations expressed depend on the conditions entailed in the situation observed and among them on the broad individuality dimensions of the observer. Despite assuming that the vectorial combination is not expressed only as a single sum or weighed average emotion, we still accept the typical dominance of more "polar" (positive/negative) and higher intensity emotions in experiences. Third, the emergence of emotions is coupled with both sensory and mind events. As was previously implied (see chap. 3, n. 32), the individual can also be flooded with emotions while experiencing situations which, to us, the outside observers, seem as incapable of changing his or her energetic-genetic state. Such events typically employ imagination-driven associative interpretations that may involve, for example, identifying with external-to-one's-own-ecosystem situations as well as projecting from the self on others. Fourth, we view fears as special negative emotions which emerge in response to experiencing, predicting, or imagining different life events. As suggested, many of these project on the energetic-impactful circumstances which trigger(ed) our core FoAA and FoD. The last, though very significant, assumption at this stage uses the above concepts to suggest that the assimilation of beliefs is strongly coupled to the psychoenergetics of the human, and as such also depends on the emotive vector distribution he or she is experiencing at the present time of the exposure (also considering the impactful projections of the core fears at this individual instant in time). This effect is eminent and determines in many cases the resistance of assimilated beliefs towards possible changes and replacement. Returning to the example concerning religious beliefs, one can accordingly ascribe their strong, almost unbreakable, grasp in many believers' minds (see chap. 3, n. 39) to being communicatively transferred at early points of their lives by guardians who have also been emotionally associated then with ultimate power and protection donating characteristics.

We now continue to assume that the individual is mostly unaware of the psychoenergetics affecting his or her responses. Somewhat similar to the belief inextricability limitation, attempts to take full control over our lives and navigate them unbiasedly of emotions are forever doomed to fail, with us being intrinsically driven to act in ways that intensify experiences rewarding with positive emotions and simultaneously avoid or minimize the impact of situations evoking negative emotions including fears. These natural drives will be referred to here as *urges*, and their direct influence on the individual's assessments and predictions regarding his or her self energetic interactions with spacetime will be considered as free from any moral concerns in this regard. Adopting a broad viewpoint, we assume that the human's life is accompanied by time-evolved circumstantial *distributions of urges*. These momentarily converge towards *dominant consciousness attractors*,[40] while forming PCEs which presumably affect the EP. Now, in spite of some reasonable connections which can be drawn between fears/urges and the (motivation to advance) genetic goals, such as correlating FoD with extending survival or FoAA with replicating and then guardianship, due to the high complexity of the factors determining in every given situation the distributions of the former, it is quite impossible to associate them to the goals accurately. In fact, we believe that fears and urges are often prioritized in a way that sabotages the I/C of some of the goals, and their attractors divert the human from "robotically" following the realization paths. With that said, one can still attribute to fears and urges a prominent contribution in motivating the human to struggle over the recruitment of energy resources in attempt to fulfill, improve, and conserve his or her goals. As such, these PCEs play a backstage role in the evolutionary processes extending beyond the individual level to the entire species. As was recently implied, motivated by different beliefs as well as by the FoD and the consequent urges to resist it and postpone our demise, we are pushed to recruit excessively and work hard towards conserving and improving our perceived "reserves". At the same time, the inner

---

40 The term "attractor" is borrowed from the mathematical world, referring to certain states to which dynamic functions tend to develop to. For example: J. Milnor, "On the Concept of Attractor". *Commun. Math. Phys.*, **99(2)**, 177–195 (1985).

struggle against FoAA urges our social behavior, which increases the probability of realizing the replication and its subsequent targets. Nevertheless, these same urges can also act as genetic inhibitors, counterproductively distracting the individual or even pushing him or her towards behaviors and efforts that could otherwise have been spent on recruitment and/or C/I processes. We believe that depending on the prevailing circumstantial conditions, such contradictions between needs and/or urges can promote "antigenetic" tendencies and behaviors. These include, for example, unwillingness to enhance a grown-up offspring, evading early guardianship, choosing not to have children, and even committing suicide. The fine emotionally influenced balance between the acceleration and inhibition of genetic motivations plays a prominent role in the self narrative of the individual human and we identify this aspect of mind activity to be fundamental in our psychoenergetic approach. Furthermore, the multilevel impact of fears and urges on energetic assessments seems to be significant to such an extent that it can be analogized to an *inner conflict* in every individual's mind, a micro-scale conflict that always precedes the macro struggle over energy resources. Using these biased dynamics, we will now attempt to describe universal mechanisms allowing every human to energetically assess his or her own life experiences.

3.2.3 Detection-reaction model. Part I: genetic consciousness foci

The next three subsections of the chapter will introduce the detection-reaction model, a hypothesized, simplified mechanistic description of the systematicness operating behind the generation of the EP as a basis for practical PbB. The model will mainly focus on behavioral functions related to recruitment of resources and conservation/improvement of genetic targets, whereas the principal characteristics of other typical types of human behaviors, referred to here as "behavioral states", will be highlighted in Section 3.3. A fair amount of attention will be given to certain considerations behind the individual's decisions of whether to respond to different experienced situations and in which way. Clearly, no model can provide pinpointed and accurate predictions to every specific situation being encountered in life, and especially when bearing in mind the wide range of influences acting on the human. Accordingly, rather than aiming for ultimate precision, we are mainly interested in generally demonstrating the concept of energetic considerations taking part in perception and PbB, and in examining it from the standpoint of the physical evolution of nature. The model starts its descriptions from where we have left the CP-based recognition of objects and dynamics in the "assessment nuclei and clusters" (see chap. 3, n. 9) associated with the basic consciousness foci (BCF), Equation 3.2, and further directs us to the evaluation of the identified elements as possible *genetic consciousness foci* (*GCF*). GCF are treated as coarsely predicted potentials of BCF to, either actively or passively, facilitate or prevent as well as ameliorate or sabotage the individual's goals following his or her possible interactions with them. We will regard the assessments as giving rise to *genetic motivation indexes*, $\mu^0{}_{GCF}(BCF)$, and recognize their transient contribution to the EP at this stage. Following the assessment of the motivation indexes of different BCF in the experienced situation, their relative genetic weights are compared and used in prioritizing subsequent energetic assessments. In view of these ideas, we further suggest that (a) as will be described, the assessments of the motivation indexes and their grading employ both the cognitive functions of the CP (including top-down processing which is relying on the BES) and PCEs of memorized emotions (relying on transmitted EMES); (b) all assessments depend on the structural distribution states of the observing individual which are hypothetically reflected by his or her ID and that project on the current influences biasing him/her; (c) an important assumption is that the assessment of the $\mu^0{}_{GCF}(BCF)$ is nearly "quantitatively independent" of the energetic self evaluations. Whereas perceptive connections between the BCF and some elements of the individual ecosystem are required and indeed being established at this stage, the EPself does not serve as a direct reference for assessments of basic genetic motivations, and partly due to that, the obtained indexes appear as coarse and general.

Let's examine a GCF assessment that is dealing with an extreme, yet possible, scenario. Imagination-assisted interpretations enable the individual to identify a substantial self-conservation danger upon waking up and watching a relative with a drawn knife bending over him or her. Clearly, we may assume that the routine presence of both the knife and the relative in the individual's kitchen would be perceived by him or her as benign.[41] Now, regardless of the exact situation experienced, whether a life-threatening hazard in the bedroom or an innocent salad-cutting in the kitchen, we assume that the "knife" element is always associated with a certain potential to become a conservation risk to the observer. Returning to the potential assault scene in the bedroom, we assume that at this point the individual has the tools to rapidly predict the evolution of complex dynamics holding a fair potential to turn into "a considerable body-conservation danger which may put my own[42] life at risk". This prediction, envisioning an undesirable self energetic change and yet refraining from directly relying on the current "pseudo-quantitative" state of EPself, can be broken down to several interlinked estimations. The first relates the possible development of the experienced situation to the self-conservation of the individual, as opposed to improving his or her ecosystem, for example, or to realizing his or her goals. The second estimation identifies a problem or a potential loss regarding this conservation, as opposed to foreseeing a clear opportunity to enhance it, for example. It almost goes without saying that from our outside spectating standpoint it seems absolutely natural to correlate such a problem with an energetic loss to the individual ecosystem. The third estimation delves deeper into analyzing the conservation issue and predicts that, at its most elementary form, the impact of the expected interaction concerns bodily harm with possible implications, as opposed to major damage in other DRS, such as to EI reserves and possessions. This prediction is believed to require CP assessments involving overarching beliefs and associative correlations between the identified BCF in the experienced situation and certain perceived elements of the individual ecosystem that do not require quantitative or qualitative assessments at this stage (and as such rely mainly on the spatial self as a reference). As a result, the individual is likely

---

41 We reemphasize the flexible capabilities of the CP in predicting development of situations and sequences of events while relying on overarching beliefs in causality, circumstantiality, and their experience-based interpretations. As a part of that, potential interactions with separately identified yet interactively connected BCF, such as in our example of the relative and the knife, are also predicted. A combination of past experiences, associations, and reasoning allows correlating in this case the locations of the relative and the knife and the grip characteristics of the knife by the relative with its role in the situation.

42 For simplicity, the example disregards any potential interactions between the attacker and other elements from the individual's ecosystem possibly present at the site of the event.

to associate the swing of the knife over him or her with self-body harm, or in a different scenario, to link a potential receival or giving of various forms of payment with his or her savings and monetary assets. We will refer to these associative connections between BCF-identified objects and specific parts of the individual ecosystem as *perceptive conjugations* and already note their prime importance in the model. The fourth estimation aims to coarsely predict the effective magnitude of the impact. In our example, and depending on the CP-decrypted identity and characteristics of the attacker, we expect the individual to predict an impact which at its most severe level fits the definition of a "considerable life threat".

We continue with our extreme example. As suggested, the reliance of the CP's predictions on a combination of event-specific and formerly experienced beliefs enables the individual to identify a potential conservation problem upon sensing another human holding a knife[43] and appearing to behave in a threatening manner, or when his or her incentive to attack is unveiled. As the CP is not only involved in assessments of static elements (and among them those interactable with the individual ecosystem), but also in estimating dynamics in spacetime. it utilizes approximate estimations of source intensities, distances, direction of motion, velocities, and so forth. The respective interpretations of these often remain generally and coarsely categorized between "high to low", "close to far", "approaching or getting farther away", "fast to slow", and the like. As such, they are presumably being used for the relative grading of the motivation indexes of the foci with regard to the general emergency of the impact and its expected magnitude. It is fairly intuitive, for instance, that upon noticing a significant fire close-by which is fast-approaching us or our resources, we tend to increase our attention to it and motivation to respond to its presence. These human impacts are expected to be greater in comparison to sensing a similar-sized fire at the far, "unrelated" distance. Another factor expected to play a similar role while grading and prioritizing situations is the CP-interpreted "spontaneity" of the interaction with regard to the individual and

---

43 It could be that certain components and properties of the assessment cluster (related in our case, for example, to the attacker, knife, location, etc.) are CP-assessed separately prior to yielding integrated predictions. As we stated, we deliberately leave the methodological exploration of this systematicness to experts in the fields of cognitive sciences and pattern recognition.

his or her ecosystem. We suspect that in many cases the motivation to respond to events—like fire, for example—which are being perceived as holding a potential to actively trigger a C/I-impactful interaction with the "physically passive" individual/ecosystem, will be graded and prioritized higher than events which require his or her own involvement and investment in forming the interaction. Our next assumption is of a correlation between certain aspects of the μ^0_{GCF}(BCF) grading and elementary, hereditary-based directions emerging from within the mind systematicness. One possible example concerns a *genetic selfishness effect*,[44] suggesting that a plain spatial recognition of other humans holding increased genetic closeness to the individual observer automatically prioritizes his or her attention to and motivation for different possible interactions with them. Further emphasized are various inherent and accrued factors which tend to bias the GCF assessments. We may exemplify these with individual time-related shifts in prioritization of human goals or the general propensity to prioritize severe conservation over improvement issues.

So far, we have emphasized the fundamental contributions of the CP to the graded assessment of the genetic motivation indexes and their prioritization. As was previously insinuated, these are also promoted by a systemic use of emotions. Emotion PCEs fit well with the current need at this stage for a prompt reaction which does not significantly rely on previous "pseudo-quantitative" EPself estimations. The seamless mind assimilation of emotion vectors while experiencing (directly and/or through communicated impressions of others) genetic-focused impacts of perceived spacetime events, turns the EMES transmissions into effective "first-impression" indicators for later-encountered situations, enabling instant, coarse assessments of the BCF detected. We believe that as the cognitive comparisons used by the CP access the BES-stored memories of experienced situations and their identified elements, they also bring up co-assimilated memorized emotions (implying an expected linkage in the BES-EMES storage characteristics) which provide a quick impression for a potentially recurring genetic impact by the assessed foci. This speculated mechanism ascribes a major systemic role to the CP-adjacent emotive

---

44 Some parts of this postulation intersect with Dawkins's works correlating certain aspects of cooperations in nature with genetic ties. For example, R. Dawkins, *The Selfish Gene*. Oxford: Oxford University Press (1976).

expressions in prioritizing the motivation indexes $\mu^0{}_{GCF}(BCF)$ and respectively screening the foci for subsequent energetic assessments. Assuming that, we return to the assault example and acknowledge the extreme emotion expected[45] during the CP-interpreted situation (possibly also reflecting the projection of an intense FoD).[46] The systemic combination between the CP interpretations and the emotive indications is assumed to provide a quick and efficient means of *genetic lensing* for screening massive amounts of sensory information. These help narrow down the number of subsequent energetic assessments and ideally focus them on the higher genetic potential BCF estimated. Nevertheless, the systematicness can still be criticized for being unreliable and overly subjective. Many factors contribute to the questionable trustworthiness of the emotion indicators and among them the dubious reliability of assimilations of past experiences (also in regard to the error-accruing nature of communicative transfers), "recalling" situations that have never occurred, forgetting relevant experiences that indeed happened, incremental structural drifts in the memories,[47] assimilation of overlapping emotion vectors in different situations and under variable individuality dimensions,[48] and biasing by emergence of emotions unrelated directly to EI events. We may add to these complexities objective variations in expression of emotions between individuals which are often associated with human traits ranging from hypersensitivity to indifference. Another complexity arises from "contradicting" experiences. A child who became used to playing with a friendly dog and has adopted a *conservation-related trust* in their interaction, which is accompanied by experiencing

---

45 We reemphasize that in order to generate the emotion, a preceding—direct or communicated—experience which can be associated with the situation is needed.

46 In a related example, the individual wakes up and suddenly notices the unexpected presence of a foreign knife in the room. Based on its CP interpretations, such situation is also expected to trigger emotions of dismay and fear, which normally increase the motivation to further assess the foci and its potential conservation risk. The case also implies our need to retain a *conservation territory* of different levels of intimacy. We assume that frequently we are willing to invest "conservation energy" in securing this territory from the possible invasion of foreigner intruders, motivated by their own triggers in the global struggle.

47 Memorized EMES might be more susceptible to such drifts and distortions than BES and thus harder to conserve.

48 This can also relate to the tendency to mix up emotions as their (vectorial) variation spectrum appears to be limited in comparison to the versatile sensory information assimilated during the exposure to spacetime events.

"positive emotions" (associated in this case with an escapist pleasure; see Section 3.3), might still become severely bitten by it under certain circumstances. We assume that in the case that such a misfortunate event has happened, the combined memory-assimilated mix of beliefs and emotions will bias the child's assessments and determine his or her behavior upon the next encounter with the same or a different dog. Based on the set of contributing factors presented, we assume that emotive influences on the assessments of the foci extend beyond a simple weighted average of different—at times of opposite polarity—vectors embedded in EMES memories of CP-interpreted EI events.

Considering the numerous inherent and external influences on the grading and prioritization of $\mu^0_{GCF}(BCF)$, as well as the systemic use of perceptive conjugations coarsely associating the examined foci with the individual ecosystem/EPself, we accept the inevitable reliability limitations and complex biased nature to which the postulated functionality are bound to. Yet, through hypothetically assuming the veracity of the processes and relying on intuitive self-observations, we believe that these mechanisms indeed allow us to screen countless environmental stimuli and navigate our lives, sometimes heuristically, by assessing and then "successfully" interacting with those which appeared, and thus remained, as more genetically important at this stage. Now, parallel to the combined CP and emotive efforts to assess and prioritize the $\mu^0_{GCF}(BCF)$ indexes, we acknowledge that the continuous actions and reactions of the individual in and to spacetime keep producing more and more BCF for him or her to evaluate. We also assume that the individual keeps monitoring and assessing the evolution of some of the previous foci, in a process we refer to as *dynamic updating*. Such activity requires mind functions promoting attention and concentration towards detecting effective changes in the genetic grading of the foci during the experienced situation. To deal with fast-changing dynamics, we assume that a temporal $\mu^0_{GCF}(BCF)$ grading is being stored in a short-term mind stack designated for this purpose (possibly connected to the sensory memory). Upon the systematic discarding of the foci with the lowest $\mu^0_{GCF}(BCF)$ assessments from the stack, the more significant BCF remaining, to now be referred to as GCF, become subjected to additional comparisons and updating. In parallel to that we assume that an all-embracing discard of GCF below a "genetic interest" threshold level $\mu^0_{GCF}(threshold)$ will take place, namely when $\mu^0_{GCF}(BCF)<\mu^0_{GCF}(threshold)$. These "genetic lensing" filtering functions save the individual precious time over countless insignificant estimations and allow him or her, for example, to "send" the static kitchen-stored knife back to the low-priority "background layer" of sensation PCEs. With that said, it should be emphasized that GCF which have been shifted back to the genetic background can still be reassessed and reprioritized, and may occasionally contribute, for example, as catalysts or inhibitors in later stages where tangible actions are considered. Interestingly, one can assume a possible dependence of $\mu^0_{GCF}(threshold)$ on the behavioral state (see Section 3.3) in which the individual is found. To summarize this section, we suggested that the determination, grading, and prioritization of the BCF depend on multiple mind processes and their biasing factors. This initial stage of energetic estimations will screen a considerable amount of information while selectively allocating "systemic attention" for subsequent assessments of more attractive GCF. As we will describe next, the process of genetic lensing is expected to lead to an increased systemic vigilance towards performing more pinpointed predictions regarding potential self-interactions with the foci. Before moving on, we also suggest the existence of a mind-body feedback between the dynamic GCF-graded layer formed in the individual's consciousness and his or her immediate motoric reactions (and their consequential implications over his or her spatial orientation as well as sensory reception and scanning). Being mostly unaware of many of these feedback reactions, accepting their existence might challenge our intuition regarding our capabilities to unbiasedly scan and monitor the surroundings.

3.2.4 Detection-reaction model. Part II: assessments of action and interaction and the perceptive physical dimension

In addition to screening information, prioritizing the GCF assists the individual in "choosing his or her battles" throughout the ongoing energetic struggle of life. Conducting the latter requires an abundance of assessments regarding possible action and reaction pathways with respect to the prioritized foci emerging. At this stage we will ascribe to the cognitive operations entailed in these assessments an energy perception operator O^0_{EP} which is believed to mechanistically direct the mind-conversion reactions determining the preferred human responses to the GCF. Viewing the mind-conversion products as incrementally contributing to the macro sensoperceptive process, we allude that O^0_{EP} enriches the energy-perception layer with genetic-based interactive estimations for the GCF assessed, Equation 3.4.

$$(3.4)\quad O^0_{EP}[\dot{k}_{mind}(CP\text{-}GCF),\ \dot{k}_{mind}(EPself),\ \dot{k}'_{mind}(BES)]$$
$$= \dot{k}_{mind}(EP\text{-}GCF)\{\dot{P}^0_{EP}(EP\text{-}GCF)\}$$

As suggested by the equation, the O^0_{EP}-directed mind process which yields the discrete-like $\dot{k}_{mind}(EP\text{-}GCF)$ contributions and their respective $\{\dot{P}^0_{EP}(GCF)\}$ PCEs, relies on $\dot{k}_{mind}(CP\text{-}GCF)$ as the mind-imprinted structural distributions of the prioritized GCF for assessing, on the mind projections of the energetic self (mainly as a subjective reference), and on the BES (for the comparative top-down processing entailed).[49] We further assume that, before contributing to the EP PCE layer, several GCF can be co-assessed in a cluster-like manner. Such operation would also be reflected by the expansion of the $\dot{k}_{mind}(CP\text{-}GCF)$ term in the equation to the distribution fitting the CP-interpreted situation assessed. Evidently, Equation 3.4 implies a combined use at this stage of the classical and energetic perceptions. We regard this dynamic interplay between the perceptions and the consequent feedback formed as participating in the GEAP-directed "$k_f(t)$" systematicness operating the mind, where O^0_{EP} triggers O^0_{CP}, for example, with "spatial inquiries" concerning different elements of the projections involved, following their perceptive conjugation to the energetic self. Indeed, the assessments at this stage demonstrate the first practical use of the mind-stored energetic self-estimations as a pseudo-quantitative (or, alternatively, semi-quantitative) reference point for the energetic interpretations. With that in mind, it is possible to view the EP too as relying on a combined cognitive processing of external and internal fluxes of data.

We now leave temporarily the formulation of the mind processes to suggest a hypothesis related to their macro mechanistic operation.

---

49 For simplicity reasons, we avoided incorporating into the equation contributions which are related to emotions (as $\dot{k}'_{mind}(EMES)$).

The hypothesis, to be referred to as the *perceptive physical dimension* (*PPD*), claims that the operating mechanisms of the core perceptions, and especially the EP (e.g., as indicated by O_{EP}), have been evolved and shaped alongside different physical (energetic/entropic) principles, and as such are expected to correlate with the physical laws of nature while reflecting them to a certain degree.[50, 51] Based on the present scientific knowledge, we assume that during the period of existence of life on Earth, the physical laws which have shaped its evolution have not changed by themselves and yet persistently directed the circumstantial conditions determining its progression paths. These processes have naturally also contributed to the formation of the specific human mind mechanisms and their current structure-functionality traits, and one may even analogize between the physical "struggles" that accompanied the evolution of life and the mind of the human, to the struggles being dealt by the latter's EP mechanisms. Accordingly, we believe that the functional cognitive "algorithms" directing the perceptive mind assessment mechanisms, with an emphasis on the energy perception, have evolved to reflect the operating principles (and logics) behind certain physical laws of nature and possibly also their combinations. We wish to emphasize that in the absence of a convincing objective proof, it may appear as if we impose our own beliefs and interpretations regarding this correlation. Yet, we still assume that behind the practical and theoretical restrictions, science may verify the veracity of the PPD through combining physics and physical observations that target the macro CP/EP guidelines. Now, while assuming that the PPD principle may apply to a wide range of physical laws,[52] we focus at the moment

---

50 We accept that our understanding of natural laws will forever remain limited and question-able. As we stated in Chapter 1, we regard O_{sci} as a dynamic function whose truths can change with time and will always stay behind belief inextricability and other perceptive limitations. It almost goes without saying that one cannot validate scientific principles from analogies found to them in perception mechanisms.

51 While this bottom-up approach might be applied generically to functional systems in nature, to the best of our knowledge, our suggestions to harness it for the decryption of mind mechanisms, and especially in postulating the operating principles of the hypothesized energetic-genomic perceptive layer in the consciousness, have not yet been described. These might complement or replace conventional top-down attempts to decipher cognitive processes by observing and analyzing the mind's emerged functionality (see also Section 3.4).

52 A future work will be dedicated to accentuating possible analogies between EP-based human behaviors and canonical laws of physics.

on those related to overcoming energy barriers which are predicted as needed to activate human reactions[53, 54] (and generally symbolize the circumstantial contingent progression which is required for reactivity and conversion in spacetime).

Abiding by the PPD, we may view $O^0{}_{EP}$ as a GEAP product whose operative functions project on the conversion reactions that enabled the evolution of the individual's human mind. As was previously noted in Equation 1.3, we can generally describe basic conversion/transformation dynamics and its necessary activation barriers by means of reactions such as $R{\rightarrow}P$ $(E_R>E_a)$.[55] Such transformations typically take place when certain reactants (R) fulfill the physical necessities (e.g., hold structural-physical/chemical/biological affinity to each other and gather closely) to form meaningful interactions and possess at this state sufficient energy to overcome the activation energy barrier E_a required for their conversion, at a certain rate, to the reaction products (P). Clearly, these dynamics conform with the energetic and entropic dictates of the general spacetime. Now, unless greater forces interfere, the fulfillment of these prerequisite spacetime conditions should objectively suffice by itself to carry out the reaction, as is evident, for example, from transformations of lifeless reactants and among them atoms and molecules. Despite these ideas and while acknowledging that many external and internal forces do bias our perceptions and behavior, most humans intuitively tend to believe that the reactions which guide their lives are not necessarily physically controlled and predetermined. As was previously mentioned, we abide here by causal determinism views which negate free will and relate our behavior to physically directed genetic incentives coupled to psychoenergetic influences.

Being particularly interested in "sensoresponsive PbB", we start considering a perceptive mechanism which relies on potential reactions of the kind (see chap. 3, n. 55).

---

53 The common energetic grounds of the EP and the energy-related laws which are expected to be dominant in its mechanisms point out on possible correlations between specific physical principles and the functionalities emerged from the systems they guide.

54 We remember that the human sensoresponding reactions also require crossing of energy barriers and among them for sensory activation and neurobiological transformations.

55 Clearly, this generalized and basic formulation can be expanded and tailored to fit more complex, specific reaction cases. As such, its preferred use in the current form does not bind our description to any types, quantities, ratios, and energies of reactants and products.

$$(3.5) \quad R_{event} + R_{self} \longrightarrow P_{event} + P_{self}$$

In this formulation,[56] the R_{event} and R_{self} "reactants"[57] respectively correspond to a *referred event* to which a human response is being considered (symbolically reflected by the projection of the highly prioritized GCF, to be referred to as $\dot{k}_{mind}(GFC)$), and to the energetic self (referring in practice to the individual's ecosystem) perceived at the time of assessment and projected via the mind distribution $\dot{k}_{mind}(EPself)$.[58] In accord with that, we treat P_{self} and P_{event} as the predicted (perceptive) products of the interaction between the individual human (his or her ecosystem) and the referred event, and in order to simplify the descriptions we will keep referring respectively to the reactants and the products using the abbreviated "R" and "P" forms. Considering the mind systematicness involved, we view these pseudo-quantitative indexes as often being linked to each other through perceptive conjugations. With that in mind, we believe that at this pivotal, pre-behavioral stage, the individual EP is intensively engaged in assessing the self-genetic implications of different interaction paths, referred to as *response channels*, between the R_{self} and R_{event} elements. With respect to different predicted implications on R_{self}, Equation 3.5 may be hypothetically split into a set of more specific potential reactions, representing the channels under consideration. Holding distinctive characteristics, each channel is expected to have its own activation barrier and to genetically affect the individual in a different way.[59] Later on, we will assume that it is possible to address the basic characteristics of all different channels using a fairly uniform, general formulation, yet before exploring that we wish to point out several principles which seem relevant to this stage. First, we emphasize

---

56 In order to distinguish the symbols of the products (P) from the perception PCEs ($\{\dot{P}^0\}$), the "0" notations were removed from the equation.

57 Despite referring to subjective perception elements, the mechanistic reaction can also be ascribed in a way to genuine "organic" interactions between the underlying structural distributions $\dot{k}_{mind}(GFC)$ and $\dot{k}_{mind}(EPself)$ which have found physical proximity in spacetime (at the individual's mind).

58 It should be noted that R_{event} may also correspond to a communication event entailing mediated information between humans (regarding spacetime).

59 At this stage we focus the discussion on channels which direct the individual to improve or conserve his or her genetic state. Various aspects of other responses with different primary incentives will be elaborated on in Section 3.3.

that no matter how "strict" the EP mechanistic guidelines are, their outcome will keep being affected by the full spectrum of influences acting, and among them fears and urges. Depending on the unique psychoenergetics of the individual, these may lead, for example, to "exaggerated" R and P predictions. Another principle suggests that the subsequent process of *prioritization of response channels* reflects natural inclinations to maximize genetic profits (IEBs) and minimize both potential losses as well as investment of energy (and particularly excessive energy) in the interactive processes. A further point highlights the mechanistic shift from relying on coarse emotive and CP-based "qualitative" estimations facilitating the determination and grading of the GCF, to more specific pseudo-quantitative assessments of the response channels. We believe that the assessments integrate the EPself at this stage as a comparative reference basis, in conjunction with the imagination-assisted perceptive conjugation processes.[60] We continue and claim that assessing the response channels requires additional CP-based evaluations and predictions of certain forces and energies expected to take part in the different scenarios. These are often ascribed to overcoming activation barriers with respect to potential actions by an individual and his or her ecosystem, the focused event, and/or to third-party participants in the situation experienced. Therefore, one may already notice some elementary PPD features in the mechanistic perception systematicness. Another point to consider is that the large variety of factors biasing the grading and prioritization of the specific response channels at this stage turns these more advanced genetic lensing processes to less predictable and "robot"-like rigid, as compared with what should be expected from the strict systematicness in use. In order to highlight and at the same time simplify the significant contribution of the biasing factors to the cognitive outcome, we unite their overarching influences under a *unified bias function* ($f(\Psi)$), to which we require a full coupling of the assessments taken at this stage. Adhering to universal physicalism, we also regard the bias function and its origins as entirely relying on physical occurrences which obey physical principles. Nevertheless,

---

60 To briefly exemplify this, we return to the possible assault case in the bedroom and suggest that in contrast to the previous, quite limited, general predictions for a potentially harmful self-impact, using these systemic tools the individual is now allowed to consider his or her own present capabilities to defend or avoid confrontation.

the function may appear to stray from the relative simplicity of the physical principles participating in the PPD and depend more on circumstantial events which serve no systematic guiding functionality.

As implied, while estimating his or her responses to the referred event, the individual is believed to assess and grade several channel-specific indexes, to be marked by $\mu_{channel}$(event), which represent *potential worthwhileness of implementation (PWI)*. Along with different other factors that we will discuss shortly, the grading of the indexes is assumed to correlate with the self-genetic implications predicted for the channel-specific interactions between R_{event} and R_{self} as well as with the respective reaction's *spontaneity*. The spontaneity refers in this context to the ability of certain events to interact with the R_{self} without requiring direct self-energy investment from the individual, who remains relatively passive in the situation. Basic examples for spontaneous interactions include some of the formerly mentioned "background" processes, such as the natural absorption of the sun's heat, or "contingent" processes like effortlessly receiving an "improving" gift from another individual. A strong hurricane heading towards a less fortunate individual exemplifies, for instance, a spontaneous conservation problem. Accordingly, we can distinguish between human reactions to spontaneous processes, and human *actions* entailing an active initiation of interactions with non-spontaneous yet possibly impactful events.[61, 62] In this regard, we assume that the necessity to work and self-invest energy and resources in altering spacetime while producing life functionality is normally being assimilated in the individual's BES from an early stage of life and continues to shape, also in compliance with the PPD-based perceptive mechanisms, his or her actions and reactions with respect to the EI world. Such a necessity clearly abides by the general spacetime laws of energy conservation, and among them the EDB.

The preliminary CP-based predictions regarding the spontaneity of the impact of the referred event in the different response channels are believed to be followed by crucial assessments predicting whether

---

61 Despite the distinction made and unless stated otherwise, we will keep referring to all inter-actions between R_{self} and R_{event} as "reactions".

62 We emphasize that different interactive processes might also be facilitated via energy co-in-vestment by both R_{self} and certain EI elements which either relate directly to the GCF under con-sideration or to third-party entities affecting the event.

the individual's own reactions can ameliorate or worsen his or her R_{self}, and for the non-spontaneous cases (see chap. 3, n. 62) what is the extent of energy, E^0_{inv}(channel), based on perceptive conjugations, which needs to be invested in the execution of these reactions. With respect to that, we will now start reviewing the main response channels to be considered at this point. The first (I) potential response refers to the *collection channel* which aims to elevate the individual's R_{self} through interacting with the event. The amelioration in this case is achieved by appropriating certain EI contents, a behavior which is normally bound to social laws and conventions regarding ownership and possession (addressed in the next section). As we previously implied, we believe that increasing our energy reserves can improve our genetic conservation. Now, regardless of if the interactions in the experienced situation require an additional external investment of energy, we tend to view the collecting response as based on an active PbB, emphasizing its overall non-spontaneous nature. In accord with our previous assumption, this estimation by itself can be meaningful for the comparative assessments to be made with the other response channels. Assisting our side-observing analysis at this stage is Figure 3.1(A), which highlights several fundamental expectation trends in regard to a non-spontaneous event involving a collecting response by the individual (it is important to note that such objectivity-seeking presentations tend to ignore the full $f(\Psi)$ spectrum of influences biasing the predictions). One possible example for such an event regards a bias-free hypothetical situation in which the individual recognizes an abandoned hoard that he or she can (legally) appropriate. An experience-based, CP-interpreted first glimpse at the discovery allows the individual to realize that ignoring it and refraining from collection will not enrich his or her own R_{self}. This simple interpretation is reflected by the predictive index of self-energetic change, generally elaborated on in Equation 3.6, whose zero value in this case, Δ_{self}(collecting)=0, suggests that the (energetic impact by the collection) event is not expected to be spontaneous.

$$(3.6) \quad \Delta_{self}(\text{channel}) = P_{self} - R_{self}$$

This expectation is further highlighted by the dashed line in Panel (i) of the figure. Ignoring the precious hoard might have personal consequences (which we ignore at the moment), and most often the individual would be interested in scrutinizing the option to invest self energy in appropriating it, Panel (ii). Such intervention of the individual in the event is expected to decrease, even marginally, for instance when it comes to the modest motoric investment by a healthy human, his or her self-resources. Past experiences of the individual in spacetime enable him or her to estimate, often very coarsely and occasionally more quantitatively, this self-effort as E^0_{inv} before deciding to interact with R_{event}. With respect to that, an arbitrary prediction of a certain amount of self-invested energy was symbolically added to Panel (ii) of Figure 3.1(A). In the next step, we relate the estimated success of the collection response to a potential increase in R_{self} value due to the appropriating interaction with R_{event}. These expectations suggest that $P_{self} > R_{self}$, as is further indicated in Figure 3.1. Now, in predicting the success or the failure of his or her own responses, the individual heavily relies on the CP's arsenal of top-down processing and other cognitive functions. These, combined with the EPself as a "pseudo-quantitative" energetic reference for the assessments, assist in determining P_{self} and, subsequently, in accord with Equation 3.6, the self-change Δ_{self}(channel) expected by the interaction. The natural aspiration, indicated in the figure, to maximize the genetic gain, correlates the PWI with the P_{self} values, and thus suggests higher motivation indexes $\mu_{channel}$(event) for channels predicted as yielding elevated Δ_{self}(channel) values.

Recalling our previous postulation regarding the overarching influences over the energetic assessments and predictions, including those described by the impact function $f(\Psi)$, we may already relate some of them to beliefs adopted by the individual (e.g., regarding social norms such as taxation, which reduces from his or her potential pessimistically compared to a reference based on others, thus revealing a certain aspect of his or her evolved personality.[63] Clearly, no solid factual correlation must exist between the practical outcome of the behavioral response and its human prediction. In the case of the collection channel, this can be demonstrated by appropriating

---

63 It is possible that the assessments of the referenced event begin with imagination-radicalized utopic and dystopic interpretations, from which the predicted energetic variables are being subsequently derived. In this regard, we also mention the ($f(\Psi)$-related) potential impact of expectations for reward or suffering and their possible connection to experiences involving release of dopamine.

an object which for certain reasons turns out to have no positive contribution to the R_{self} as had been initially predicted.

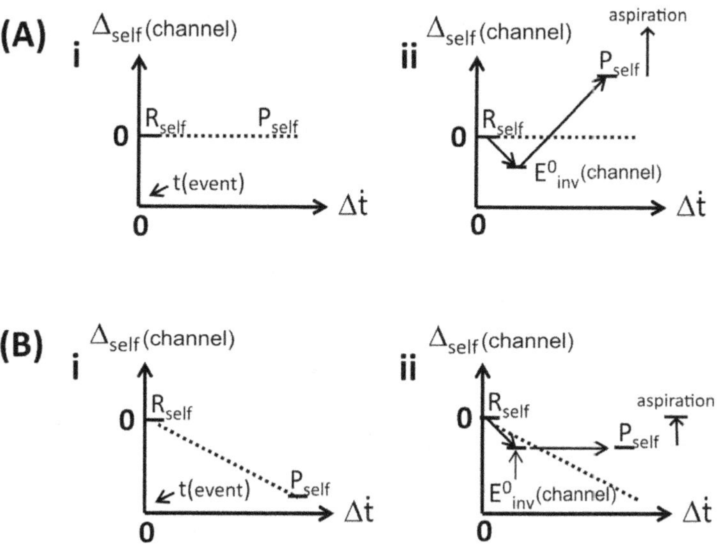

Figure 3.1. Basic patterns of predicted energetic self (individual ecosystem) changes caused by possible responses to referenced events. (A) shows an "ideal" non-spontaneous event perceived as holding a potential to improve the energetic self. Panel (i) is without self-intervention. Panel (ii), predicting a successful response which leads to self-amelioration. (B) shows a spontaneous event which is perceived as holding a potential to worsen the energetic self and thus become a conservation problem. Panel (i) is without self-intervention. Panel (ii), predicting a successful response minimizing the potential losses in (i). All estimated energy levels and changes shown are arbitrary and might not necessarily correlate with the physical consequences of the applied interactions in effect.

personal gain) and to his or her psychoenergetic profile. With respect to these, it is reasonable to believe, for instance, that the present specific state of the individual's mind affects his or her tendency to assess the response parameters optimistically or pessimistically. Hence, an uncertainty regarding the practical outcome is naturally expected to accompany the predictions in all possible response channels at this stage of assessments. The next concept, which is also encompassing all assessed channels, deals with the systematic normalization of the expected reaction variables with respect to the present energetic self-resources of the individual relevant to the experienced situation. Assisted by the perceptive conjugation cognitive operations, this normalization is presented in regard to a specific R_{event} as:

$$(3.7) \quad \Delta_{self}(relative) = \Delta_{self}(channel)/R_{self} = (P_{self}-R_{self})/R_{self}$$
$$= P_{self}/R_{self} - 1$$

We already note that $\Delta_{self}(relative)$, the estimated index of *relative change expectancy*, is an important factor in our simplified mechanism. Relying on the normalization, a rich individual who is aware, for example, of his or her bountiful possessions may ascribe a low $\Delta_{self}(relative)$ value to collecting a resource perceived as marginal compared to them. In contrast, the exact resource might be more likely perceived by a poor individual as worth collecting. In accord with these seemingly unbiased propensities, it is possible to correlate the PWI motivation index with, among other parameters, the relative self-change expectancy through the general formula:

$$(3.8) \quad \mu_{channel}(event) = |P_{self}/R_{self}-1| \cdot [\varphi^0(channel)/E^0_{inv}(channel)]$$

Lacking an empirical validation at the time of its writing, Equation 3.8 is algebraically treated with considerable care,[64] and its generic formulation suggests that we ascribe it to a broad range of responses extending beyond $\mu_{collecting}(event)$.[65] Examining the equation, one may observe that it contains a multiplicity of two expectancy factors, the index of relative self-change by the response, and a term referring to elementary practical considerations regarding the interaction. In

---

64 We reemphasize that the equation does not attempt to precise mathematically the "algorithm" behind the estimation but to provide us with some perspective of the physical assessments which hypothetically govern it. We also recall our assumption regarding the coupling of the cognitive assessments to $f(\Psi)$, a dynamic which may divert the results yet is deliberately omitted from the equation.

65 Relative adjustments to the formulation are probable when the response involves, among other possible cases, a combined investment of efforts by the individual and others. Some basic energy-related characteristics of cooperations between individuals will be discussed in Chapter 4.

accord with the presumed tendency to minimize self-investment of energy in the responses (which can also contribute to maximizing the relative profit), the formulation alludes a reciprocal correlation between the PWI and the predicted E^0_{inv}(channel). The second factor refers to the individual's estimated *self-potency to succeed*, φ^0(channel). The latter can be regarded as a pseudo-quantitative prediction based on assessments of a person's own body and mind physical/mental capabilities and present readiness to successfully ameliorate R_{self} in the situation using the response channel under consideration. While the two measures, E^0_{inv} and φ^0, may be interrelated, they can also be respectively addressed as the self-effort required to initiate the response, and the individual's potency, for example, in terms of skills and feasibility, to successfully respond in a way that will hopefully yield the highly anticipated $\Delta_{self}>0$ results (such as carefully digging, collecting, and securing the hoard as a part of its appropriation in the example above). In the case of the collection channel, for instance, Equation 3.8 implies that the attractiveness of this response elevates with predictions of increased profit, diminished self-resources relative to it, decreased self-investment of energy, and enhanced capabilities to perform the action and establish an IEB. Now, considering the influence of $f(\Psi)$ and its ID manifestations during the experience on these different predictive parameters, we can describe several exemplary "contradictions" or "trade-offs" between them which often divert the $\mu_{channel}$(event) evaluations and affect their follow-up prioritizations. One such case concerns assessment of responses at times of experiencing poor, or alternatively overexaggerated, *confidence* in the self-performance. These are being respectively reflected by remarkably low, or otherwise high, biased values of the φ^0(channel) expectancy index. Quite often, the latter appear to be more critical to the prioritizations of the motivation indexes preceding the chosen response than predictions of high Δ_{self}(relative) or low E^0_{inv}(channel). In addition to circumstantial momentary influences on the confidence levels, we may also intuitively relate them to experiences gained and assimilated by the individual regarding the reliability of his or her energetic estimations. This psychoenergetic impact can be achieved through persistent comparisons between past assessments and subsequent observations of their genetic outcomes.[66] Another example relates to assessments made in the case of collecting resources whose potential profits to the individual seem to overcome his or her estimated needs by a great extent. An ordinary human would be doubtfully appreciably over-motivated to collect, for example, 1.01 over 1.00 billion dollars and, therefore, is unlikely to change his or her predictions regarding the practical factors E^0_{inv} and φ^0 with respect to the difference between these opportunities. In most cases we can assume that this individual would gladly settle on collecting the smaller amount despite the fact that even the difference between the sums would be significant in terms of his or her current self-resources. Possibly also challenging the straightforward "unbiased" trends shown in the equations is the frequent inclination to prioritize responses which aim to yield smaller profits yet are being perceived as easier to achieve (thus maintaining a sort of trade-off between Δ_{self} and φ^0) or sustain, and as such are treated as holding a potential to gradually lead to higher IEBs with time. A further tendency concerns the prioritization of channels associated with a faster realization of self-gain. In this case we indicate a possible trade-off between the estimated profit and the shortening of the effective time predicted for implementation. One can assume that a main contribution to this tendency comes from the FoD which is fuelling the uncertainty regarding the prolongation of the individual's life. Looking from a broad perspective, these and possible other examples should be considered if the possible refinement or development of Equation 3.8 are to be made.

So far, we have suggested that the incentive behind the collection responses lies at an appropriation of perceived elements from R_{event} to elevate R_{self}. Before moving on to discussing other interaction pathways, we wish to acknowledge a specific type of PbB related to the collection channel, which is the *collection-oriented migration* contributing to the specific roaming of humans in the accessible spacetime. We ascribe the spatial directions and several other characteristics of this migration to following "gradients" of potential human energy resources which are

---

66 It is also intuitive for us to believe that different experiences change our estimations regarding the activation barriers of specific interactions. Accordingly, it is possible to generalize that all humans tend to shift with time their personal assessments of the response parameters involved in Equation 3.8.

being perceived as collectable.[67] In this context, the collection-oriented migration is viewed as distinct from several other motoric responses as a PbB-directed translocation that is based on direct energetic-genetic amelioration considerations. Let's now move on to another interaction path occasionally considered by the individual; the *enriching receival channel* (II). Although in many cases the individual can trigger the receival of energetic resources him- or herself by properly manipulating different identified objects,[68] we will generally regard the effective interaction represented by this channel as facilitated by an external force that controls R_{event} or is operating from within it. This allows us to predominantly perceive the event as spontaneous from the perspective of the individual while we still consider his or her engagement in the assessment and acceptance stages. As expected, during a successful receival process, resources are being transferred to the individual and enrich his or her R_{self}. Scrutinizing the reaction from the standpoint of the expectancy parameters presented in Equation 3.8, the enriching receival resembles to some extent an optimized form of a "passive collection", where the individual is mostly free in this case from investing energy in the interaction while accepting the externally transferred resources. Despite our intuitive expectation that such an "ideal" situation, supported by highly graded and potentially prioritized $\mu_{receiving}$(event) indexes, would be "automatically" favored at nearly all times, we remember that $f(\Psi)$ influences may inhibit the individual from persistently and habitually proceeding with these interactions. Somewhat inverse to the enriching receival is the *giving channel* (III). In this case, the individual actively transfers from his or her own resources to other objects, often humans, which are identified as external to his or her R_{self} in the referred event.[69] Recalling our suggestion from Chapter 1 assuming that "spending without gaining" is merely an illusion, the act of giving can be associated with an asymmetric exchange process which yields reorganizations in R_{self}

---

67 In conjunction with the previous suggestion (chap. 3, n. 34) that the psychoenergetics of the individual also directs him or her to follow gradient pathways of social attention.

68 Sometimes also through adopting a catalyst-like behavior, attempting to minimize one's own efforts to achieve the resources by convincing or manipulating others to help or to give away resources.

69 A complementary act of giving corresponds to controlled redistribution of self-resources within members of the individual ecosystem. This behavior may involve for instance, acts of guardianship and enhancement.

and R_{event}. Now, in a similar way to the other channels, the assessment of the motivation index, in this case $\mu_{giving}(event)$, is accompanied by prediction of Δ_{self} changes. In some cases where the individual purposely plans on gaining a profit from the giving, the interaction can also be viewed as a present self-investment of E^0_{inv} in future receival/collection reactions. Next is the *diversion channel* (IV). This behavioral response mainly applies to events predicted as holding a spontaneous impact (Figure 3.1(B), Panel (i)), which can be "deflected" via an intervention of the individual (Panel (ii)). Changing the course of the spontaneous reaction requires investment of resources and, if successful, the response can be viewed as leading to alternative (spontaneous) products, such as P'_{self} and P'_{event}. The interest of the individual in diverting such reactions typically stems from identifying conservation problems in R_{event} which are predicted to yield significant $\Delta_{self}(event)<0$ without further intervention. Possibilities to divert the event's dynamics in ways which aspire to minimize the expected losses are then considered (Panel (ii)). Naturally, during all assessment stages, the self-losses and their potential minimization can be hard to quantify and, as such, often rely on coarse and subjective imagination- and $f(\Psi)$-biased assessments.[70] We should also emphasize that due to the expected loss of self-energy as a result of the spontaneous conservation-threatening event, the relative genetic change $P_{self}/R_{self}-1$ is assumed in this case to reflect a negative fraction whose absolute-value limits range between unity (upon estimating a maximal loss, $P_{self}=0$, implying death) and zero (for an ideal, harmless conservation, $P_{self}=R_{self}$). Regardless of such channel-specific variations, we assume that the entire set of elementary response parameters determining $\mu_{channel}(event)$, and thus the responses' indirect genetic attractiveness, is being EP-evaluated for all relevant cases using "algorithms" similar to Equation 3.8.

Another response to be typically considered following a CP/emotive recognition of a conservation problem relates to active attempts to reduce self-damages through *escaping* (V). As we know, in certain situations these attempts coerce the individual to sacrifice and leave behind self-resources, as acts which by themselves are expected to decrease the R_{self}. In accord with that, we may approach the common

---

70 While still attempting to remain linked to certain reference points in the EP$_{self}$ through the perceptive conjugation.

"fight or flight" dilemma via the reduced comparative assessments of the Δ_{self}, φ^0, and E^0_{inv} parameters in regard to the diversion and escape channels, while still considering that these can be affected by the $f(\Psi)$-based biases. In the case of this dilemma, typical relevant biases include, for example, the individual's self-image, susceptibility to others' judgement, personal beliefs shaping his or her own principles and morality, emotional connections to resources and/or acknowledgement that they were earned by hard work and prolonged efforts, and others. While these occasionally push the individual to favor fighting as an instance of diversion, substantial fears from physical, social, or legal consequences of possible confrontations often lead him or her in other cases to escape. The next optional channel refers to the somewhat passive behavior of *awaiting vigilantly* (VI). This response is being generally considered upon facing substantial difficulties to decisively prioritize other response paths, often due to overall low-value assessments of different $\mu_{channel}(event)$ or lack of sufficient information to reliably back up the predictions. While waiting for a change which may resolve this situation, the individual continues sensing the environment and is accordingly updating and/ or reinitiating his or her spatial assessments. Furthermore, depending on the genetic potentials detected and estimated, an increase in the activity levels of the individual's vigilance-concentration functions may occur. This might help him or her improve the predictions of the possible upcoming changes while waiting for the situation to further develop. To our modest list of potential responses, we wish to add the seemingly passive behavioral channels of *acceptance* (VII) and *ignoring* (VIII). In a similar manner to the awaiting response, acceptance may follow different low PWI assessments concerning a (spontaneous) referred event of a reasonable expected impact. In this case the reduced attractiveness of several channels pushes the individual, under the influence of the overarching biases acting on him or her, to accept potentially upcoming self-losses while giving up on immediate attempts to divert the situation or escape from it. In this regard, one may also mention the case of delayed acceptance of lower profits than initially expected. Unlike acceptance, ignoring applies to cases where the motivation indexes estimated for the different channels do not cross the threshold levels required for their genuine practical consideration. Now, considering the various responses listed,[71] and their possible assessment and prioritization mechanisms, we still believe that no simple and straightforward methodology to "select our own struggles" in the global energetic struggle can be easily formulated. The complexity-related implications of the unique individuality dimensions of every person as well as his or her exposure to the dynamic EI environment thwart any attempt to generate a reduced algebraic algorithm that can precisely and globally predict the outcome of specific assessments with respect to all events experienced. Despite accepting that such limitations will remain valid even if we find better ways to decrypt the $f(\Psi)$ impact function and tailor it to the specific experiences, we still believe that simplified models can help trigger new perspectives and hypotheses, for example, regarding energetic considerations which might have been rooted in perceptive mechanisms through the evolution of nature. As we previously implied, these "big picture" assumptions are far more interesting to us than the precision of this or another preoptimized formula, and accordingly we will continue our descriptions abiding by these concepts.

3.2.5 Detection-reaction model. Part III: Overarching influences

So far, we have mostly portrayed the mechanism behind the EP as some sort of a "serial" mind systematicness which leads the individual in selecting his or her responses to interpretations of received sensory inputs. Such depictions may evoke a false impression that the human PbB automatically follows a pure, "algorithmic" type of unbiased conversion. While adhering to the concepts behind the suggested formulation, we wish to expand the descriptions of the biasing effects and refer to some of the factors assumed to be participating in the impact function $f(\Psi)$. Increasing the complexity associated with the processes entailed, such factors provide to the sensoresponses a more varied and "parallel-like" character. Furthermore, viewing

---

71 The reader is warmly encouraged to add from his or her own ideas to the list of response channels. One can think of, for example, additional "secondary" reaction paths involving mediated and/or catalyzed operations to improve or conserve the R_{self}. These naturally add up to many other responses by the individual which are not necessarily genetically focused (see next section).

the different influences as converging in spacetime[72] allows us to describe this process as "integrative" and physically imposed on the individual via a restricted-contingent deterministic dictate. Given that, we wish to distinguish between two types of biases: those which affect the treatment of the event foci prior to their assessments (including their clustering) and those which impact the later selection of the appropriate response path. We start with the first type. As we postulated, the sensoperceptive conversion of physical stimuli arriving to our body's sensory systems triggers a systematic mind evaluation in search of potentials of genetic interest and value for the individual. Based on hereditary-shaped cognitive abilities to interpret and predict spacetime changes which further rely on accrued mind-encoded assimilations, the CP serves as the prominent functional tool for indicating causal/circumstantial connections and associations between the assessed foci. These, we believe, continue to affect the subsequent energetic assessments. In one example, upon a CP-based recognition of two freely wandering lions close-by, an unprotected individual who ran into the situation is likely to CP-assess the lions' presence and behavior from both clustered and separated GCF viewpoints. The predicted spatial dynamics, also considering, for instance, the behavior of the lions, their sizes, distances, and so on, will further affect the subsequent energetic estimates of the situation and the prioritization of the respective response. This clearly also applies to multiple foci dangerous scenarios (such as a combined presence of lion and fire), to dangers associated with distinct implications on different R_{self} elements (a fire which is endangering me, my offspring, my house), to situations entailing both spontaneous and non-spontaneous dangers (a lion chasing me towards a steep cliff), to situations holding mixed, sometimes contradicting, C/I implications (noticing a fruit hanging on top of a hard-to-climb tree, while I am starving), and so forth. Unsurprisingly, the association of assessment foci to clusters relies on many perceivable and emotive parameters. Returning to the bedroom assault example, we indicate that the potentials of the attacker, allegedly providing the motive and energy to trigger the event, and the knife, which is believed to be capable of inflicting the body damage, are being united during the evaluation of the

---

72 Converging into the individual's mind at the present time of assessment.

situation. Related to that, we also wish to mention the contribution of associations, emerging alongside the intensive use of the imagination function at this stage, to the clustering and assessments of the foci. The associations blend into additional considerations regarding exposure factors which themselves normally have little or no direct impact on the experienced event itself and are frequently biased by momentary consciousness attractors evoking in the individual's mind. Combined with the broad "database" of BES-assimilated beliefs, we also acknowledge the contributions of imagination-based manipulations to assessing foci at times when the existence of certain objectives in the experienced situation is only perceptively insinuated. One intuitive example for that is predicting the presence of fire upon seeing or smelling smoke. We also note the connections between the individual's awareness (and vigilance) and the assessment of the foci. Let's consider, for example, an individual who is sensing the presence of a fruit which is readily available for collecting, yet seemingly skips its assessment while processing the pre-perceptive sensory projection. One possible event that could have potentially reverted this situation is contraction of the individual's stomach muscles, signaling a hunger sensation to his or her consciousness and awareness and consequently increasing the attention to the BCF. It is thus easy to see that the interplay between needs, sensations, and awareness plays a tangible role in triggering and ignoring foci assessments, some holding a genuine potential to affect human behavior. As a part of that, we can also relate the ongoing focal assessments to the individual's concentration and the distraction or fixation of the concentration by different consciousness attractors, including those which are based on surfacing urges and emotions.

As we mentioned, we also presume that certain processes specifically impact the prioritization of the response channels under consideration and eventually lead the individual to prefer specific reaction paths over others. Within this complex dynamic, one can accentuate, for example, effects related to imbalances formed by contradicting urges/needs (some of which have already been mentioned or insinuated in the examples above). Such common situations account for dilemma-evoking "inner-struggles" in the individual, which we believe can also be occasionally correlated with the absolute or relative assessments of the DRS-specific contributions to the EPself reference. Further playing a significant role in the prioritization processes are emotional influences. We find this to be quite intuitive, as we occasionally notice changes in our or others' responses when taken under different emotional (vector distribution) states. One may also presume that emotions intensify the use of the imagination function in exaggerating (see chap. 3, n. 63) the predictions regarding the experienced event, which often leads to over- or underestimating Δ_{self}, E^0_{inv}, φ^0, and the implementation times, among other possible factors relevant for the interaction.[73] Interestingly, we believe that one fundamental origin for experiencing negative emotions lies within experiences in which the individual identifies high potential self-gain values, yet they coincide with his or her own predicted obstacles to implement due to different estimated reasons. These apparent discrepancies between high and positive Δ_{self} values and low self-potency estimates of φ^0 (including unmatching response times regarding the interaction), are often short-term manifestations of psychoenergetic effects impacting PbB. Moving on, some biases can also be associated with cognitive activity related to *reasoning*. The emergence of reasoning is assumed to pertain, at least in part, to background mind processes attempting to impose instinctive/inherent or assimilated order patterns on predictions and prioritizations. The order patterns seemingly aim to strategically assist the individual's survival and self-amelioration (occasionally by restricting some C/I aspects), and as such often take the form of objectivity-inspired cause-and-effect beliefs and interpretations regarding potential implications of his or her intervention in spacetime dynamics. Some basic examples include the general tendency to prioritize conservation issues over improvement potentials, or to favor reliance for the assessments on one's own sensory observations over adopting self-serving and/ or misguided beliefs communicated by others.[74] Clearly, the last example does not contradict the idea that as long as there is no sharp dissonance between our beliefs and those of others—defying our core life narratives, for instance—our assessments can consider the

---

73 A prolonged, accrued emotive impact can contribute to a persistent long-term biasing effect. Retrospectively examining correlations between predictions and the respective gains or losses which they have effectively led to may indicate, for example, personal inclinations towards (acquired) optimism or pessimism in human assessments.

74 It should be noted that other biases and circumstances can overcome these tendencies.

latter and, when applicable, even benefit from the wisdom of the crowds. These ideas naturally relate to a social factor that frequently affects the estimations, which is trust. Trust can be approached from different perspective levels related to the energetic struggle between humans. Here, we favor to mainly associate it with certain emotion vectors evoked in individuals who are willing to share and/or invest resources (including potential energy-related information) with others. The willingness is often empowered/incentivized by a genetic affinity between them or by rewards expected from the interaction.

Communicated information and the beliefs it triggers and encodes in the human indeed play a prominent role in the grading and prioritization of the PWIs. Obedience to orders, listening to others' suggestions, succumbing to social pressure, and abiding by social norms, provide plain examples for such communication-mediated biases.[75] Employing a feedback system of rewards and penalties with respect to the human responses, and assisted by various means of communication, societies and groups attempt to direct their individual members to adhere to certain behavioral laws. Some of the latter aim to serve as a moral compass which is uniting, normalizing, and allowing distribution of normalized beliefs regarding the good, the bad, and what lies between them with respect to different behaviors and related topics.[76] Such beliefs can oppress, for example, collecting responses when the objective GCF in the event is being recognized as legally belonging to others, and they frequently prioritize paths of escape or avoidance over diverting reactions which seem nonmoral in the view of social conventions. With respect to that, the detection-reaction model suggests that upon assessing the self-genetic-based transition of R_{self} to P_{self}, not only does the individual consider the feasibility and the self-consequences of possible interactions between R_{self} and R_{event}, but he or she also estimates and reckons with the change of R_{event} to P_{event} (and its additional effects on P_{self}). With respect to that, in the presence of other individuals, either constituting a part

---

75 One can even play with the idea of an analogy between the biasing effect resulting from the presence of other (interacting) humans during the individual's response assessments and the collapse of a wavefunction to a single eigenstate due to the presence of a nearby detector observing the process.

76 We assume that beyond their mind-projected interpretations which are directly and indirectly related to the energetic struggle, the terms "good" and "bad" lack any absolute meaning in the general spacetime.

of R_{event} or as third-party spectators, the individual can be additionally engaged with "game theory-like" estimations such as: How will the others estimate my response? How do they assess the situation themselves? and even, How do they estimate my own estimations? The answers to these questions often stay uncertain and imprecise in view of the unique IDs and differences in the $f(\Psi)$ functions of the people present in the situation, and considering their alien subjective "selves" estimates from the individual's perspective. Yet, in light of the energetic struggle, the importance of such estimations to the individual remains high. We also intuitively accept that upon recognizing other individuals and associating them with our life narrative, we tend to refine the way in which we evaluate their beliefs, assessments, and responses to events. Our strong inclination to assess achievements by others and compare them with ours yields beliefs and emotions that, often without our awareness, push us towards social status-biased and/or acting behaviors fueled by clear self-interest. Furthermore, depending on the circumstances, jealousy in the achievements of others[77] or hedonic adaptation[78] may elevate or suppress motivations to self-accomplish and accordingly impact the selection of behavioral responses.

The examples which have been mentioned so far suggest a psychoenergetic interplay between certain influence factors, projected through consciousness-traversing dynamics, and mechanistic responses that are cognitively biased by them and which attempt to realize, ameliorate, and conserve the individual's achievements. Assisted by his or her cognitive interpretations, imagination, and reasoning, the human can assess complicated events consisting, for example, of multiple C/I or C+I potentials. Under the right conditions, he or she may further identify in the experienced situation the presence of certain catalysts holding a potential to reduce the activation energy E_a required for the interaction with R_{event}. As expected, such abilities also apply to identifying inhibitors which elevate the energetic barriers

---

77 One may generally view relative self-underachievement as triggering jealousy and affecting—either positively or negatively—the motivation to self-ameliorate, and overachievement as typically evoking positive emotions like self-content or often leading the individual to ignore the comparison.

78 Hedonic adaptation is discussed, for example, in S. Frederick, and G. Loewenstein, Hedonic Adaptation. In *Well-Being: Foundations of Hedonic Psychology*, edited by D. Kahneman, and E. Diener, N. Schwarz. Russel Sage Foundation (1999).

of the possible response channels or compete with the individual on crossing them.[79] We also note the special assessments occasionally made by the individual with respect to deficiencies in self-resources to overcome a certain channel's barrier, and to opportunities to co-invest resources with others for this matter or to share with them future gains/losses. Further acknowledged is the basic desire to profit at a modest self-investment. The propensity extends beyond the general tendency to deprioritize and dismiss immoderate E_a channels and is particularly valid for minimizing excessive E^0_{inv} investments in regard to the E_a barriers required. Some other factors biasing the processing of the potential responses are time-related. Among these we highlight the cursory CP predictions of the times required for the gains or losses to take effect in the different interaction channels under consideration. The impact of the assessments is expected to be complex, as it might demonstrate contradicting prioritization affinities, such as between the basic desire to expedite gains (before spacetime dynamics may change and/or others utilize R_{event} for their own goals) and reasoning-biased inclinations to postpone[80] a potential amelioration. A different time-related impact on the sensoresponses concerns the progression of the individual time, which correlates with the incremental BES and EMES mind assimilations affecting the CP and emotive indicators/biases, respectively. Gaining experience related to spacetime dynamics may further ameliorate the time assessments of the response channels and affects their prioritization in regard to the individual's readiness and the maturation of the external conditions to provide him or her an optimal benefit. Adhering to the mind/brain correlation, we also believe that EI processes and their time constants contingently impact (also in physiological terms) the assessments and responses. This kind of physically driven time "equilibration" between the mind biases and EI spacetime is quite intuitive, for example, when scrutinizing the impact of tiredness on our decisions with respect to our sleeping habits synchronized to Earth's rotation around its axis. Another time effect concerns the age-dependent shifts in the energetic dependency

---

79 Inhibitory actions by other individuals constitute an inevitable part of the human struggle and are usually self-justified from the energetic narrative viewpoints of their executors.

80 Allowing possible trade-offs between energy gain and effective amelioration time from the present perspective of the reference state of R_{self}. The trade-offs are also bound to the momentary needs and urges attractors.

of the individual on others. These are often maximal during infancy, decrease after adolescence, and rise again at an old age, as was illustrated in Figure 1 of the Appendix.

Bound to the inextricability limitations, the detection-reaction model associates several perceived characteristics of potential response pathways with physical characteristics of reactions in spacetime.[81] Accordingly, the PPD hypothesis suggested that elementary physical principles directing general spacetime reactions have been assimilated through the long evolutionary process into the human CP/EP operational mechanisms and, as such, they play a prominent role in dictating the mind-processed reactions to sensory stimuli, and consequently direct the genetic-based PbB of the individual. Based on our scientific beliefs, crossing the "organic" implementation barriers of the response reactions along the anticipated way to conserve and ameliorate the individual requires contingent compatibility conditions. While the biased predictions of these are mostly unreliable, we believe that the assessments of the different response reaction parameters presented will always continue to be carried out through the perceptive mechanisms. Indeed, the human is constantly affected by internal and external "side/secondary reactions"[82] which occasionally divert his or her assessments, decisions, and responses. Such reactions cause the PbB to appear to the outside world as slightly more "stochastic" and less "robotic", and based on the biased energetic considerations, entailed to reflect some kind of an *energetic qualia* effect in perceiving, prioritizing, and responding to events and opportunities. Naturally, most biasing reactions evade the individual's awareness and thus extend beyond the reach of his or her EPself assessments. Before moving on, we wish to emphasize that due to our primary interest in this book in the energy perception as a hypothetical core element shaping the PbB, we refrain from further elaborating

---

81 Adopting a broad viewpoint, we also note that in a similar way to other reactions in nature that require spatial convergence of components to initiate conversion, prior to the processing reaction the mind content distributions reflected by the perceptive projections R_{self} and R_{event} (subjective and biased as they are) also coincide during the time of assessment at the individual's mind "reactor".

82 Some of these reactions, including the impacts we regard as related to the $f(\Psi)$ function, can be viewed as exerting an inner struggle—as opposed to the external struggle between humans—that is abundant with needs, urges, and apparent contradictions between them (acting as catalysts or inhibitors to the sensoresponsive process).

the well-studied motoric stage of the sensomotoric response despite acknowledging its vital role in the process. Whereas we now shortly divert the discussion to the behavioral states of the human, we note that the last subsection of the chapter will return to describing some fundamental aspects of the PPD.

3.3 Behavioral states

So far, we have focused on the individual energy perception of spacetime and its hypothesized role in guiding the human's responses to experienced events with respect to his or her inherent genetic aims. Such descriptions insinuate that the individual is mostly occupied with self (ecosystem)-serving PbB which is also taking a modest part in the global energetic struggle of humanity. Assuming that, we ask, Are we solely and permanently engaged with C/I and realization attempts? Inspecting our entire spectrum of activities in our daily lives indicates that we dedicate parts of our time to interactions holding other purposes. While clinging to the elementary detection-reaction principles proposed, we can still associate the behavioral aspects of these interactions and the functionalities emerged from them to typical *behavioral states* recurrently being switched by every individual throughout his or her life. Abiding by our fundamental belief in structural-functional correlations, we may even regard the possibility that the behavioral states employ different mind mechanisms within the $k_f(t)$ entire operative mind dynamics. Considering these ideas, we begin by referring to a prominent *genetic-focused state*, which is believed to be focused on realizing, conserving, and improving the individual's own ecosystem and requires attention/concentration to these matters. As expected, such activity entails the aforementioned reactions associated with the collection, receival, giving, diversion, and escape channels, as well as conversion of resources and realization of targets, collection-oriented migration, and possible other behavioral responses.[83] Another elementary behavioral state is

---

83 One may also associate, for example, to this genetic-focused behavior socially accepted conventions such as seeking employment and working. Modern expressions of working can be perceived as an evolutionary product of the energy struggle and communicated beliefs. Generally speaking, we can see the work itself as investing energy and time in reordering parts of spacetime in ways that are believed to benefit us and often also other benefiters who can reward us for these actions.

ascribed to *sleeping*. Contrary to states of wakefulness, during sleep the individual's body shows an elevated passivity as his or her motoric control is relatively restricted. These observations are commonly associated with reorganizational physiological processes taking place while in this rest state, and which are believed to be necessary for sustaining the appropriate operation of the human functions. Beyond the body rest and particularly the relaxation of the muscles, which appear to be crucial from a homeostatic point of view, we further correlate the mind activity taking place at this stage with several systemic processes. One way to approach this activity is by paralleling it to controlled charging and discharging of (mind) capacitors. Viewing the short-term memory (STM) as a functional stack temporarily storing encoded sensory, perceptive, and emotive assimilations, we may analogize it to a mind capacitor in which assimilated information (memories) replaces the accumulated charge. At every given moment the memories present in the STM correspond to recent assimilations into it (since the last charge cycle) and previous assimilations (from past charging cycles) which still reside there for different reasons. The STM is presumably interacting, especially during the sleep state, with another capacitor-like mind array, the long-term memory (LTM), to which some of the memories are transferred. This is carried out through a systemic—yet unique, as it considers multiple factors related, for example, to the type/nature of the information and to its urgency to the individual—updating process. Presumably facilitating subsequent access to the BES and EMES information necessary for the top-down processing, we believe that such capacitor-like charge/discharge activity is required for the continuity of the conversion and thus for the spacetime perceptions and PbB.[84] By following the inherent systematicness demanding basic compatibility for the STM-LTM transitions, and through an extensive reliance on the imagination function in facilitating it,[85] the consequent reorganization of the mind will shape the individual's spatial/energetic self and participate in the

---

84 It should be emphasized that the top-down processing used in our perceptive interpretations further relies on STMs, including the sensory memory, for example, and as such does not necessarily require preliminary updating of the LTM in the sleep state.

85 We may hypothetically associate the PCEs experienced during dreams with attempts of the imagination function to fluidly match parts of the memory arrays along the way to charge the LTM and reorganize the self. This is the finest hour of the mind events (see Chapter 2) enabling us to have a possible glimpse into the individual's subjective world of associative connections.

interpretations of spacetime.

Another central behavioral state is related to *escapism-focused activity*. The human behavior in this case is associated with different interactions which are not directly intended to enable, conserve, or improve the individual's ecosystem and its continuation, yet are often deliberately chosen by him or her to engage in. Escapism-focused activity takes up a significant time from the human's life and includes a wide range of activities which are quite often pleasurable, such as creating, playing, reading, staring, thinking, and many others. One may notice that some of these are covert behaviors and, as such, do not necessarily exhibit motoric expressions. Moreover, certain leisure time activities, such as engaging in sports, socializing, and others, occasionally share both genetic and escapist characteristics. We also believe that some escapism-focused activities might themselves circumstantially impact the individual's EPself. Despite the possible connections between the two major wakefulness behavioral states, we still view the engagement of the human in escapist activities as free of a clear intention to invest main attention, energy-resources, and time in the C/I of his or her individual ecosystem during their practice. Now, we know that during the escapism-focused and sleep states, the sensory systems of our body remain active. The continuous sensing of the environment allows us,[86] in case the now-elevated (during these states) motivation thresholds $\mu^0{}_{GCF}$(threshold) are being crossed by a proper focal trigger, to revert our attention to it and promptly refocus on the genetic-based activity and energetic struggle. With respect to that, we can further distinguish between the behavioral states based on the levels of attention and concentration allocated in each of them to potential genetic C/I interactions with spacetime or through the different thresholds set for these assessments (supporting reversion from the other behavioral states). Looking at the entire systematicness entailed, one may ask, Why is the human being engaged at all in activity which does not necessarily help him or her realize or ameliorate the inherent targets? One possible answer relates to the need to mitigate prolonged body and mind efforts invested in the genetic-focused behavior. This applies, for example, to the relaxation required for the muscles and for the revitalization of the mind's attention/

---

86 As we refer to comatose states and the like as circumstantial pathologies triggered by different events, we deliberately omit them from the discussion.

concentration functions which tend to decline following a sustained focused activity. Therefore, unless other forces interfere, sleeping and escapism-oriented activities aid the individual in performing better and staying sharp upon reverting from them to the genetic-focused state. Now, from a broad perspective, one may regard the escapism-focused activities as a sort of gamble to the individual and potentially also for the species. As insinuated by their name, escapism-focused activities enable the individual to temporarily escape from or repress fears and other negative emotions associated with genetic behaviors and, thus, to reduce potential inhibitions along the way to promoting his or her self-goals. This powerful positive distraction effect is seemingly also incentivized by the experience of rewarding emotions while engaging in carefree activities. Nevertheless, such rewards can easily turn into addictions that lead the individual to overspend precious time on escapist behaviors while relatively neglecting his or her genetic targets. Furthermore, as leisure provides the individual with more free time to think abstractly, it can further raise by itself awareness to the fears or even trigger them. Such contrasting effects also apply to thoughts about the essence of life and our meaning in nature. Adopting an emotionless scientific viewpoint, we speculate that the fundamental essence of our existence and all our actions is set to "serve" the greater physical evolution of the general spacetime which was assumed to extend beyond our ecosystems and perceptions. Within this generalization, one may point out different levels of human "subordination", which also include being "enslaved" to the (bio)physical dictates of the hereditary process and its genetic goals.[87] While these interpretations are clearly "organic" and therefore emotionless, motivated by his or her psychoenergetic needs to find order patterns, the human appears to project from them on his or her own emotions and illusions-biased narrative and often finds self-significance in raising children or in other ecosystem-related, emotionally rewarding dynamics.[88] Despite all these, acknowledging our insignificant role in the total development of the universe can

---

87 And from another interesting perspective, we might be genetically enslaved to leaving behind physical trails of sequential individuality through reproducing and supporting, as much as we can, our next generations.

88 Some humanistic-based propensities related to finding self-essence are discussed in Y. N. Harari, *Homo Deus: A Brief History of Tomorrow*. London: Harvill Secker (2016).

possibly pose a demotivational effect in some believers. Considering the various merits and risks associated with escapism-focused activities, it is interesting to look beyond conventional anthropological perspectives and consider them while attempting to analyze different aspects of human behavior, including the evolution of this behavioral state itself.

We now wish to refer shortly to the times dedicated to the different behavioral states and to the patterns of switching between them. The first point to consider is that the distribution of the time being spent in the different behavioral states correlates to a certain degree with notable changes in the dynamic balance of the individual human energy (Equation 2.1), which in turn affect the individual. Next, we suggest that, in a manner somewhat resembling the energetic assessments, the switching between behavioral states is also affected by urges, needs, emotions, and beliefs. An acquired practical experience in life allows the individual to develop "trustful" beliefs, for instance, which aid him or her to partially detach from the full genetic-focused state whenever no immediate attention to C/I potentials is needed.[89] Naturally, the switching between wakefulness and sleep states further depends on bio-signaling of tiredness/sufficient rest levels. This physiological mechanism itself is normally affected by the individual's age and habitual synchronization to certain natural events. Also worth mentioning is the assumption that the human keeps memorizing his or her recent switching history between the behavioral states, which can be used in assessing the authenticity of situations experienced. Accordingly, no matter how realistic a film can appear from the sensory viewpoint of watching it, how deeply it triggers us to immerse in its storyline, or how strong the emotions it evokes in us as we project its plot on our narrative and identify with it, using this memory we remain subconsciously alert that it is "just" an artificially mediated, and often acted, projection of certain spacetime dynamics. Another hypothesis suggests that the sleeping state provides an effective opportunity to reduce the potential buildup of "excess charging" of sensory energy dE_{st}^{in}(sensory) in the human during the wakefulness states. This might be carried out by a sleep-induced increase, potentially peaking

---

89 Nevertheless, and as we intuitively know, overspending time in non-genetic-focused activities can earn the individual a social image of a "slacker", which can also impact his or her behavior patterns.

during the rapid eye movement phase, in the relative emission of consciousness-coupled neural oscillations to sensory reception. To end this part, we highly encourage any possible extension to the reduced, symbolic list of behavioral states suggested herein.

3.4 Basic implications of the perceptive physical dimension-directed energy perception

So far, we have assumed that the human mind is systematically triggered to elicit different layers of perception atop basal pre-cognitive sensory projections, promoting the spatial interpretations of their stimuli. In many cases, and especially when the individual is immersed in the genetic-focused behavioral state, the interpretations turn to further rely on predictions of C/I and other potentials ascribed to identified objects in the experienced situation. According to the detection-reaction model, these potentials are used as a substrate for subsequent energetic-genetic assessments which often yield the decisions regarding the execution of the responses. As was previously hypothesized, the macro-level cognitive guidelines behind the EP mechanism of assessment and prioritization applied at this stage correlate with some fundamental physical laws of nature, thus reflecting what we regard as a perceptive physical dimension in mind processing. Now, from a broad perspective, an existence of PPD, reflecting, for example, restricted-contingent progression principles in nature, should not be surprising. Footprints of barriers to reactions and the need to invest energy to cross them along the way to produce spatial changes (and occasionally functionality) are all around us and can be easily observed in individual human behavior and in the macro human struggle. We can even generalize and claim that bound to causal deterministic dictates, all these contingently progressing reactions, over their energetic-, structural-, symmetrical- and kinetic-related aspects, facilitate the evolution of general spacetime and its observable dynamics, including the observations themselves. This universality should hence also apply to the mind processes discussed here and to the (probably physiology-emerged) perceptive mechanisms directing them. Scrutinizing the evolution of the mind to its current state, scientists commonly believe that since the early emergence of its distant biological origins on Earth, and through the appearance of primordial and then more advanced life forms, the process has been shaped by circumstantial changes in environmental conditions. Such changes further impacted the energetic struggles between the organisms while catalyzing transformations in their structures/functions and behavioral traits.[90] We believe that the circumstantial "struggles" (analogous to competing reactions) which have been accompanying the prolonged, restricted-contingent physical evolution of the human mind shaped its perceptive mechanisms in a way that reflects some of their most basic fundaments. These include the core physical principles and the susceptibility to biasing forces facilitating the progress and environmentally (including psychoenergetically) shifting it out of equilibrium, respectively.

Next, we refer to the scientific claim that during the evolution of life as we know it, the universal physical laws have remained unchanged, and ask, Could their allegedly correlated perceptive mind mechanisms have evolved themselves? Such a question is important, as scientific evidence indicates persistent changes in the human brain ever since our early ancestors' days[91] and, as was recently mentioned, differences between brain structures and cognitive abilities of humans and other species are clearly visible. Given that all mind/brain-owning life-forms have been shaped under the same laws of physics and share some of the fundamental genetic goals,[92] we assume that their various EP mechanisms would also share "core" PPD features

---

90 Adhering to scientific beliefs in structure/functionality and mind/brain correlations, we suggest that specific GEAP dissimilarities in the brains of humans and other species prevent the latter from possessing the entire set of cognitive capabilities necessary for performing the full range of assessments and predictions involved in the human EP, and from being susceptible to the same wide range of influences acting on these estimations. Whereas many living creatures excel and outperform us in sensing, moving, navigating, camouflaging, and many other traits, they are still not fully capable of imagining and predicting complex implications of potential interactions with the environment (including various $R_{event} \longrightarrow P_{event}$ transitions, for example) or its independent evolution. Furthermore, the energetic self-reference points of other mind/brain-owning organisms might be considerably more elementary, and so are their assessments, arsenal of potentially invested resources, and communication skills. These are likely to limit the variety and versability of the nonhuman response channels in tailoring self-favored solutions to different situations experienced. It should be emphasized that such assumptions do not contradict the existence of PPD-directed EP in other species as well.

91 For example: S. Neubauer, J. J. Hublin, and P. Gunz, "The Evolution of Modern Human Brain Shape". *Sci. Adv.* **4(1)**, eaao5961 (2018).

92 While taking into account the different environmental impacts which have accompanied the specific evolution paths of the different species and shaped their functionalities in regard to realizing the (common) hereditary-directed life goals.

irrespectively of their species-specific evolutionary pathway and/or its duration. The reliance of the EP on both inherent PPD mechanisms and environmentally impacted mind structure distributions, such as BES and EMES, shapes the PbB that is being reflected from the human. Accordingly, the susceptibility of the assessments to the external (and, consequently, the internal) influences and the intensive use of the cognitive imagination function at this processing stage, make the functional outputs appear less "robotic" or "conservative" than what might be expected in light of the strict PPD-directed core mechanisms. Interestingly, we also seem to fluidly adjust certain aspects of our energetic assessments, including those concerning our own "energetic selves" and interaction potencies, to the presently evolved standards of the world we live in and experience. It is also important to note that we assume that the EP matures to a full functional state upon the infant acquiring a critical level of assimilated experiences and following a sufficient development of impactful functions such as imagination (clearly required for the effective top-down processing).[93] This naturally follows chronologically the emergence of basic cognitive activity at t_{0mind}, where prior to this time we may view the inherited mind functionality related to the PPD as genetically unexpressed yet, or potentially degenerated.

The biasing of the matured EP by different factors, and environmental influences among them, can help explain, for example, why many of us tend to believe in "non-scientific" ideas. Such "counter-physical" beliefs defy the restricted-contingent progression principles represented by some of the most basic elements of the PPD-directed mechanisms.[94] Attempting to resolve the apparent contradiction, we recall the strong natural urge to search for and adopt order patterns which help us mitigate our core and incidental fears and needs (as one manifestation of biases included in $f(\Psi)$). Unsurprisingly, this "inner systemic struggle" between the strict scientific orientation of the PPD-directed mechanisms versus psychoenergetic as well as other biasing

---

93 One potentially critical experience in this regard is the sensation of one's own birth event, which we have previously assumed as providing the individual with a first impression of something analogous to a physical reaction in the general spacetime.

94 One representative example is the popular belief in astrology and its science-contrasting, physically nonrestricted views concerning the influence of (the alignment of) far-away celestial objects on our behavior.

factors,[95] may easily incline in favor of the latter.[96] In fact, the potentially superior strength of the psychoenergetic influences not only can lead to non-scientific beliefs but also may unfocus our genetic-oriented decisions and occasionally even drive us to anti-genetic responses contradicting the fundamental aims of the EP mechanisms (see also the discussion at the end of Chapter 1). We should remember that in parallel to the influences, many deviations from genetic-favored behavior are established on "fully reasonable" restricted-contingent perceivable grounds which frequently include self-energy-related considerations. Another point to consider is whether there are, upon excluding imagination-induced non-"organic" perceptive expressions, different PbB patterns or perceptive traits which appear to defy basic scientific principles yet ostensibly rely on a PPD-directed mechanism. At a glance, for example, the motivation of the human to recruit potential resources might seem odd given the natural tendency to get rid of local excesses of potential energy. Yet, and as we remember from the introduction section, the energy recruited by the human is further being utilized to stabilize his or her structures, emerging functionality which increases the entropy in the general spacetime and, thus, supporting natural physical tendencies. Generally speaking, we believe that no instances of physical contradictions exist, and proper ways will always be found to justify questionable functionality expressions reflected from the human. Next, we wish to compare between a human being whose PbB is presumably bound to the perceptive concepts suggested and a hypothetical human-made robot. Assisted by a set of algorithms controlling its optimized hardware, the ideal robot is designed to act in its own "artificial self" favor, which is made to imitate some of the human genetic goals. As such, it is programmed to look for and identify energy resources and, upon finding them, manipulate them to recharge its power, self-repair its components, and even dedicate time for replication-like activity by constructing other robots with similar functions. Furthermore, the robot may fight over the resources, attempt to protect itself and the

---

95 Including some of the biases mentioned in Subsection 3.2.5, and highlighting the intense reliance of assessments at this stage on imagination functions which challenge the physical reliability of the perceived world.

96 It should be noted that many other experiences and $f(\Psi)$-related influences do support the restricted-contingent physical principles of spacetime evolution (and their projected perceptive reflections).

other functional assemblies it has created, and even take actions to maintain the latter. While at present this scenario seems far-fetched and entirely hypothetical, we do not rule out the possibility that technological advances in artificial intelligence and computer engineering will enable it in the future. If ever made possible, one may even think of tuning to such a functional machine a certain level of phenomenological experiences as a precursor to consciousness, and biases to the main algorithm, as analogous to the human's $f(\Psi)$. While accepting that structural, mechanistic, and phenomenological dissimilarities will always exist between humans and such "ideal" machines, in accord with our views here we can still theoretically regard both types of entities as localized evolutionary states in general spacetime, holding certain functional similarities, and which in the latter case emerged through circumstantially branching (from DNA-based heredity) physical reactions. Despite perceiving ourselves special and unique as a part of our energetic self narrative, such physical similarities might provide an important perspective of us being nothing but plain and replaceable conversion systems in the universe.

Behind the inextricability limitations we interpret spacetime from, it is quite reasonable that our scientific beliefs themselves lead us to suggest the existence of the PPD and to impose it on the mind-operation model. Additionally, we have already acknowledged that one can generally ascribe a physical dimension to any functional system evolved by nature and attempt to analyze it from this standpoint. By itself, these possibilities do not contradict the potential veracity of the PPD or its special association with the mechanistic guidelines of the (energy) perception as a potential tool for their bottom-up exploration on physical grounds. Having said that, we further believe that the PPD and all possible mechanistic elements relevant to our perceptions are independent of our scientific knowledge. As such, and though we clearly wish that they could be indicated and empirically validated, we view the perceptive guidelines as not necessarily being bound to current interpretations of physical laws, and among them to our own simplified model's non-empirical equations. Nevertheless, assuming that the PPD indeed exists, it is expected to be ingrained in the mind mechanisms of every individual, independent of his or her beliefs in its validity.[97] These all lead us to a pivotal claim in this book. Looking from a wide perspective, we view the persistent efforts to empirically study perceptive mechanisms via observing human traits and reducing these observations into operational principles and algorithms, as top-down exploration attempts. Based on the (quantized-like) layered detection-reaction model and the assumed PPD control over the perceptive (EP) mechanisms, we suggest *a bottom-up exploration approach based on tailored algorithmizing of fundamental laws of spacetime*. As this modeling strategy has to correlate with the observable macro human EP and PbB traits, one may suggest that at its first step, *a comprehensive search for instances of parallelism between fundamental physical laws and the functional perceptive/behavioral human reflections should be conducted.* Whereas in the subsequent step *the candidate physical algorithms found should be bottom-up-integrated in fitting commonly observable human sensoresponses.* Being related to the evolution of the mechanisms, some PPD "building blocks" physical laws need to involve, for example, the energetic barriers to spacetime progression, while variations and combinations of these can be tested in increasing levels of complexity. Now, among different possible merits, discovering and studying such analogies is expected to reformulate (hopefully more correctly) our intuitive, representative detection-reaction model, advance current machine-learning algorithms attempting to mimic human cognition,[98] and help predict individual responses in various situations. Besides attempting to look for common grounds for human functionalities and laws of nature (such as describing EP mechanisms using principles involving energy transfer and its barriers in nature), one might further prefer to focus the search on analogies to physical principles which (also) operate on spatial stimuli of perceivable scales and among them many related to classical mechanics descriptions of bulk spacetime content. Nevertheless, the PPD approach might

---

97 One should be aware that in case the evidences for the veracity of the PPD are discovered, possible reversed insights on natural laws projected from perception-based human traits should be treated with a grain of salt due to the reliability-veridicality restrictions. Despite this alleged asymmetry, the PPD is in a way also mechanistically uniting physics and beliefs by intersecting their "partly dual" nature. Upon believing that the deterministic channel connecting these two is reflected by the ID, one can further contemplate extended philosophical meanings in regard to individuality.

98 With some additional efforts directed to the integration of enhanced AI algorithms in robots, allowing them, for example, to process the environment and respond to it in a more human-like manner.

further assists us in hypothesizing mechanistic transitions, which do not always entail macroscale physical principles. One interesting hypothesis is that close to dying and to the collapse of the human individuality, certain changes occur in the macro mind mechanisms (possibly also upon considering the speculation presented in Section 3.2.1 regarding the existence of self-sensing mind functions). These relatively short-term yet fast boundary effects, which using some imagination or intuition can be paralleled to transitions from reliance on "classical" physical principles associated with bulk mind states to quantum principles applicable to less dense and more discrete (?) states, might be considered in the exploration of reported near-death experiences and/or terminal lucidity in certain dementia patients. In parallel to the efforts to comprehend the physical guidelines of the cognitive mechanisms and to find their analogies, we should also remember the required complementary efforts to decrypt the $f(\Psi)$ bias function. While ID-related psychoenergetic factors will always remain a substantial hurdle in the model, finding similar physical laws-perceptive trait equivalents (PPD patterns) among many individuals is expected to overcome in a way the analytical problems associated with the subjective individual impacts. We are also fully aware that a possible progression/changes in our scientific beliefs and/or technologies can affect the decryption progress. Despite the challenges, we believe that following the suggested structuralist-reductionist directions—extending beyond conventional macro-behavioral and meso-neurobiological interpretations—can facilitate a better understanding of our minds as wonders of nature which allow us to observe, interpret, and respond to spacetime while maintaining our lives in it.

Chapter 4

Expansion to the Macro/Future: Some Elementary Ideas

4.1 Elementary energetic considerations in human groups

So far, we have been mainly interested in the individual human's perceptive and behavioral responses to external spacetime events. One basic question that can be further asked is: In what ways are decisions and behaviors of groups[1] different than those taken by their individual human members? As one may expect, in our context here this question is mainly directed at the energetic aspects of realizing the genetic goals of the groups' members. Prior to our attempts to address this question, we wish to note that the ideas to be presented in this short subsection cannot and definitely do not aim to cover the entire range of sociological and anthropological considerations in regard to human groups and the behaviors reflected from them. The main goal here is to highlight elementary differences between the individual's EP and the *group's energetic considerations* (GECs) accompanying a given executable reaction, and to inquire the validity of the PPD principles with respect to them. One central idea to which we will adhere suggests that due to the "fermionic-like separation" of minds in spacetime, GECs can only exist as a spatially distributed, convoluted set of communication-mediated mind "outputs". Under these conditions, the energetic considerations behind executing the group's reaction, which are encoded within this macro structure, differ from the plain sum of EP outputs of its members regarding the same operation.

Considering our common GEAP-directed mind mechanisms and

---

1 We consider a human group as consisting of two or more individuals. None, some, or all of the groups' (other) members might belong to the individual ecosystem of a specific member. Each individual in such a group can be simultaneously a member in other groups, and we refer to the largest human group that we know of as "humankind" (regardless of the significant heterogeneity in the beliefs of its members and their awareness to being a part of this human assembly).

functional traits, the actions of connecting with others and forming groups seem to be both likely and reasonable despite the global energetic struggle between us. Formation of groups of cooperating people, for example, often requires certain interactions which typically rely on shared motivations to realize, conserve, and improve individual genetic goals and achievements, as well as on finding stabilizing order patterns in order to quench psychoenergetic fears and satisfy different needs. Naturally, all individuals become exposed at an early stage of their lives to certain kinds of human interactions. These start with the "bosonic condensed state" in the mother's womb and continue with the connection to the guardians and others. As we mature, we are being further pushed into social behavior by the inherent urge to reproduce and by the energetic struggle around us, which also often lead us to adopt different social norms and conventions that increase our social exposure. As a matter of fact, all genetic goals relate to human interactions, and we might accordingly speculate that as such, they inherently urge us into connecting and associating with other individuals. Regarding the energetic struggle, unless discovered to be otherwise, it is commonly believed that human life is confined to Earth, a habitat of a relatively constant area $S_{habitat}$, on which a certain number of humans, to be referred to as $N(t_{present})$, dwell at any fixed observation time $t_{observed} \equiv t_{present}$. At this specific observation instant, we can describe a limited spatial content that can potentially be utilized by humanity for its needs. Part of the content has already been present in the habitat while another is arriving to it from an external source. Its usability depends on the species' present practical capabilities to collect and convert it. To such content, holding an energy projection of $E_{PU}(t_{present})$, we ascribe a practical *potential usability* (PU) for humankind. That is, under the proper circumstances that enable it, some of these potentially usable resources can be realistically received/collected by the living individuals who turn them into genetic benefits. Now, one of the basic ideas overlooked by this simplified presentation is that both $N(t_{present})$ and $E_{PU}(t_{present})$ are unevenly distributed over $S_{habitat}$, which is reflected by different densities of population and potential resources across the planet. While from the global geographics perspective we expect a relative correlation between the two densities, we also assume an additional link between the local concentrations of the humans and the availability of *catalysts* in these areas which increase their accessibility to the resources and/or allow them to convert them in ways that require less invested efforts. As we implied in Chapter 3, one factor contributing to changes in population densities is migration towards destinations believed to be abundant with resources and catalysts.[2] The closeness formed by the gathering of the population in the coveted areas accelerates human interactions and exchange of beliefs,[3] and thus is a prominent factor in the assembly and development of social groups, societies, and cultures.[4] Thus, one may point out on the interplay between beliefs-catalyzed gathering and gathering-catalyzed exchange of beliefs as contributing to the roaming of humans across the habitat and to formation of groups, while it can also help explain the correlated distributions of habitants and energy resources.

As separated minds communicate through transferred beliefs, cooperation between humans is naturally often considered (typically via high-cognition processes). Depending on the bilateral energetic considerations and interpretations of the participants involved, these might evolve into *association processes* and formation or expansion of functionality-oriented groups. Once formed, the human assemblies are potentially subjected to a dynamic competition between association and *dissociation processes* which tend to reduce their size and can even disintegrate them. The balance between the opposing trends plays a critical role during the initial growth of the assemblies from their social nucleation cores, impacting their sizes, inner structures, and stability as properties that may affect the operational decisions taken and implementation of their subsequent actions. As expected, we believe that regardless of their capabilities to implement them, the inclinations to stay associated or dissociate apply to all members of a group, each with his or her own unique

---

2 We also expect that, unless effective and constructive cooperation between individuals is formed, upon the arrival of a large, critical number of people to the attractive destinations, the potency of the local resources and catalysts to ameliorate the entire expanded population start eventually to decline. Under such conditions, an escalation in the local struggle is expected to lead to a subsequent emigration of weaker populations from the energy hub.

3 Resembling in some aspects the need for a certain proximity between entities in nature in order for physical forces to trigger interactions and reactions between them.

4 From the prehistoric times and up to the current day, the evolution of humankind is believed to have always obeyed similar as well as other related trends. The latter have been described from various viewpoints; for example, in Y. N. Harari, *Sapiens: A Brief History of Humankind*. New York: Harper (2015).

individuality states and EPself perceptions. Many of these personal decisions are significantly biased by the psychoenergetics of the members as a part of their ever-changing influences united under $\mathfrak{f}(\Psi)$, as well as by beliefs and expectations regarding the group itself and concerning, for instance, its proven and potential functionality and functions, specific participants, structure, and so on. At this point we may ask, What can be a basic incentive for a human to team up to a given group?[5] While the glue-like shared beliefs uniting the group members around it cannot entirely supress the natural forces driving the energetic struggle inside it, the overall functionality generated by the assembly often appreciably ameliorates the members' individual energetic-genetic states. This is normally achieved via a synergistic collaborative effect increasing the group's accessibility to potential resources or catalysts and accelerating shared recruitment processes. Among others, additional advantages of associating in groups concern the potential improvement to the members' internal stability and their confidence. These are often related to the order patterns found in the narratives of the groups, and their implications are likely to assist the members in their struggle for gaining an increased share in the global $E_{PU}(t_{present})$ and implementing it. A related specific element propelling us towards social behavior and association in groups is the FoAA. In the last chapter, we attributed the beginning of this psychoenergetic fear to experiencing the sharp "bosonic to fermionic" transition during our birth and ejection from the protective and nourishing environment of our mother's womb. Combined with the delayed realization that we might lose our protective guardians as well, we develop a strong urge to minimize the extent of negative emotions aroused by these abandonment associations. Accordingly, the urge increases the individual's dependency on socializing as a means of mitigating the FoAA and self-stabilizing. Considering all these, we suggest that in addition to the intuitive, passive affiliation of every individual to different groups,[6] he or she is also being pushed by the genetic targets and psychoenergetic influences to actively

---

5 Whereas the question deliberately disregards certain possible energetic and entropic explanations along the lines of the preferred dictates of nature, we still wish to mention the possibility that association with other people intensifies emotions in the human, thus helping him or her to further discharge excessive sensory energy through such PCE expressions.

6 An affiliation which is based, for example, on beliefs concerning heredity, geography, religion, and others.

associate to different collectives holding a potential to ameliorate his or her energetic state. It should also be noted that in light of the global struggle, every decision to join a group holds a risk for its taker and, as such, requires a certain degree of the aforementioned conservation-related trust.

Contrary to association are also *refrainment* (*from associating*) and dissociation, which refer to inhibition to the assembly and catalysis to the disassembly of groups, respectively. Both seem natural to the energetic struggle and also somewhat to our human aspirations of being, similar to our IDs, unique. Refrainment and dissociation often follow EP-based estimations that association to a given group cannot or does not ameliorate the individual enough, can harm him or her, or that there are better options than joining or staying affiliated to this assembly. Among the parameters which are typically being considered at this stage, we find the perceived impacts of past and present activity of the group, its size and composition, the human interactions operating within the collaboration, external influences, and so on. Dissociation often requires overcoming resisting forces, and among them subtle or pronounced expressions of FoAA. Despite these difficulties, the decisions to separate and disengage occasionally benefit the individual with a mutative-like relative advantage in the struggle. While some of these concepts are also applicable to refrainment from association, we believe that decisions against binding also entail significant social inhibitions, including in some cases a *fear of rejection* and an initial *fear of difference*. Before moving on to discussing several mechanistic aspects of collaborated generation of functionality, we wish to highlight several complementary ideas. The first suggests that compared to the individual's EP and PbB, GECs and group functions emerge from an even more complex structure in spacetime which often supports heterogeneous componential functionality contributions from its physically separated human members. These include, for example, receiving inputs, their processing, and performing decisions before the collective reaction is produced. The increased complexity and diversity involved in these cases, and to a certain extent also their impact on the converted outcome, normally increase with the group size and can further be ascribed to the collection of discrete mind structures and IDs of its members, each biased by his or her own $f(\Psi)$.[7] As such, some personal motivations and propensities of the members are expected to balance out or become attenuated due to different inner forces acting inside the group. In other cases, belief exchange inside the group and other causes lead to individuals adopting certain parts of self energy perceptions and reference points of others while assessing different matters.

The energetic struggle in which all members of cooperating assemblies keep being engaged in is not only directed towards the external-to-the-group (EG) world but also invades its inner dynamics and structure. As a matter of fact, we believe that this inner struggle often has substantial biasing implications on the collaborated functionality produced. One important property which emerges from the struggle is *polarity*.[8] Several types of polarities are assumed to impact the functionality of the group assembly. One is attributed to *genetic polarity*, which corresponds to perceived differences between the genetic achievements of the members, with a special focus on the possession of potential resources, $E_{st}(p)$. Assessing such differences typically involves each individual using his or her own EPself reference in determining superiority or inferiority relative to others while believing that some external resources can be converted to promote the realization of all genetic targets from survival to offspring enhancement. Genetic polarity often exists in groups without being clearly visible to the EG world. Nevertheless, under certain conditions its effects might be dramatic and as such can even lead to establishment of distinguishable classes amongst humans. Either subtle or dramatic, we argue that inner group comparisons indicating unequal achievements and substantial energetic (genetic) gaps between them produce an effect of *agitation*. Upon crossing a certain ($f(\Psi)$-related) threshold, this unbalanced state is assumed to trigger internal group reactions with a potential to unfold to an extent, which impacts its overall observed functionality or catalyzes its

---

7 And yet the spatially-separated macrostructure is united around common beliefs reflecting a relative resemblance in certain mind parts of its human components.

8 Quite clearly, polarity also applies in general to gaps between different (perceived) states of individuals regardless of their association to any specific groups. Yet we believe that polarity effects from within a group can hold meaningful implications to its functions. We should also note that perceiving polarity in regard to others occasionally induces a strong $f(\Psi)$-related influence on the individual.

dissociation.[9] Another type of polarity, which is assumed to be related to the former, is *leadership polarity*. As we all know, throughout history, and probably ever since the dawn of humanity, some individuals and groups have either taken it upon themselves to lead others or have been crowned by others to rule them. Many circumstantial factors have been involved in determining the identity of these leaders, including struggles and investment of efforts, psychoenergetic effects, and etheoses.[10, 11] Leadership polarity leads to formation of distinct classes among humans which are usually more pronounced than in the case of genetic polarity. Natural aspirations to advance in these drive different individuals to occupy intermediate leadership and influential positions holding different functions in the assembly (including managing, commanding, inspecting, etc.). Clearly, one can categorize the polarized groups with respect to their specific motivations and functionalities, or in regard to different aspects of their inner hierarchal organization, control by the leadership, internal paths of communication and interaction (including sharing resources), and other related parameters.

Significant polarity effects can be regarded as contributing to an *extended bias function* ($f(\Psi)_{extended}$), which in this case affects the functionality of the entire group.[12] As expected, the function introduces broader influences than in the case of the individual member, extending beyond the personal (including psychoenergetics) biases to social interactions inside the group and with the EG world. Now, we believe that this broad range of influences, including the polarities, affect both the energetic considerations of the whole group and the individual functional throughputs in the collective effort. Individually assessed disturbances appear to propagate through agitated individuals and subgroups on their way to affect the GECs and operative decisions

---

9 Some dynamic aspects of a possible inner reorganization which follows the agitation can be paralleled to structural changes made in a functional system by the propagation of (several) TDs.

10 While leading does not necessarily turn the leader into the strongest in the local energetic struggle, it may benefit him or her with several relative advantages in comparison to his or her subjects.

11 It should also be noted that all of us become exposed to basic aspects of leadership polarity through experiencing—and responding to—the behavior of our guardians at the early stages of our lives.

12 Polarities are also found between groups, and as such they play a role in the energetic struggle up to the level of the entire humanity.

taken.[13] Unless getting cancelled out or dissipated, these often reach a leadership/management level whose relative contribution to setting out the GEC is normally greater than the other collaborators yet in many cases is still affected by their reactive states. Above a certain threshold of agitation and when appropriate conditions are met, the process is also believed to induce reorganizational-functional changes in the group and, under extreme conditions, it may even trigger disassembly or lead to overall reactions which bypass the leadership. Moreover, as we regard the emerged functionality to depend on *individual functional contributions* (IFCs) by the collaborating members, we also assume that these personal work investments[14] are susceptible to the propagating disturbances and other factors in $\smallint(\Psi)_{extended}$. It is thus clear why many collaborations attempt to track some of the biases and optimize self-performance with respect to their predicted reoccurrences. These often add to artificial attempts, including implementation of targeted behavioral rules and social norms to resist or regulate the responses to the emerging polarities. Various "socioenergetic" factors therefore affect the structure, stability, operative considerations, and performance of different human groups. Adding to this complexity are also the natural inclinations of the individual members to prioritize the amelioration of their own ecosystems over the profits of groups consisting of genetically less related members.[15] This "selfish" propensity also holds when the individual fully identifies with the group's goals and narratives, and upon considering the "pure altruistic illusion" mentioned in Chapter 1. Another important point is that we expect the GEC to direct the group towards implementing its plan in ways that intersect with some of the individual response channels

---

13 Somewhat resembling the TDs crossing the sensoresponsive pathways.

14 Depending on the functions of the group and the conversion processes involved in its operation, IFCs can include, for example, reception of information or physical content, processing-producing, managing-leading, stabilizing-regulating, recruiting from the EG environment, and so forth.

15 Other profit-based prioritizations and the logics behind them are known to stand in the focus of the mathematical field of game theory. For example, in C. F. Camerer, *Behavioral Game Theory: Experiments in Strategic Interaction*. Princeton, NJ: Princeton University Press (2003) and H. Gintis, *The Bounds of Reason: Game Theory and the Unification of the Behavioral Sciences*. Princeton, NJ: Princeton University Press (2009). Interestingly, some contributions in this field have also utilized neuroscience principles to explore decision making, such as in A. G. Sanfey, "Social Decision-Making: Insights from Game Theory and Neuroscience". *Science* **318(5850)**, 598–602 (2007) and D. Lee, "Game Theory and Neural Basis of Social Decision Making". *Nat. Neurosci.* **11**, 404–409 (2008).

discussed in Chapter 3, implying a certain extent of resemblance in some of the energetic considerations made. Such response channels add up to new opportunities, including implementing inner group reorganization (while applying, for example, new policies regarding conversion/response channels, sharing gains and losses, etc.), adding or dismissing individuals to or from the assembly, as well as disseminating, compartmentalizing, or encrypting communicated data, to name a few. With respect to all these, we identify several functional and operational similarities between basic responses of individuals and groups as well as differences between them.

Scrutinizing the GEC, we suggest that despite every biased, discrete EP within it appearing as some sort of a reduced contribution to the group's functional layout, due to emergence effects and the extended involvement of the $f(\Psi)_{extended}$ biases in them, it might be hard to recognize the exact role of each EP in the total generated functionality (with some fractal-like resemblance to the difficulty of pinpointing the contribution of a single receptor to the individual's behavior). This suggests that GECs are never simple sums of the members' EPs in a group. Also interesting to assume is that regardless of the differences between the individual and the group, the GEC and its correlated collaborative behavior keep reflecting some physical laws of nature (thus obeying PPD-like patterns). Despite the possibility that the functionality reflected from the more complex human assembly is abundant with them,[16] the laws might be harder to detect due to their partial masking by the strong $f(\Psi)_{extended}$ influences (analogous to attempts to formulate a physical principle for a sensitive system operating under rapidly changing environmental conditions). One may also notice that some contributions to $f(\Psi)_{extended}$, including the aforementioned human polarities, possess physical analogies in nature as well, and that "organic" polarity-based reactions further contribute to the contingently evolving spacetime, also through the human sensoresponsive functionalities.[17] It almost goes without saying that these views, suggesting the fundamental assimilation and

---

16 An extended follow-up work will be dedicated to demonstrating analogies between human behavior in groups and macroscopic (including thermodynamics-based) physical laws.

17 One relevant example refers to the critical physiological importance of polarity in receptor cells' membranes and its function in activating neural firing and initiating the sensoresponsive process.

integration of physical principles in responses reflected from different human association scales, conform with our deterministic approach to the causal evolution of nature alongside the energetic struggle emerging between the living.

4.2 Progression under deterministic dictates

Adhering to our previous assumptions, we believe that predetermined physical processes have evolved our minds to depend on systematic sets of physical reactions in projecting, observing and interpreting changes in spacetime. Adopting a physicalistic-deterministic standpoint, we believe that not only these reactions, projections, and changes are predetermined, but also the objectivity-seeking explanations of science for them and to all other universal occurrences.[18] One may therefore accept that at any point in time we individually and collectively understand what has been determined for us by the physical evolution of nature. Conforming to these views, we regard each human as a "deterministic reactor" converting energy on the way to change nature's entropy, and whose inner conversion processes and their trajectories (including the sensoresponsive projections presented in Chapter 2 and down to the "ID microscopic level") are causally connected (physically). These and other related processes lead to destined emergence of behaviors and struggles which are modestly contributing from our local habitat to changes in general spacetime. The predetermined nature of the mind mechanisms, sensation and perception PCEs, and reactions to the environment clearly contradicts our intuition, which for our own survival and genetic benefits is inclined to illusively portray a fundamental self-control over one's own wills, actions, and many consequent experiences in life.

Next, we argue that causal determinism leads us to different unavoidable catastrophes[19] that are not necessarily foreseen by

---

18 As beliefs that to the best of our knowledge cannot change the universal laws of nature and which in this sense are somewhat inferior to the physics behind their existence (and thus in a way breaking the symmetry needed for a genuine physics/belief duality).

19 We emphasize that a "catastrophe" is a human-made term which does not exist in the inanimate nature lacking such emotive connotations.

fundamental-level laws of nature.[20] One prominent catastrophe relates to *extinction*, in our case of the entire human race, which overcomes the forces attempting to oppose it and conserve the lives of its reproducing members. Quite clearly, extinction can occur either by the impact of external forces which are not triggered by human intervention or through human-catalyzed actions. One scenario refers to a situation in which humans are unable to capture and convert over time enough E_{PU} to satisfy the basic genetic demands of their expanded population. This might happen due to limitations on their capability to do so or when the total amount of accessible E_{PU} during this period becomes critically insufficient for mass utilization.[21] Such situations are also expected to escalate the energetic struggle and lead to multiple chain reactions, some with a potentially anarchistic nature, which hold deadly consequences. Sadly, we might make ourselves extinct even before facing an immediate energetic crisis. Wars employing mass destruction weapons, careless or vicious actions that harm the protective nature of the habitat or which give critical advantage to competing species (viruses, for example), mass-manipulation of minds against their self-functions, and other misconducts, provide potential hazards which can eventually cost humanity its life.

Given some of the scenarios above,[22] humanity attempts to devise plans for preventing its own potential demise. Though unevenly, regulations and social laws are being legislated and enforced around the globe in an attempt to provide welfare and safety to the inhabitants and restrict anarchism, wars, theft, violence, and the like. These require an investment of appropriate resources and, in a sense, act counterintuitively to the direct and emotionless propensities of the natural struggle in favor of the species. Also frequently implemented

---

20 Yet occurrence of catastrophes might be implied from more complex sets of rules tailored to certain circumstances and conditions.

21 Interestingly, some researchers believe that such energetic limitations and the deficiencies they bring about inevitably trigger the extinction of possibly existing extraterrestrial civilizations before they can reach Earth: M. L. Wong, and S. Bartlett, "Asymptotic Burnout and Homeostatic Awakening: A Possible Solution to the Fermi Paradox?". *J. R. Soc. Interface.*, **19(190)**, 20220029 (2022). One should also consider Hawking's and others' warnings regarding the severe threats posed by a possible invasion of advanced alien civilizations to Earth due to interactions humankind trigger with them.

22 We encourage our readers to read the views of Harari, complementing in different aspects some of the topics covered in this subchapter: Y. N. Harari, *Homo Deus: A Brief History of Tomorrow*. London: Harvill Secker (2016).

are effective strategies to reduce overconsumption of global resources. In one example, entire populations are convinced or forced to limit the number of their offspring. While these changes contribute to preserving the energetic states of existing populations and relatively (to the poverty expected in their absence) mitigate the human struggle, a critical mass of such ostensibly anti-genetic behaviors would naturally harm the growth of the species. Unsurprisingly, from a psychoenergetic perspective, such a strategy can also be viewed as conflicting the FoAA of its followers. Alternative to restricting the human size of the individual ecosystem is the choice to limit the energetic consumption from within its existing assembly, which is somewhat unnatural to our basic C/I aspirations. Despite both of these reproduction and consumption limiting behaviors seem to oppose immediate genomic propensities, we emphasize that nature does not punish, in short life expectancy for instance, those who do not comply with the genetic targets the second to the fourth. We speculate that one of the reasons for this[23] is an absence of a genetic achievement feedback mechanism which might currently be evolutionarily degenerated. Another core strategy attempting to keep us away from energy crises-driven extinction employs technological aids and solutions. Some current advances in technology are specifically directed towards enhancing the collection, conversion, and storage efficiencies of energy resources for Earth's expanding population. Now, converting more implementable E_{PU} into implemented "genetic energy" that supports the continuation and growth of humankind requires a considerable investment in ongoing research and development. Such efforts persist despite the ideas that the scientists, engineers, industry workers, entrepreneurs, and other officials engaged in the practices might not find any immediate extinction scenarios to be probable and while not being able to emotionally relate to more than a few following-up generations. It is thus unsurprising that the active involvement in the efforts and identifying with their noble goals are normally triggered by personal energetic rewards. Another intriguing opportunity that

---

23 We recall that one possible justification for an absence of shorter-life punishment is the entropic contribution towards general spacetime from the life of every individual who has already been born (and thus became invested with nature's energy resources), regardless of his or her achievements with respect to the entire species. Contrary to that, we assume that certain punishments, such as emotional (e.g., loneliness) or lack of individual ecosystem-based energetic support, are more likely to be expressed among those who age without offspring.

might come true with the help of modern and future technologies is to massively colonize currently nonpopulated regions on Earth and, hypothetically, also on habitable exoplanets in our galaxy. Combined with possibilities of finding additional energetic resources in the extended habitats, the expected increase in $S_{habitat}$ in case of successful colonialization attempts might provide key factors in preserving our rapidly expanding species.

Devising the right strategies to save ourselves from potential extinction brings us back to the topic of beliefs and their changes. Hand in hand with the development of various capabilities and skills, some of our beliefs evolve as well. Looking from a wide perspective, one may parallel this process to a "struggle" between spatially separated mind structures whose fate is (deterministically) shaped by certain natural selection rules. Such perspective relates to Dawkins's ideas and the works that followed them regarding memes as carriers of communicatively replicated cultural units.[24] Whereas social and cultural influences on and by the evolving memes have been mainly ascribed to communication dynamics involving different threshold conditions and selection rules, we wish to complement these views and focus here on the bidirectional correlation between internal changes in the BES of the communicators and their external energetic struggle. As implied, a prominent factor affecting in recent years both the energetic and belief struggles is the technology-assisted advance of communication, demonstrating the increasing power of remote "copy-paste" dissemination of BES in believers' minds regardless of the PCEs they evoke. The development of easily accessible modern communication tools and social media enabled their use as catalysts for both serial and parallel, and often exponential, relaying of beliefs that can rapidly reach significant parts of humanity. This effective distribution methodology provides a clear indication for the power of communication to gather (or separate) spatially separated humans around beliefs (relative similarities in BES), and consequently often also catalyze their genetic amelioration. Indeed, following the foundation of the solid infrastructure required for the communication,

---

24 R. Dawkins, *The Selfish Gene*. Oxford: Oxford University Press (1976). With the ideas expanding to the memetics field of study—for example, in R. Brodie, *Virus of the Mind: The New Science of the Meme*. Integral Press (1996) and S. J. Blackmore, *The Meme Machine*. Oxford: Oxford University Press (1999).

current dissemination of beliefs to the masses has become a far more facile and routine process, requiring a significantly reduced energy investment in instantly "bridging" many minds. With respect to that, we can hypothetically relate any momentary distribution state of specific beliefs to present (and past) contributions to their dissemination and BES assimilation. These contributing efforts are affected by the contributors' subjective energy states, EPselves, relative polarities, as well as psychoenergetics and other individual parameters. Hence, one may generally and causally connect the struggle between beliefs to the human struggle over energy resources and attempt to identify some impactful, relating behavioral trends within their coupled evolutions. As we know, some BES are being replicated throughout many generations and reach numerous individual ecosystems unless a dramatic energetic change concerning the involved persons introduces a significant enough force to affect this inertia-like progression. Currently, some significant force is held by *strong distributors* (*influencers*), who are typically well-connected socially and are often invested in and rewarded for considerably impacting the assimilation. Strong distributers trigger and/or exponentially amplify the spread of their own or others' (energetically biased) beliefs using special skills in operating communication catalysts. While a strong distributor does not necessarily have to possess exceptional energy resources or a high leadership potency,[25] his or her contributions may still leave a remarkable energetic impact on those being affected by them. Accordingly, we may refer to another type of polarity between humans, a *communication polarity*, reflecting their relative potencies to distribute beliefs and energetically impact others, and which gives a relative advantage in this regard to the strong distributors in the general struggle. Before moving on, we would also like to briefly note the influence of flaws in the consistency and reliability of the BES copying process on the development of beliefs. Some of the flaws can be viewed as divergent mutations which are related to the unique mind states of the communicating people and to the environmental conditions biasing them during the transfers. These all take part in

---

25 Regardless of the intuitive correlation between power and influence which is reflected by the idiom "He who holds the gold makes the rules". As we know, desirable characteristics of distributors can also relate to being charismatic, sociable, vibrant, ambitious to leave a mark or legacy, and others.

the deterministic connection between the biophysical struggles which have shaped our minds and their mechanisms and the struggles for the distribution and survival of the beliefs they have created.

Examining current effects of communication on humans raises several concerns. One of them relates to the potential increase in relative mind structure similarities due to the extensive use of over-normalized communication patterns. For example, using emojis, emoticons, gifs, stickers, and the like narrows down the spectrum of vectorial expressions one is naturally employing while articulating emotions and feelings. The same applies to the automated, succinct text messages which now often replace richer and more comprehensive ways to interact and exchange beliefs. Additionally is the increased, mainly escapist, time being spent on "limited choices" social media, which is also potentially contributing to minimizing BES differences among humans and to a relative unification in their response patterns. Despite humanity's expected loss of certain aspects of subjectivity and creativity among its interacting individuals through prolonged and intensive exposure to such evolved communication products, we also wish to acknowledge the latter's beneficial contributions to exposing the users to knowledge (also requiring less effort on their part to obtain it) and to reducing some of the mutative flaws throughout its distribution. We are also aware that communication provides leaders and strong influencers who master it with immense potential power. While this power can serve humanity in different ways, it can also be viciously abused—for instance via deliberately spreading disinformation, incitement, and propaganda—upon promoting narrow (usually energy- and/or leadership-related) interests of groups and individuals. A different kind of threat is posed by escapist addictions attempting to over-satisfy different urges. If we scrutinize, for example, the current addiction of many people to digital screens, we find that not only does it shorten the time they spend on genetic-focused activities in their own favor, but it also significantly competes with experiencing the "external-to-screen spacetime" with its additional important implications. Namely, in parallel to the apparent advantages of the electronic media, these humanmade attention attractors might dangerously turn into "black holes" for the genetic-favored behavioral states of some individuals and as such will slow down to a certain extent the macro-level progression of the species. Another problematic topic relates to the hazards in sharing sensitive human information such as biometric and other personal details. Despite these risks, a complete avoidance/disengagement from the communication traffic exposes its seekers to some risks and increases their chances of missing energetic opportunities. In this complex mosaic of energy-oriented inclinations and biological drives, exchanged beliefs, and developing technologies, we can only hope that future advances in communication will turn out to be unharmful and mostly beneficial for the human race.

One interesting merit of combined modern technologies and contemporary beliefs is that they assist us in finding complementary realization solutions to our genetic goals, and occasionally also catalyze their fulfillment by overcoming the natural barriers. Given the right circumstances and investment of adequate resources in the matter, individuals who wish to have children but are temporarily or permanently incapable can practice different present-day options related to fertilization or adoption. In the case of the latter, we notice that despite the relatively increased genetic dissimilarity between the adopting individuals and the adopted infants, the act may still lead to fulfillment of the guardianship and enhancement targets from both the standpoint of the adoptive parents and the standpoint of the evolving species.

In another example, guardians rely on other humans, often upon rewarding them with $E_{st}(p)$ resources, in temporarily taking care of their offspring, thus "freeing up" time for alternative genetic- or escapist-focused activities. Now, as in the case of communication, many other technological advances hold a potential to harm humanity. One fundamental concern is the "piracy of privacy" regarding the decryption of the mind (see chap. 4, n. 22). Our increasing understanding of physics and brain sciences, combined with gradually improving engineering- and computing-based skills (and, among the latter, machine learning and artificial intelligence, for example), draw us nearer to developing sensor systems and cognition models that might eventually unveil the mechanisms behind the core mind functions. From basic polygraphs to brain-implanted electrodes "listening" in-vivo to communicating neurons,[26] and from

---

26 E. Musk, Neuralink, "An Integrated Brain-Machine Interface Platform with Thousands of Channels". *J. Med. Internet Res.* **21(10)**, e16194 (2019).

advances in quantum computers capable of effectively analyzing the unprecedented amount of data associated with such experiments to noninvasive decoding of cortical semantic presentations by fMRI,[27] we envisage a gradual progress in the abilities to read and control human minds. All these provide an explosive potential for vicious, selective "mind reading, copying, and writing" activities that can sharply imbalance the energetic struggle through altering the mind states and behaviors of the victims in ways that benefit the abusers. And indeed, in an absence of strict legislation and enforcement to limit such knowledge from being obtained, disseminated, and abused, it might fall into the wrong hands and pose a serious threat to humanity. Considering this possible scenario, a few assumptions can be made. The first suggests that nature has intentionally evolved the complex mind/brain functional system to be hard to decipher (allowing it, for example, to be highly susceptible to the overarching biasing effects) as a means to struggle "piracy of privacy" attempts holding energetic incentives. Another possibility, which nevertheless seems quite challenging from several mechanistic and time perspectives, is that as a part of this strong decryption mechanism, close to the "event horizon" of physiological-mechanistic mind decoding, a (BES structural distribution-based feedbacked?) mutation will be formed and proactively trigger (dormant?) evolutionary processes to strengthen the encryption of some of its operational principles. From the brain's perspective, such process might entail changing firing mechanisms, thresholds, processing tracts, and so on. Irrespective of this scenario, in case of a fierce energetic struggle over a prolonged time, we might also expect an evolutionary branching of mind structures and functions within humans. Such branching could be based on severe objective polarities between "stronger" and "weaker" populations which are persistently manifested in their and their ancestors' specific energetic intakes from the environment.

---

27 J. Tang, A. LeBel, S. Jain, and A. G. Huth, "Semantic Reconstruction of Continuous Language from Non-Invasive Brain Recordings". *Nat. Neurosci.* **26**, 858–866 (2023).

Epilogue

Along the journey between physics, beliefs, and mechanistic interpretations of human behavior, we have encountered numerous challenges. Limitations imposed by belief-inextricability issues, subjectivity, veridicality, latency of the mind, and objective physical uncertainties have all become an inevitable part of our story. Being aware of these obstacles and believing that basic physical principles govern our emergent biology and all its products, including perception and belief, we attempted to approach the sensoresponsive systematicness of the human by generically referring to it as a set of sequential and coupled micro-scale reactions, progressing contingently via overcoming physical compatibility constraints and energy barriers on the way to form critical life functionalities. Our particular interest in the mind-processing mechanisms directing perceptive-based responses to circumstantial triggers has led us to suggesting several interesting assumptions regarding possible connections between their inherent guiding principles of operation and some physical laws of the evolving nature.

While believing that the book offers many additional—related and unrelated—insights and interpretations that deserve the full attention of the reader, we have selected to mention at this concluding stage only a few "crux of the matter" concepts, referring to the following postulations:

- In a somewhat similar and upscaled manner to the environmental effects of sensory stimuli on shaping memory arrays and impacting human responses, deterministic-physicalistic progression in spacetime has locally driven "struggling" reactions that obey the laws of nature to evolve the human mind and its abilities to projectively observe, process, and respond to changes in spacetime. As a part of this process and in order to satisfy the growing energetic demands of the evolved biosystems, the ongoing struggle has shaped the pristine mind mechanisms behind the human behavior (which keeps inducing local changes in nature) in compliance with its favorable energetic and entropic propensities.

- Environmentally triggered perception-based behavior is established through the formation of a sequence of "layered" phenomenal expressions involving sensation, different perceptions, and higher cognition processes including thinking and behavioral decisions. Within these, the individual energy perception is a prominent cognitive tool, harmonically operating with other core perceptions in predicting and grading the implications of the individual's potential interactions with spatially recognized elements on his or her realization of fundamental genetic targets, and particularly on the conservation or improvement of his or her achievements in this regard.

- The mechanisms determining our hypothesized genetic lensing, perception, and perception-based behavior responses are coupled to psychoenergetic biases reflecting certain circumstantial aspects of our individual experiences and impressions from the "organic" struggle over realization of the genetic goals. Such experiences also affect our beliefs, and thus further impact the processing stage of the sensoresponsive conversion and its behavioral implications. In addition to that, some life events that shape the psychoenergetic biases—including, for example, our birth—introduce us to projections of certain physical principles in nature, which we also assimilate as distributions of emotive vectors.

- With an emphasis on the energy perception, the cognitive operators ("algorithms") directing the perceptive mechanisms have been evolved (see first postulation above) to correlate with physical laws of nature and as such (biasedly) reflect their fundamental principles. Thus, in attempt to decipher the mechanisms, one may seek and is expected to find analogies between basic laws of physics related to the progression of nature (as we know them) and perception/behavior patterns in individuals. Potential findings should then be followed by a systematic bottom-up integration of the physical algorithms to fit commonly observable human sensoresponses. This reductionist approach may complement the current neurobiological and behavioral studies attempting to analyze cognition processes involved in human responses from the meso and macro levels, respectively. It is further assumed that, despite being emergent and deviating from simple upscaled projections of discrete energy perceptions, energetic considerations in human groups also tend to reflect (higher complexity) bottom-up products made of physical laws "building blocks".

Upon looking for potential analogies between human perception-based responses and elementary physical laws as a first potential step in the attempt to decrypt responsive mind mechanisms, one may use his or her vivid imagination. Among countless possibilities, we suggest paying attention to human parallels to the fundamental forces and polarity in nature, and in a broader sense to (CP-interpreted) similarities in physical manifestations, such as between the complex arrays of the brain's neural connections and the cosmic web, the "birth, life, and death" of celestial objects like stars, the possible latency of dark matter and dark energy, and so on. Another possibly interesting direction to follow is developing a combined deterministic-psychoenergetic approach as a psychological aid directed to explaining energetic/genetic assessments, responses, and struggles in one's life. Awareness to such factors clearly cannot change the inherent mind mechanisms of the patient, yet it might affect his or her biasing function while reshaping the energetic self perception towards evaluating the environment and life events differently. Finally, we reemphasize our call for further development and debate in regard to the ideas presented in order to improve the understanding of our self-functions and functioning. We wish that all these insights will assist in mitigating some aspects of the human struggle and contribute to the formation of a nicer place for future generations to live in.

Appendix

We wish to postulate the possible contribution of the fundamental core fears FoAA and FoD to fears which are raised by incidental events experienced throughout the human's life. Given that fears are circumstantial, can lead one to another, and intensify or fade away due to different reasons, we try to adopt a simplified approach which can later be refined to fit these observations. Our first assumption is that at an individual time such as t_{young}, following the birth of a human and prior to him or her becoming aware of the concept of death, his or her prominent fear is FoAA. We believe that the birth experience is not the only factor responsible for the prominence of this fundamental fear at this stage, but also the strong energetic dependency of the infant or child on the guardians which triggers his or her imagination of the implications of losing them. On the other side of the timeline, an elderly person is expected to be more preoccupied with death. The awareness to the upcoming transformations[1] which will terminate his or her life, consciousness, and the experience of genetic achievements he or she is emotionally connected to, elevate[2] the contribution of the fundamental FoD element. Nevertheless, we expect that many humans who have reached an old age would also experience a relative increase in FoAA. This is due to the often-increasing energetic dependency of elderly people, even if not necessarily as dominant as it was during their period of infancy, on external human mediators and the fear of being abandoned by them at this stage. Hence, looking from a broad perspective, one may generally suggest a connection between the relative magnitudes of the core fears (projecting as we remember on the significantly $\dot{E}_{human}$-changing "energetic events" of birth and death) and the individual time. With respect to that we believe that every incidental event which triggers a fear emotion in the individual

---

1 Probably further contributing to the awareness is the perception of time speeding among elderly people.

2 Regardless of frequently contradicting emotions in elderly people who face a substantial decrease in life quality, or upon denial of the fear itself.

carries individual time-correlated contributions from this rough "core fear distribution function". Given that, we suggest that the projective contributions of the major "energetic events" provide a long-lasting background influence to the assessments and operative decisions of the individual.

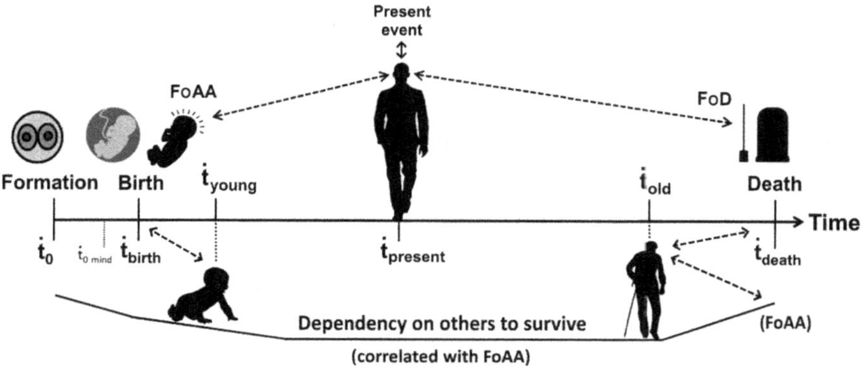

Figure 1. Typical individual time-dependant background influences by fundamental "core" fears originating from experiencing/perceiving significant "energetic events" during the individual's life.

Abbreviations and Acronyms

BCF	Basic consciousness foci
BES	Beliefs-encrypting structures
C/I	Conservation/improvement
CCF	Construction-conservation functionality
CP	Classical spacetime perception
DOS	Dynamic operational states
DRS	Distinct reference site
EDB	Equation of the dynamic balance
EG	External to the group
EI	External to the individual
EM	External to the mind
EMES	Emotions-encoded structures
EP	Individual energetic perception
EPself	Energetic self perception
FoAA	Fear of absolute abandonment
FoD	Fear of death
FRU	Frontal reception unit
GC	General construction
GCF	Genetic consciousness foci
GEAP	Genetic expressions in the forms of anatomy and physiology
GECs	Group's energetic considerations
IBE	Individual energetic benefit
ID	Individuality dimension
IEGP	Individual external genetic possession
IFCs	Individual functional contributions

LTM	Long-term memory
OCA	Overarching cognitive assessment
PbB	Perception-based behavior
PCE	Phenomenological conscious experience
PPD	Perceptive physical dimension
PU	Potential usability
PWI	Potential worthwhileness of implementation
st	Spacetime
STM	Short-term memory
TCA	Transient cognitive assessment
TD	Travelling disturbance

Projections

$PoA_{st\text{-}body}$	Projection of arriving EI spacetime content
$sPoR_{body}$	Body projection of sensory reception
$sPoA_{body\text{-}mind}$	Projection of impactful body responses arriving to the mind
$sPoPPS_{mind}$	Mind projection of pre-perceptive sensations
$sPoP_{mind}$	Mind projections of generated perceptions
$sPoOD_{mind}$	Mind projection of operational decisions directed to the body
$sPoEff_{body\text{-}st}$	Projection of activated effectors

Symbols

x'	Referring to a specific part of "x"
x^*	"x" is activated
$\{x\}$	Mind projection of "x"
x^0	"x" involves cognitive processing
$\dot{x}$	Individuality applies to "x"
Δ_{self}	Estimated self energetic change
E	Energy (also in a perceptive form)
F	Functionality
$f(\Psi)$	Unified bias function
$f(\Psi)_{extended}$	Extended bias function
H	Energy operator
I	Intensity
φ^0	Estimated self potency to succeed
k	Structure function
κ_{sci}	Scientific interpretation for an O_{sci}-based operation
μ	Motivation index
N	Number (of habitants)
ν	Frequency
O	Operator (beliefs-based, also for cognitive operations)
$\dot{P}$	Perception
P	Product
θ	Spatial angle
R	Reactant
$S_{habitat}$	Area of habitat
t	Time

Index

www.ingramcontent.com/pod-product-compliance
Lightning Source LLC
LaVergne TN
LVHW011006200726
843509LV00011B/1007